Step-by-Step
COOKERY

Step-by-Step COOKERY

a Salamander book
Published by Salamander Books Limited
LONDON

Published by Salamander Books Limited
129-137 York Way
London N7 9LG
United Kingdom

1 3 5 7 9 8 6 4 2

ISBN 0 86101 840 0

Printed in France

CREDITS

Recipes by: Pat Alburey, Jo Craig, Linda Fraser, Annette Grimsdale, Kerenza Harries, Kathryn Hawkins, Lesley Mackley, Janice Murfitt, Louise Pickford, Lorna Rhodes, Lyn Rutherford, Anne Sheasby, Louise Steele, Beverley Sutherland Smith, Sally Taylor, Hilaire Walden, Elizabeth Wolf-Cohen.

Photographs by: Steve Baxter, Simon Butcher, Ken Field, Paul Grater, David Gill, Ray Joyce, Jon Stewart, Alister Thorpe, Philip Wymant.

CONTENTS

INTRODUCTION

Do you need inspiration for another quick supper to please all the family or for a simple-to-make but special dinner party starter? Are you looking for the perfect, failsafe recipe for a Christmas cake or a low-calorie sauce? Do you plan to try your hand at creating some authentic Thai, Chinese or Indian dishes? Or do you want to delight your family and friends with some home-made food gifts, such as a special preserve or hand-made chocolates? With 448 delicious recipes, *Step-by-Step Cookery* is the only recipe book you need.

For those with a love of food, this is a book to pour over; as well as classic favourites, it also contains recipes from cuisines around the world, ranging from Greek meze dishes, such as Imam Bayaldi, to Chinese salads, such as the traditional Eight Treasure Salad; from Cajun Crabcakes to the alcohol-rich Scottish Atholl Brose; from Indian breads, such as nan and chapati to Japanese Teriyaki Steaks. For those who have been nervous of gourmet cooking, this is a book to ease the fear – the layout of each recipe ensures that the instructions are easy to follow; all the ingredients you will need are given at the beginning of each recipe, each finished dish is beautifully photographed, and step-by-step photographs and accompanying text instructions clearly explain how to achieve a perfect result every time.

SOUPS

CONSOMMÉ

1.2 litres (40 fl oz/5 cups) homemade chicken stock (see Note)
115 g (4 oz) raw chicken breast
2 large eggs
4 tablespoons finely chopped fresh parsley
salt and pepper
1 teaspoon vegetable oil

Put the stock in a large pan and bring to the boil. In a blender or food processor, finely chop chicken. Separate 1 of the eggs and beat the white with a fork. Crush the shell. Mix together chicken, egg white, shell and 3 tablespoons parsley. Add to the stock.

Bring stock to just below boiling point, stirring. Lower heat and simmer very gently for 25 minutes. Beat remaining egg with remaining yolk and parsley and season with salt and pepper. In a small omelette pan, heat the oil, pour in the egg mixture and cook until set. Turn out and roll up like a Swiss roll, then cut into thin strips. Strain soup through a sieve lined with muslin or cheesecloth, pour into bowls and add strips of omelette.

Serves 4.

Note: To make your own stock, put a raw or cooked chicken carcass, 1 quartered large onion, 2 halved carrots, 2 halved leeks, 2 sliced celery sticks, 1 bay leaf, some parsley stalks, 1 bunch of thyme and 6 peppercorns in a large pan with enough cold water to cover. Bring to the boil, then reduce heat and simmer for 2-3 hours. Skim off any scum. Strain into a large bowl and cool as quickly as possible. Chill in the refrigerator, then remove any fat that has set on the surface. Use within 2-3 days or freeze in convenient amounts.

VICHYSSOISE

30 g (1 oz/6 teaspoons) butter
3 leeks, trimmed, sliced and washed
1 shallot, finely chopped
250 g (8 oz) potatoes, sliced
785 ml (1¼ pints/3 cups) light chicken stock
pinch ground mace or grated nutmeg
salt and pepper
155 ml (5 fl oz/⅔ cup) single (light) cream
snipped fresh chives, to garnish

Melt butter in a large saucepan, add leeks and shallot, then cover and cook gently for 10 minutes without browning. Add potatoes, chicken stock and mace or nutmeg.

Bring to the boil, cover and simmer for 20 minutes. Purée in a blender or food processor, then pass through a sieve. Season with salt and pepper.

Set aside to cool, then stir in two-thirds of the cream. Chill until ready to serve. Ladle into bowls, swirl in remaining cream and garnish with snipped chives.

Serves 6.

SUMMER AVOCADO SOUP

2 ripe avocados
3 teaspoons lemon juice
1 clove garlic, crushed
155 ml (5 fl oz/⅔ cup) single (light) cream
625 ml (20 fl oz/2½ cups) cold chicken stock
dash Tabasco sauce
salt and pepper
½ avocado, diced, and snipped fresh chives, to garnish

Halve avocados, discard stones and scoop flesh into a blender or food processor. Add lemon juice, garlic and cream and work to a purée.

Blend in stock and season with Tabasco and salt and pepper.

Turn into a bowl, cover with plastic wrap to prevent discoloration and chill for 1 hour. Serve garnished with diced avocado and snipped chives.

Serves 4-6.

GAZPACHO

750 g (1½ lb) beefsteak tomatoes
½ Spanish onion, chopped
1 green pepper (capsicum), chopped
1 red pepper (capsicum), chopped
2 cloves garlic, chopped
2 slices firm white bread, crusts removed, broken into pieces
300 ml (10 fl oz/1¼ cups) tomato juice
3 tablespoons virgin olive oil
2 tablespoons sherry vinegar
salt and freshly ground black pepper
about 8 ice cubes, to serve
ACCOMPANIMENTS:
1 diced small red pepper (capsicum), 1 diced small green pepper (capsicum), 1 diced small onion, 1 chopped hard-boiled egg and croûtons

Peel, seed and chop tomatoes. Put in a food processor or blender with remaining soup ingredients, except ice cubes. Mix until smooth. Pour soup through a nylon sieve, pressing down well on contents of sieve. If necessary, thin soup with cold water, then chill well.

Place accompaniments in separate bowls. Adjust seasoning of soup, if necessary, then pour into cold soup bowls. Add ice cubes and serve with accompaniments.

Serves 4.

Variation: Do not sieve the soup if more texture is preferred.

COURGETTE & TOMATO SOUP

30 g (1 oz/6 teaspoons) butter
1 onion, finely chopped
375 g (12 oz) courgettes (zucchini), coarsely grated
1 clove garlic, crushed
625 ml (20 fl oz/2½ cups) vegetable stock
440 g (14 oz) can chopped tomatoes
2 tablespoons chopped fresh mixed herbs, if desired
salt and pepper
60 ml (2 fl oz/¼ cup) double (thick) cream and basil leaves, to garnish

Melt butter in a saucepan, add onion and cook until soft. Add courgettes (zucchini) and garlic and cook for 4-5 minutes.

Add stock and tomatoes with their juice, then bring to the boil, cover and simmer for 15 minutes.

Stir in herbs, if desired, and salt and pepper. Serve the soup in individual bowls, garnished with teaspoonfuls of cream stirred in or floating on the surface and basil leaves.

Serves 4.

CURRIED PARSNIP SOUP

45 g (1½ oz/9 teaspoons) butter
1 onion, chopped
1 teaspoon chopped fresh root ginger
1 teaspoon curry powder
½ teaspoon ground cumin
500 g (1 lb) parsnips, peeled and chopped
1 potato, chopped
940 ml (1½ pints/3¾ cups) beef stock
155 ml (5 fl oz/⅔ cup) plain yogurt
salt and pepper

CURRIED CROÛTONS: ½ teaspoon curry powder
squeeze lemon juice
30 g (1 oz/6 teaspoons) butter
2 thick slices bread

Melt butter in a saucepan, add onion and cook gently until soft. Stir in ginger, curry powder and cumin and cook for 1 minute, then add parsnips and potato and stir over a medium heat to coat vegetables with spicy butter. Pour in stock and bring to the boil, then cover and simmer for 30 minutes or until vegetables are very tender. Purée in a blender or food processor, then return to saucepan. Ladle a little soup into a bowl and whisk in yogurt, then pour back into pan.

Add salt and pepper and while reheating, make croûtons. Preheat oven to 200C (400F/Gas 6). Beat curry powder, lemon juice and butter together in a bowl. Spread on bread, then remove crusts and cut into cubes. Place on a baking tray and bake until crisp and golden. Serve with soup.

Serves 4-6.

FRENCH ONION SOUP

30 g (1 oz/6 teaspoons) butter
6 teaspoons olive oil
500 g (1 lb) onions, thinly sliced
pinch caster sugar
1.2 litres (2 pints/5 cups) beef stock
1 bay leaf
salt and pepper

TO GARNISH: 4 thick slices French stick
1 teaspoon Dijon mustard
90 g (3 oz/¾ cup) Gruyère cheese, grated

Heat butter and oil together in a large saucepan. Add onions and sugar.

Cook over medium heat for about 20 minutes, stirring occasionally, until onions are deep golden brown. Add stock and bay leaf and slowly bring to the boil, then cover and simmer for 25 minutes. Remove bay leaf and add salt and pepper.

To make garnish, toast bread on each side, then spread with a little mustard. Ladle soup into 4 flameproof bowls and float a slice of bread in each. Pile cheese on to each slice and place bowls under a hot grill until cheese has melted and is bubbling. Serve at once.

Serves 4.

WINTER VEGETABLE BROTH

30 g (1 oz/6 teaspoons) butter
1 onion, sliced
250 g (8 oz) carrots, diced
250 g (8 oz) swede, diced
1 potato, diced
2 large parsnips, diced
500 ml (16 fl oz/2 cups) vegetable stock
1 bay leaf
3 teaspoons cornflour
500 ml (16 fl oz/2 cups) milk
salt and pepper
90 g (3 oz) frozen peas
2 small bread rolls and 60 g (2 oz/½ cup) Cheddar cheese, grated, to garnish

Melt butter in a saucepan, add vegetables, except peas, cover and cook gently for 10 minutes. Add stock and bay leaf, re-cover and simmer for 30 minutes. Blend cornflour with a little milk, then add to soup with remaining milk and cook, stirring until thickened. Remove bay leaf and add salt and pepper.

Stir peas into soup and simmer for 2-3 minutes while making garnish. Cut bread rolls in half, divide the cheese between them and grill until melted. Place on top of each portion of soup just before serving.

Serves 4.

SPICED BLACK BEAN SOUP

225 g (8 oz/1¼ cups) dried black beans, soaked overnight in cold water to cover
2 tablespoons olive oil
1 onion, chopped
1 clove garlic, chopped
1 dried red chilli, seeded and chopped
2 carrots, chopped
1 stick celery, chopped
1.2 litres (40 fl oz/5 cups) vegetable stock
1 teaspoon each toasted coriander seeds, cumin seeds and allspice
1 bay leaf
115 g (4 oz/½ cup) unsalted butter, softened
zest and juice ½ lime
1 tablespoon chopped fresh coriander
salt and pepper

Drain the soaked beans and rinse well. Heat the oil in a large saucepan and fry the onion, garlic, chilli, carrots and celery for 5 minutes until browned. Add the drained beans and stock and bring slowly to the boil. Boil for 10 minutes. Tie the spices and bay leaf in a small piece of muslin and add to the pan. Cover and simmer gently for 1-1¼ hours until beans are cooked. Discard the muslin bag.

Meanwhile, prepare the lime butter. Cream together the butter, lime zest and juice, chopped coriander and salt and pepper to taste. Roll into a log shape about 2.5 cm (1 in) thick, and chill until required, then cut into 12-16 slices. Purée the soup in a blender, spoon into bowls and serve topped with slices of lime butter.

Serves 6-8.

HOT & SOUR SOUP

1.2 litres (2 pints/5 cups) chicken stock
9 teaspoons rice vinegar
3 teaspoons dry sherry
2 teaspoons soy sauce
1 small clove garlic, finely chopped
½ teaspoon finely chopped fresh root ginger
5 dried Chinese mushrooms, covered with hot water and soaked for 20 minutes
1 carrot, cut into thin strips
90 g (3 oz) canned bamboo shoots, rinsed and cut into thin strips
½ teaspoon Tabasco or chilli sauce
6 teaspoons cornflour
125 g (4 oz) tofu, cut into strips
2 spring onions, shredded

Put the stock into a saucepan and bring to the boil, then add rice vinegar, sherry, soy sauce, garlic and ginger. Drain mushrooms, remove stems, slice and add to pan with carrot, bamboo shoots and Tabasco or chilli sauce. Bring to the boil, then simmer for 10 minutes.

Blend cornflour with 9 teaspoons water, and stir into soup with tofu, then simmer for 2 minutes to thicken. Scatter over spring onions and serve at once.

Serves 6.

CREAM OF MUSHROOM SOUP

60 g (2 oz/¼ cup) butter
375 g (12 oz) mushrooms, finely chopped
60 g (2 oz/½ cup) plain flour
500 ml (16 fl oz/2 cups) chicken stock
155 ml (5 fl oz/⅔ cup) milk
1 tablespoon chopped fresh parsley
3 teaspoons lemon juice
salt and pepper
155 ml (5 fl oz/⅔ cup) single (light) cream
75 ml (2½ fl oz/⅓ cup) double (thick) cream and 1 tablespoon finely chopped fresh watercress, to garnish

Melt the butter in a large saucepan, add mushrooms and cook gently for 5 minutes.

Stir in flour and cook for 1 minute, then gradually add stock and milk. Bring to the boil, then cover and simmer for 10 minutes. Add parsley, lemon juice and salt and pepper, then stir in single (light) cream and reheat gently.

When ready to serve, whip double (thick) cream until holding its shape and stir in watercress. Float a spoonful of the watercress chantilly on each portion, and serve at once.

Serves 4.

WATERCRESS & ALMOND SOUP

2 large bunches watercress
30 g (1 oz/6 teaspoons) butter
1 small onion, finely chopped
500 ml (16 fl oz/2 cups) vegetable stock
60 g (2 oz/⅓ cup) blanched almonds, toasted and ground
4 teaspoons cornflour
500 ml (16 fl oz/2 cups) milk
salt and pepper
flaked almonds, lightly toasted, to garnish

Wash watercress and reserve a few sprigs for garnish. Cut away any coarse stalks and chop remainder.

Melt butter in a saucepan, add onion and cook gently until soft. Add watercress and cook for 2 minutes, then stir in stock, cover and simmer for 10 minutes.

Purée in a blender or food processor and return to rinsed out pan with the ground almonds. Blend cornflour with a little of the milk, then add to pan with remaining milk and cook gently over a low heat for 5 minutes, stirring, until smooth. Remove from heat and set aside to cool. Refrigerate for at least 4 hours or overnight. Season, then serve garnished with a few toasted flaked almonds sprinkled on top and the reserved watercress sprigs.

Serves 4.

TOMATO, OLIVE & BREAD SOUP

900 g (2 lb) very ripe tomatoes
3 tablespoons olive oil
1 onion, chopped
2 cloves garlic, crushed
115 g (4 oz) stale Italian bread, cubed
1 tablespoon chopped fresh sage
150 ml (5 fl oz/⅔ cup) dry white wine
550 ml (20 fl oz/2½ cups) vegetable stock
1 tablespoon tomato purée (paste)
1 teaspoon balsamic vinegar
55 g (2 oz/½ cup) stoned black olives, finely chopped
15 g (½ oz/3 teaspoons) finely grated Parmesan cheese

Skin and seed the tomatoes over a bowl to catch any juices and finely chop the flesh; set aside. Heat the oil in a large saucepan and stir-fry the onion, garlic, bread and sage over a medium heat for 5 minutes until the bread is golden.

Add the wine and boil vigorously until almost evaporated, then stir in the tomatoes with any juices, stock, tomato purée (paste) and vinegar. Bring to the boil, cover and simmer for 15 minutes. Blend the olives and cheese together and use to garnish the soup.

Serves 6.

– THAI PRAWN & NOODLE SOUP –

425 ml (15 fl oz/scant 2 cups) fish stock
2 stalks lemon grass, crushed and chopped
2 small star anise pods
2 cloves garlic, chopped
425 ml (15 fl oz/scant 2 cups) coconut milk
8 large raw prawns, shelled
4 shelled scallops, halved horizontally
85 g (3 oz) clear vermicelli, soaked in cold water for 10 minutes then drained
2 spring onions, thinly sliced
2 fresh red chillies, seeded and sliced
juice 1½ limes
1 tablespoon fish sauce
1 tablespoon chopped fresh coriander

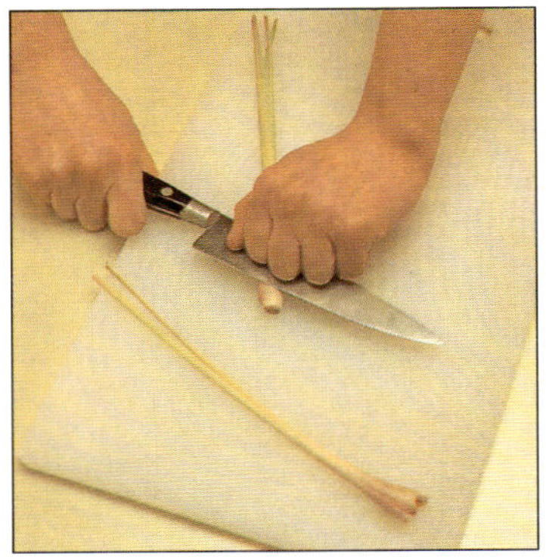

Bring stock to the boil in a saucepan, add lemon grass, star anise and garlic, then simmer, uncovered, for 5 minutes. Cover and leave to stand for 30 minutes.

Add coconut milk to pan and heat to simmering point. Add prawns and scallops, poach for 1 minute, then add noodles, spring onions and chillies and cook for a further minute until prawns are pink. Remove pan from heat and stir in lime juice, fish sauce and chopped coriander.

Serves 4.

MEDITERRANEAN FISH SOUP

1.15 kg (2½ lb) mixed fish and shellfish, such as monkfish, red mullet, bass, bream, snapper, prawns, mussels, cleaned
pinch saffron threads, toasted and crushed
5 tablespoons olive oil
2 Spanish onions, sliced
1 stick celery, sliced
3 cloves garlic, chopped
3 large tomatoes, peeled
bouquet garni of 1 bay leaf, sprig each dried thyme and fennel, 3 parsley sprigs and a strip dried orange peel
1.2 litres (2¼ pints/5½ cups) fish stock
salt and pepper
torn basil or chopped fresh parsley, to garnish
French bread, to serve

Skin and fillet fish and cut into fairly large pieces. Remove shellfish from their shells. Soak saffron in 2 tablespoons warm water for 10 minutes. In a large saucepan, heat oil. Add onions, celery and garlic and cook gently until softened. Chop tomatoes and add to pan with bouquet garni. Arrange fish on vegetables, add saffron liquid, then pour in sufficient stock to cover fish. Simmer, uncovered, for 6 minutes.

Add shellfish and mussels to pan and cook for a further 3-4 minutes until shellfish are just tender and mussels open; discard any mussels that remain closed. Season with salt and pepper. Serve garnished with basil or parsley and accompanied by French bread.

Serves 6.

CRAB & SWEETCORN SOUP

940 ml (1½ pints/3¾ cups) chicken stock
1 small knob fresh root ginger, peeled
2 teaspoons light soy sauce
3 teaspoons dry sherry
470 g (15 oz) can creamed sweetcorn
salt and pepper
2 teaspoons cornflour
125 g (4 oz) crabmeat, well drained if canned
2 eggs, beaten
2 spring onions, finely chopped, to garnish

Put stock into a saucepan with ginger, cover and simmer for 15 minutes. Remove ginger, then stir in soy sauce, sherry, sweetcorn and salt and pepper and simmer for 5 minutes.

Blend cornflour with 6 teaspoons water and stir into soup with crabmeat, stirring over medium heat until thickened.

With soup at a gentle simmer, slowly pour in beaten eggs in a thin stream, stirring constantly: do not boil. Serve garnished with chopped spring onions.

Serves 4-6.

CREAM OF CHICKEN SOUP

25 g (1oz/6 teaspoons) butter
1 small leek, washed and diced
45 g (1½ oz/¼ cup, plus 6 teaspoons) plain flour
850 ml (30 fl oz/3¾ cups) chicken stock
150 ml (5 fl oz/⅔ cup) dry white wine
115 g (4 oz) cooked chicken, finely chopped
pinch of ground nutmeg
150 ml (5 fl oz/⅔ cup) single (light) cream
2 teaspoons chopped fresh chives
150 ml (5 fl oz/⅔ cup) thick sour cream and croûtons, to serve

In a saucepan, melt the butter and gently sauté the leek until soft. Stir in the flour and cook over a low heat for 1-2 minutes.

Remove the pan from the heat and slowly add the stock, a little at a time, stirring well. Return to the heat and bring to the boil, stirring until thickened.

Add the wine, cover and simmer gently for 15 minutes; add the chicken and nutmeg and simmer for a further 5 minutes. Pour in the cream and heat gently without boiling, then stir in the chopped chives. Serve in warmed bowls with spoonfuls of thick sour cream and croûtons.

Serves 4.

MULLIGATAWNY

500 g (1 lb) piece shin of beef
5 cm (2 in) piece fresh root ginger, peeled
2 bay leaves
1 onion, chopped
1 teaspoon turmeric
½ teaspoon chilli powder
2 teaspoons coriander seeds, crushed
2 teaspoons cumin seeds, crushed
8 black peppercorns, crushed
1 small cooking apple, peeled, cored and chopped
1 carrot, sliced
30 g (1 oz/2 tablespoons) red lentils, rinsed
2 cloves garlic, chopped
salt
3 teaspoons lemon juice

Put beef into a large saucepan, pour in 1.9 litres (3 pints/7½ cups) water and bring to the boil. Skim surface, then add all remaining ingredients except lemon juice. Cover and simmer very gently for 2½-3 hours, until the beef is tender. Remove beef from the pan and set aside. Sieve soup into a bowl, rubbing vegetables through; discard pulp. Cool, then chill both the meat and stock.

To serve, remove solidified fat from surface of soup, then put into a pan and reheat. Cut beef into small pieces, add to soup with lemon juice and salt if necessary. Simmer for 5 minutes.

Serves 6.

COCK-A-LEEKIE SOUP

6 skinned chicken thighs
1 litre (35 fl oz/4½ cups) chicken stock
3 leeks

Place the chicken thighs in a large pan with the chicken stock and simmer gently for 35-40 minutes.

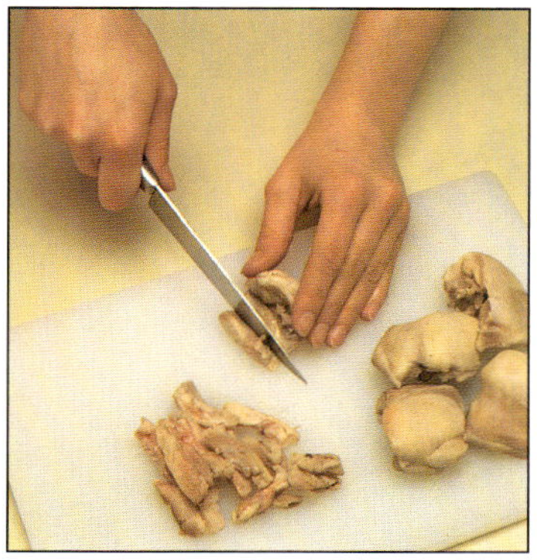

Meanwhile, trim the leeks and slice into rings. Remove the cooked chicken from the stock with a slotted spoon. Remove the meat from the bones and cut into bite-sized pieces. Put to one side.

Increase the heat and bring the stock to a fast simmer. Add the prepared leeks and cook for 3-4 minutes until the leeks are just tender. Add the chicken to the pan and simmer for 2-3 minutes. Serve hot with warm rolls.

Serves 4.

Variation: Add 12 ready-to-eat stoned and quartered prunes with the chicken in Step 3.

PHEASANT & LENTIL SOUP

1 small pheasant, cleaned
1 onion, thickly sliced
1 large carrot, thickly sliced
2 sticks celery, chopped
1 bay leaf
thyme sprig
8 black peppercorns
125 g (4 oz/⅔ cup) continental brown lentils, rinsed
2 small leeks, trimmed and chopped
salt and pepper

Put pheasant into a large saucepan with 1.9 litres (3 pints/7½ cups) water. Bring slowly to the boil, skimming off any scum which rises to the surface.

Add onion, carrot, celery, bay leaf, thyme and peppercorns, cover and simmer for 45 minutes. Lift out pheasant, and when cool enough to handle remove breast meat. Return carcass to pan and cook for a further 2 hours. Strain stock and when cool, place in the refrigerator with the reserved breast meat and best bits of leg meat. Leave overnight. Next day, remove fat from soup. Measure soup and return to pan. Bring to the boil, reduce to 1.5 litres (2½ pints/6 cups) by simmering, or make up with water if not enough.

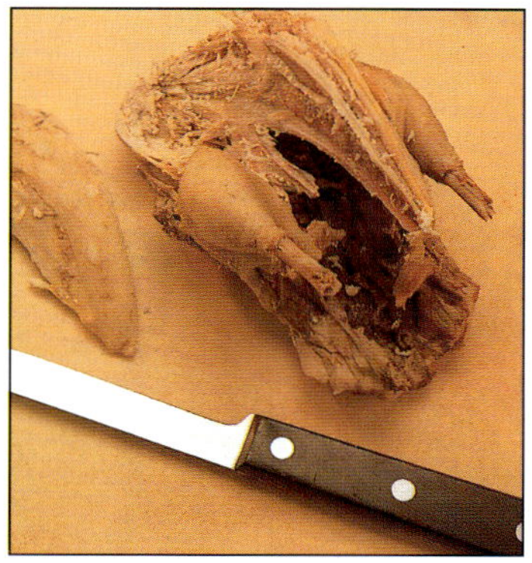

Add lentils and leeks to pan, cover and simmer for 45 minutes, or until lentils are tender. Meanwhile, dice reserved meat. Add to soup with salt and pepper and simmer a few minutes to heat through.

Serves 6.

SCOTCH BROTH

1 kg (2 lb) neck of lamb, cut into pieces
1.5 litres (2½ pints/6 cups) light stock
60 g (2 oz/¼ cup) pearl barley
salt and pepper
1 large onion, chopped
2 leeks, trimmed and chopped
2 sticks celery, chopped
1 small turnip, diced
1 large carrot, sliced
bouquet garni
1 tablespoon chopped fresh parsley, to garnish

Put lamb into a large saucepan with stock and slowly bring to the boil. Skim off any scum that rises to surface.

Add barley and salt and pepper, cover and simmer for 2 hours. Lift out lamb and take meat off bones. Discard fat, then return meat to pan.

Add remaining ingredients except parsley to soup and bring back to simmering point. Cover and cook for 30 minutes, or until the vegetables are tender. Discard bouquet garni, season if necessary and serve garnished with chopped parsley.

Serves 6.

GOULASH SOUP

6 teaspoons vegetable oil
500 g (1 lb) lean stewing meat, cut into 0.5 cm (¼ in) cubes
1 large onion, thinly sliced
1 clove garlic, crushed
½ teaspoon ground cumin
2 teaspoons paprika
3 teaspoons plain flour
1.2 litres (2 pints/5 cups) beef stock
1 large potato
440 g (14 oz) can chopped tomatoes
salt and pepper
thick sour cream and paprika, to garnish

Heat oil in a large saucepan; add beef cubes and onion.

Cook over medium heat for 4-6 minutes until meat is browned and onion soft. Stir in garlic, cumin, paprika and flour and cook for 1 minute. Gradually add stock and bring to the boil, then cover and simmer for 2 hours.

Dice potato and add to soup with tomatoes and their juice and salt and pepper. Continue cooking for 30 minutes, until potatoes are tender. Serve garnished with spoonfuls of sour cream, sprinkled with paprika.

Serves 6.

APPETIZERS & STARTERS

MINI QUICHES

1½ quantities Shortcrust Pastry
3 egg yolks
1 egg
salt and pepper, to taste
300 ml (10 fl oz/1¼ cups) whipping cream
MUSHROOM FILLING:
15 g (½ oz/3 teaspoons) butter
115 g (4 oz) mushrooms, finely chopped
PEPPER FILLING:
15 g (½ oz/3 teaspoons) butter
1 red pepper (capsicum), seeded and chopped

Preheat oven to 200C (400F/Gas 6). Grease 12 individual 6 cm (2½ in) flan tins.

To make mushroom filling, melt butter in a small pan. Add mushrooms and cook gently until soft and liquid has evaporated. Set aside. To make pepper filling, melt remaining butter in another small pan. Add the pepper (capsicum) and cook gently until beginning to soften. Set aside. On a floured surface, roll out pastry to 0.3cm (⅛ in) thick. Use to line prepared tins; prick bases with a fork.

Press a square of foil into each one; bake blind for 15 minutes, removing foil after 12 minutes. In a bowl, beat together egg yolks, egg, salt and pepper and cream. Put half the mixture in a bowl with the mushrooms and half in a bowl with the pepper (capsicum). Divide the 2 fillings between pastry cases. Return to the oven and cook for a further 15 minutes until just firm.

Makes 12.

SESAME CHICKEN TOASTS

2 large spring onions
2 cloves garlic, crushed
2.5 cm (1 in) piece fresh root ginger, finely chopped
225 g (8 oz) skinned and boned chicken
2 tablespoons cornflour
2 teaspoons light soy sauce
2 teaspoons oyster sauce
10 slices day-old white bread
55 g (2 oz/⅓ cup) sesame seeds
vegetable oil for frying

In a blender or food processor, process the onions, garlic, ginger, chicken, cornflour and the soy and oyster sauces until smooth.

Cut the crusts off the bread and spread each slice with a generous layer of chicken mixture. Sprinkle with a layer of sesame seeds and place in the refrigerator for at least 20 minutes.

Half-fill a deep fat pan or fryer with oil and heat to 190C (375F) or until a cube of day-old bread browns in 40 seconds. Cut each slice of bread into 3 and fry, a few at a time, until golden. Drain on absorbent kitchen paper and serve hot.

Makes 30.

CHICKEN APRICOT FILOS

½ tablespoon oil for frying, plus extra for brushing
½ onion, finely chopped
55 g (2 oz/½ cup) dried apricots, finely chopped
100 g (4 oz) cooked chicken, finely diced
4 tablespoons Greek yogurt
2 tablespoons chopped fresh coriander
salt and pepper
3 sheets filo pastry

Preheat oven to 190C (375F/Gas 5). In a small pan, heat the oil, add the onion and cook gently for 3-4 minutes without browning. Add the dried apricots and cook for a further 2 minutes.

Put the onion mixture into a bowl, add the chicken, yogurt, coriander and salt and pepper and mix well. Cut each sheet of filo pastry in half, then cut each half into 4 to form sixteen 10 cm (4 in) squares.

Brush each square with a little oil and place a spoonful of the chicken mixture in the centre. Gather up the corners of the filo pastry and pinch together to form a loose bag. Place the filo bags on 2 greased baking sheets and bake for 10-12 minutes or until the pastry is crisp and golden. Serve warm.

Makes 16.

ANGELS ON HORSEBACK

4 bacon slices, rinds removed
8 oysters, shelled
4 slices bread
unsalted butter for spreading
pepper
lamb's lettuce and lemon twists, to garnish

Preheat grill. Cut each bacon slice across in half, then stretch each piece with the back of a knife. Wrap a piece of bacon around each oyster and place on a grill rack with ends of bacon underneath.

Toast bread, then place oysters under grill until crisp, turn over and crisp the other side.

Meanwhile, cut 2 circles from each slice of toast and butter circles. Place an oyster on each circle, grind over black pepper and serve garnished with lamb's lettuce and lemon twists.

Makes 8.

CHEESE & HERB TRIANGLES

115 g (4 oz) feta cheese
115 g (4 oz) cottage cheese
½ egg, beaten
1 tablespoon chopped fresh parsley
1 tablespoon chopped fresh mint
1 tablespoon chopped fresh chives
pepper
4 sheets filo pastry
55 g (2 oz/¼ cup) butter

Crumble feta cheese into a bowl. Add cottage cheese, egg, parsley, mint, chives and pepper. Blend together with a fork.

Preheat oven to 190C (375F/Gas 5). Butter a baking sheet. Lay the sheets of filo in a pile on a work surface. Keep covered while working with one sheet at a time. In a small saucepan, melt butter. Brush one sheet of filo with butter. Cut it into 4 long strips.

Place a teaspoon of filling in one corner of filo strip. Fold a corner of pastry over filling. Turn triangle over and over to the end of the strip. Repeat with remaining pastry. Brush tops of triangles with butter. Bake in the oven for 10-12 minutes until crisp and brown.

Makes 16.

IMAM BAYALDI

2 small aubergines (eggplants)
salt
55 ml (2 fl oz/¼ cup) olive oil
1 large onion, chopped
1 clove garlic, crushed
1 red pepper (capsicum), seeded and chopped
6 teaspoons tomato purée (paste)
55 g (2 oz) sun-dried tomatoes in oil, drained and chopped
½ teaspoon sugar
1 teaspoon wine vinegar
pepper
toasted pine nuts and coriander sprigs, to garnish

Cut aubergines (eggplants) into 0.5 cm (¼ in) slices. Sprinkle with salt and put in a colander to drain for 30 minutes. Preheat oven to 180C (350F/Gas 4). In a frying pan, heat 2 tablespoons olive oil, add onion, garlic and red pepper (capsicum). Cook for about 10 minutes until onion is soft. Add tomato purée (paste), sun-dried tomatoes, sugar, vinegar and pepper.

Wipe aubergine (eggplant) slices dry with absorbent kitchen paper. Arrange slices in a baking tin. Put a teaspoonful of tomato mixture onto each aubergine (eggplant) slice. Drizzle remaining olive oil over and around aubergines (eggplants). Cover dish and bake for 40-50 minutes until aubergines (eggplants) are tender. Serve garnished with toasted pine nuts and sprigs of coriander.

Serves 6.

STUFFED ARTICHOKE BOTTOMS

6 hard-boiled eggs, finely chopped
7 - 9 tablespoons extra virgin olive oil
2 tablespoons white wine vinegar
½ red pepper (capsicum) packed in wine vinegar, drained and chopped
2 tablespoons capers in wine vinegar, drained and chopped
2 tablespoons chopped fresh Italian parsley
Salt and freshly ground black pepper
400 g (14 oz) can artichoke bottoms, drained
3 tablespoons extra virgin olive oil
Juice ½ lemon
1 teaspoon coriander seeds, crushed
Fresh Italian parsley sprigs to garnish

Place eggs in a bowl then, using a wooden spoon, gradually stir in 4 tablespoons of the oil and the vinegar; the mixture should be stiff enough to hold its shape but if too dry add a little more olive oil. Stir in pepper, capers and parsley and season with salt and freshly ground black pepper.

Divide egg mixture between artichoke bottoms and arrange on a serving plate. Trickle over remaining olive oil and lemon juice and sprinkle with coriander seeds. Chill for at least 1 hour. Serve garnished with Italian parsley sprigs.

Serves 4-6.

LEEKS À LA GRECQUE

8-10 young thin leeks
9 teaspoons olive oil
6 teaspoons lemon juice
1 clove garlic, crushed
salt and pepper
1 tablespoon chopped fresh mint
slivers of sun-dried tomatoes and mint leaves, to garnish

Cut root end off leeks and trim tops down to white part. Wash very carefully.

In a saucepan, put olive oil, lemon juice, 115 ml (4 fl oz/½ cup) water, garlic, salt and pepper. Bring to the boil. Add leeks, cover and cook for 10-15 minutes until leeks are tender.

Transfer leeks to a serving dish. If there is a lot of liquid, boil to reduce and thicken slightly, then pour it over the leeks. Scatter chopped mint over the top and leave until cold. Serve garnished with slivers of sun-dried tomatoes and mint leaves.

Serves 4-8.

Variation: Button onions may be cooked in the same way.

FRITTO MISTO

85 g (3 oz/¾ cup) plain (all-purpose) flour
Salt and freshly ground black pepper
2 eggs, beaten
225 g (8 oz/2 cups) dry white breadcrumbs
4 lamb's kidneys, halved and cored
225 g (8 oz) calves liver, cut into strips
1 small aubergine (eggplant) sliced
225 g (8 oz) spicy fresh Italian sausages, cut into bite-size pieces
2 medium courgettes (zucchini), thickly sliced
Sunflower or groundnut oil for frying
Fresh Italian parsley sprigs to garnish

Put flour and seasoning into a shallow dish. Put eggs in a separate dish and breadcrumbs in a third. Dip kidneys, liver, aubergine (eggplant) and courgettes (zucchini) first in flour then in egg and finally in breadcrumbs to coat evenly.

Half-fill a deep-fat frying pan with oil. Preheat to 180C (350F). Deep fry meat and vegetables in batches in the hot oil for 2-4 minutes, turning once, until crisp and golden. Using a slotted spoon transfer to absorbent kitchen paper to drain. Serve hot garnished with fresh Italian parsley sprigs.

Serves 6-8.

SPRING ROLLS

2 tablespoons vegetable oil
1 clove garlic, finely chopped
2.5 cm (1 in) piece fresh root ginger, finely chopped
115 g (4 oz) chicken breast, shredded
55 g (2 oz) mange tout (snow peas), finely sliced
175 g (6 oz) shiitake mushrooms, sliced
8 spring onions, finely chopped
55 g (2 oz) cooked peeled prawns, chopped
1 tablespoon soy sauce
1 teaspoon sesame oil
300 g (10 oz) filo pastry
1 egg white, for brushing
oil for deep frying
bottled chilli and hoisin sauces, to serve

In wok or large frying pan, heat the oil, add the garlic and ginger and stir-fry for 15 seconds, then add the chicken breast and continue cooking for 2-3 minutes. Add the mange tout (snow peas), mushrooms, spring onions and prawns, followed by the soy sauce and sesame oil. Mix well and transfer to a bowl to cool. Cut the filo pastry into sixteen 17.5 cm (7 in) squares. On a board, place one square of pastry diagonally towards you and cover with another square of pastry to give 2 layers.

Place a large tablespoon of mixture just below the centre of the pastry. Fold the bottom corner over and then the 2 side flaps to give an elongated open envelope. Brush with egg white and roll up, pressing gently. Repeat with the remaining filo pastry and filling. Half-fill a deep fat pan or fryer with oil and heat to 190C (375F). Fry the rolls, in 2 batches, for about 4 minutes or until golden Leave to drain on absorbent kitchen paper. Serve with chilli and hoisin sauces.

Serves 4.

DOLMADES

20 vacuum-packed vine leaves in brine
85 g (3 oz/½ cup) long-grain rice
salt and pepper
2 tablespoons olive oil
1 small onion, finely chopped
55 g (2 oz/⅓ cup) pine nuts
25 g (1 oz/¼ cup) raisins
2 tablespoons chopped fresh mint
¼ teaspoon ground cinnamon
2 teaspoons olive oil
6 teaspoons tomato purée (paste)
2 teaspoons lemon juice
lemon slices and fresh mint, to garnish (optional)

Rinse vine leaves and place in a saucepan of boiling water. Simmer for 5 minutes. Drain. Put rice into a pan of boiling salted water, cover and simmer until rice is almost cooked. Drain. In a frying pan, heat oil, then add onion and cook until soft. Add pine nuts and cook until lightly browned. Stir in raisins, mint, cinnamon, salt, pepper and rice. Leave to cool.

Trim stalks from vine leaves. Place a little filling on each leaf. Fold sides over and roll up. Line a saucepan with any damaged leaves. Place dolmades side by side in pan, to fit tightly. In a bowl, mix 300 ml (10 fl oz/1¼ cups) water, 2 teaspoons olive oil, tomato purée (paste) and lemon juice. Pour over dolmades. Place a plate on top. Cover pan and simmer for 1-1½ hours until liquid is absorbed and leaves are tender. Garnish with lemon and mint, if desired, and serve hot.

Makes 20.

FENNEL WITH FETA & PEARS

2 fennel bulbs
4 tablespoons olive oil
175 g (6 oz) vegetarian feta cheese
1 ripe pear
4 sun-dried tomatoes in oil, drained and sliced
25 g (1 oz/¼ cup) stoned black olives
a few basil leaves
1 teaspoon lemon juice
½ teaspoon clear honey
salt and pepper

Preheat grill. Trim the fennel, discarding any damaged outer leaves. Cut each bulb, lengthways, into 6 thin slices.

Brush with a little of the olive oil and place under the hot grill for 2-3 minutes until browned. Turn fennel, brush with oil and grill for a further 2-3 minutes until charred and just tender. Leave to cool slightly.

Slice the feta into thin slabs and quarter, core and thinly slice the pear. Arrange the fennel, cheese and pear on serving plates and top with the tomatoes, olives and basil. Blend the remaining oil, lemon juice, honey and seasonings together, drizzle over the salad and serve.

Serves 4.

PRAWNS WITH MELON

12 cooked Mediterranean prawns
1 small Charentais melon
1 small Galia or Ogen melon
Juice 1 small lemon
Salt and freshly ground black pepper
Fresh mint leaves, to garnish

Peel prawns leaving tail tips on, if desired.

Cut melons into thin wedges and remove skins.

Arrange prawns and the two varieties of melon on a serving plate or individual plates and sprinkle with lemon juice. Season with salt and freshly ground black pepper. Serve garnished with fresh mint leaves.

Serves 4-6.

CRAB & GINGER TRIANGLES

200 g (7 oz) can crabmeat, drained
6 spring onions, finely chopped
2.5 cm (1 in) piece fresh root ginger, peeled and grated
2 teaspoons soy sauce
salt and pepper
6 large sheets filo pastry about 35 cm (14 in) square
85 g (3 oz/1/3 cup) butter, melted
TO GARNISH:
spring onion slivers or tassels

In a bowl, mix together crabmeat, spring onions, ginger, soy sauce and salt and pepper. Set aside.

Preheat oven to 180C (350F/Gas 4). Lightly grease a baking sheet. Work with 1 sheet of pastry at a time, keeping the rest covered with a damp cloth. Cut sheet of pastry in half. Brush each half with melted butter and fold in half lengthways. Brush pastry all over with melted butter. Put a portion of crab mixture in 1 corner of 1 strip of pastry. Fold pastry and filling over at right angles to make a triangle and continue folding in this way along strip of pastry to make a triangular parcel.

Repeat with remaining pastry and crab mixture. Brush each parcel with melted butter. Bake in the oven for 20-25 minutes until crisp and golden brown. Serve warm, garnished with spring onion slivers or tassels.

Makes 12.

PRAWN & FETA TARTS

175 g (6 oz) peeled cooked prawns
115 g (4 oz) feta cheese
fresh basil leaves, to garnish
PASTRY:
175 g (6 oz/1½ cups) plain flour
½ teaspoon salt
9 teaspoons olive oil
1 egg, beaten
TOMATO SAUCE:
6 teaspoons olive oil
1 onion, chopped
1 clove garlic, crushed
200 g (7 oz) can chopped tomatoes
3 teaspoons chopped sun-dried tomato
2 teaspoons chopped fresh basil
salt and pepper

To make the pastry, sift flour and ½ teaspoon salt into a bowl. With a fork, mix in olive oil, egg and 1-2 teaspoons water to make a firm dough. Knead lightly, wrap in plastic wrap and chill for 1 hour. Make tomato sauce. Heat oil in a frying pan, add onion and garlic; cook until soft. Add tomatoes and sun-dried tomato. Cook for 5-10 minutes until sauce is very thick. Stir in basil, salt and pepper. Preheat oven to 200C (400F/Gas 6).

On a floured surface, roll out pastry thinly. Line four 10 cm (4 in) loose-bottom flan tins with pastry and press a piece of foil into each. Bake in the oven for 10 minutes. Remove foil; cook for a further 5 minutes. Divide prawns between pastry cases. Crumble cheese over. Spread tomato sauce over cheese and prawns. Bake for 5 minutes. Serve garnished with basil leaves.

Serves 4.

SEAFOOD PARCELS

85 g (3 oz/⅔ cup) butter
25 g (1 oz/¼ cup) flour
150 ml (5 fl oz/⅔ cup) milk
6 teaspoons lemon juice
1 clove garlic, crushed
1 tablespoon each chopped fresh mint, chopped fresh coriander and chopped fresh parsley
pinch cayenne pepper
pinch paprika
½ teaspoon ground cumin
salt
85 g (3 oz) cooked mussels
55 g (2 oz) cooked peeled prawns
55 g (2 oz) cooked squid or white fish
6 sheets filo pastry

Preheat oven to 190C (375F/Gas 5). In a saucepan, melt 25 g (1 oz/6 teaspoons) butter. Stir in flour, then gradually add milk. Stirring, heat sauce until thick. Stir in lemon juice, garlic, mint, coriander, parsley, cayenne, paprika, cumin and salt. Add mussels, prawns and squid or white fish.

Melt remaining butter. Brush over 1 sheet filo pastry, place another sheet on top and butter it. Repeat with 2 more layers of pastry. Cut into 12 squares. Butter remaining 2 sheets of pastry. Place one on top of the other. Cut in half. Pile the 4 sheets together; cut into 6 squares. Place some filling in middle of each square. Draw pastry up and pinch together to form pouches. Bake for 30 minutes or until brown and crisp.

Makes 18.

STUFFED MUSSELS

1.5 kg (3 lb) large mussels in their shells
85 ml (3 fl oz/1/3 cup) dry white wine
85 ml (3 fl oz/1/3 cup) olive oil
25 g (1 oz/1/2 cup) fresh breadcrumbs
3 tablespoons finely chopped fresh parsley
1 tablespoon finely chopped fresh oregano
2 cloves garlic, finely crushed
pinch cayenne pepper
salt and freshly ground black pepper
1 large lemon, quartered
parsley sprigs and lemon slices, to garnish

Scrub mussels and remove beards. Discard any mussels that remain open when tapped firmly. Put in a large saucepan with wine.

Cover and boil for 4-5 minutes, shaking pan occasionally, until shells open. Strain and reserve liquid. Discard any shells that do not open. Discard top shells, leaving mussels on remaining shells. In a small bowl, stir together 3 tablespoons oil, the breadcrumbs, herbs, garlic, cayenne and salt and pepper. Moisten with a little of the reserved mussel cooking liquid, if mixture is dry.

Preheat grill. Divide breadcrumb mixture between mussels on their shells. Place on a baking tray. Sprinkle with remaining olive oil and place under hot grill for 1-2 minutes until topping is crisp and golden. Squeeze over plenty of lemon juice and serve garnished with parsley sprigs and lemon slices.

Serves 4-6.

PIQUANT SALMON ROLLS

60 g (2 oz) cream cheese
30 g (1 oz/1/4 cup) walnuts, chopped
1 tablespoon chopped fresh chives
1 stick celery, chopped
2 teaspoons lemon juice
several pinches of cayenne pepper
1/4 teaspoon ground coriander
8 thin slices of smoked salmon, about 5 cm (2 in) wide and 10 cm (4 in) long
8 thin slices brown bread
a little butter for spreading
8 thin slices of cucumber
freshly ground black pepper
sprigs of dill and chives, to garnish

In a bowl, soften cream cheese.

Stir walnuts, chives and celery into cheese. Add 1 teaspoon lemon juice and spices and mix well, then divide equally into 8 and spread each portion on a slice of salmon and roll up to form neat rolls.

Toast bread and cut out eight 6 cm (2½ in) rounds, using a biscuit cutter. Spread thinly with butter. Arrange a cucumber slice on each one and put a salmon roll on top. Drizzle with remaining lemon juice and sprinkle with pepper. Garnish with dill and chives.

Serves 4.

Note: The salmon rolls can be prepared several hours in advance and kept chilled. The toast bases however, are nicer eaten freshly made.

TUNA PÂTÉ

45 g (1½ oz) butter
4 spring onions (scallions), white part only, chopped
2 sticks celery, finely chopped
200 g (7 oz) can tuna in brine, drained
2 tomatoes, skinned, seeded and chopped
2 tablespoon prepared mayonnaise
1 teaspoon lemon juice
1 teaspoon white wine vinegar
Salt and freshly ground black pepper
Chopped fresh Italian parsley and stoned green olives to garnish
Crusty bread or toast to serve

Melt butter in a small frying pan. Add spring onions (scallions) and celery and cook gently for 5 minutes, to soften. Leave to cool.

Put cooled spring onions (scallions) mixture in a food processor or blender with remaining ingredients and process until fairly smooth. Transfer to a serving dish, cover and refrigerate for at least 30 minutes. Garnish with chopped Italian parsley and stoned green olives and serve with crusty bread or toast.

Serves 4-6.

SIZZLING PRAWNS

100 ml (3½ fl oz/scant ½ cup) olive oil
4 cloves garlic, finely crushed
1 small fresh red chilli, seeded and chopped
350 g (12 oz) raw prawns, peeled
sea salt
2 tablespoons chopped fresh parsley
lemon wedges and bread, to serve

Heat oil in 4 individual flameproof earthenware dishes over a high heat. Add garlic and chilli, cook for 1-2 minutes, then add prawns and sea salt.

Cook briskly for 2-3 minutes. Stir in parsley. Serve quickly so the prawns are sizzling in the oil, and accompany with lemon wedges and bread to mop up the juices.

Note: One large dish, or a frying pan, can be used instead of individual dishes.

Serves 4.

CHICKEN & HAM MOUSSE

175 g (6 oz) cooked chicken, finely minced
115 g (4 oz) cooked ham, finely minced
1 tablespoon lemon juice
1 tablespoon chopped fresh parsley
1 tablespoon chopped fresh chives
150 ml (5 fl oz/⅔ cup) mayonnaise
2 teaspoons powdered gelatine
3 tablespoons chicken stock
150 ml (5 fl oz/⅔ cup) double (thick) cream

In a bowl, mix the chicken with the ham, lemon juice, chopped herbs and mayonnaise.

In a small pan, sprinkle the gelatine over the chicken stock and leave for 5 minutes to soften. Melt very gently over a low heat until gelatine dissolves, then cool and fold into the ham and chicken mixture.

Lightly beat the cream to form soft peaks and then carefully fold into the chicken and ham mixture. Pour the mixture into a 1 litre (35 fl oz/4½ cups) mould and leave to set in the refrigerator for 2-3 hours. Unmould carefully and garnish with fresh herbs. Serve with hot crusty rolls.

Serves 4.

CHICKEN SATAY

1 tablespoon grated fresh root ginger
1 teaspoon ground coriander
1 teaspoon turmeric
½ teaspoon chilli powder
1 teaspoon brown sugar
2 tablespoons light soy sauce
2 tablespoons seasame oil
2 cloves garlic, crushed
juice of 1 lime
350 g (12 oz) skinned and boned chicken breasts, cut into long, thin strips
85 g (3 oz) onion, chopped
55 g (2 oz) creamed coconut
1 teaspoon chilli powder
150 ml (5 fl oz/⅔ cup) boiling water
55 g (2 oz/3 tablespoons) crunchy peanut butter

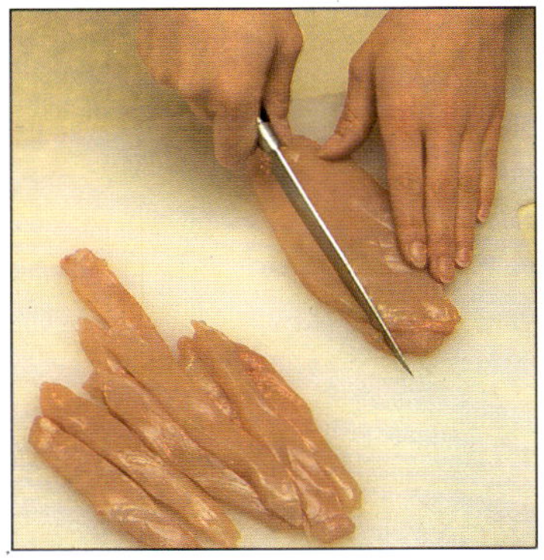

In a blender or food processor, blend together the ginger, coriander, turmeric, chilli, sugar, soy sauce, 1 tablespoon sesame oil, garlic and the lime juice; pour over the chicken strips and leave to marinate for 3-4 hours. To make the sauce, sauté half the onion in the remaining sesame oil until soft.

In a blender or food processor, blend the remaining half of the onion, creamed coconut and chilli powder with the boiling water. Add this paste to the sautéed onion, stir in the peanut butter and 2 tablespoons of the marinade, bring to the boil and simmer for 5 minutes until thickened. Preheat grill. Thread the chicken onto skewers and cook under the hot grill for 15-20 minutes turning frequently. Serve with the peanut sauce for dipping.

Serves 4.

GRILLED FIVE-SPICE CHICKEN

2 x 175 g (6 oz) skinless, boneless chicken breasts, trimmed
2 small red peppers (capsicum), halved
2 small yellow peppers (capsicum), halved
chopped fresh chives, to garnish
MARINADE:
1 clove garlic, crushed
1 fresh red chilli, seeded and chopped
3 tablespoons light soy sauce
1 teaspoon five-spice powder
1 teaspoon brown sugar
2 teaspoons sesame oil

Using a small sharp knife, score the chicken breasts on both sides in a criss-cross pattern, taking care not to slice all the way through. Place in a shallow dish with the peppers (capsicum). Mix together the marinade ingredients, pour over the chicken and peppers (capsicum) and turn to coat. Cover and chill for 1 hour.

Preheat grill. Remove chicken and peppers (capsicum) from marinade, place on grill rack and grill for 4-5 minutes on each side, basting with marinade, until chicken is cooked through. Slice chicken breasts and serve with a piece of red and yellow pepper (capsicum), garnished with chives.

Serves 4.

CHICKEN LIVER TOASTS

3 tablespoons olive oil
1 stick celery, finely chopped
2 cloves garlic, crushed
225 g (8 oz) chicken livers, chopped
1 teaspoon chopped fresh sage
4 tablespoons marsala
2 anchovy fillets canned in oil, drained
1 tablespoon capers in wine vinegar, drained
Freshly ground black pepper
1 medium stick French bread
Capers and sage leaves to garnish

Preheat oven to 190C (375F/Gas 5). Heat oil in a large frying pan. Add celery and garlic and cook for 2 minutes to soften.

Add chicken livers and fry over a high heat, stirring occasionally, for about 3 minutes until crisp and brown on the outside but just pink inside. Using a wooden spoon, stir in sage and marsala, scraping up all the cooking juices; transfer to a blender or food processor and add anchovy fillets and capers. Season with freshly ground black pepper and process until fairly smooth. To keep hot transfer to a warmed plate, cover and put over a saucepan of hot water.

Cut bread diagonally into thick slices and lay on a baking tray. Bake in the oven for 6-7 minutes, until golden. Serve chicken liver paste on the baked bread, garnishing each piece with capers and a sage leaf.

Serves 6-8.

SOUVLAKIA

2 cloves garlic, crushed
55 ml (2 fl oz/¼ cup) lemon juice
2 tablespoons olive oil
4 tablespoons chopped fresh oregano
salt and pepper
450 g (1 lb) lean lamb
6 bay leaves
oregano sprigs, to garnish
RED PEPPER SAUCE:
3 teaspoons olive oil
1 small onion, chopped
2 red peppers (capsicums), seeded and chopped
225 ml (8 fl oz/1 cup) chicken stock

In a bowl, mix together garlic, lemon juice, olive oil, oregano, salt and pepper. Cut lamb into 2 cm (¾ in) cubes. Put lamb into marinade. Mix well to coat lamb with marinade. Leave in a cool place for 2 hours. To make the sauce, in a saucepan, heat oil, add onion and cook until soft. Add red peppers (capsicums); cook over low heat for 5 minutes. Pour in stock and simmer for 10 minutes. Push through a sieve or purée in a blender or food processor.

Thread lamb onto skewers, placing bay leaves on skewers at intervals. Grill on a barbecue or under a hot grill, turning from time to time, for 10 minutes or until lamb is brown and crisp on the outside and pink and juicy inside. Garnish with oregano and serve with the sauce.

Serves 6.

PORK & LIVER PÂTÉ

350 g (12 oz) unsmoked streaky bacon slices
225 g (8 oz) pork shoulder, chopped
225 g (8 oz) pigs liver, chopped
225 g (8 oz) pork sausagemeat
1 small onion, chopped
2 cloves garlic, chopped
1 tablespoons chopped fresh thyme
1 tablespoon chopped fresh oregano
3 tablespoons marsala
Salt and freshly ground black pepper
Fresh herb sprigs to garnish

Preheat oven to 170C (325F/Gas 3). Grease a 450 g (1 lb) loaf tin. Lay bacon slices on a board and stretch using the back of a knife.

Line the loaf tin with the bacon slices, reserving a few slices to cover top. Place pork shoulder in a blender or food processor and process until finely chopped. Add remaining ingredients and process briefly until well blended but not smooth. Put pork mixture into prepared loaf tin, smooth top and cover with remaining bacon. Cover tightly with foil.

Place loaf tin in a roasting tin half-filled with boiling water. Cook in the preheated oven for 1½-1¾ hours until firm. Remove foil. Cover pâté with greaseproof paper then put a plate or board and a heavy weight on top; leave until cold. Chill overnight. Serve sliced, garnished with fresh herb sprigs.

Serves 6-8.

PORK SATAY

350 g (12 oz) lean pork, cubed
juice 1 lime
1 stalk lemon grass, finely chopped
1 clove garlic, chopped
2 tablespoons vegetable oil
SAUCE:
4 tablespoons vegetable oil
85 g (3 oz/$\frac{1}{2}$ cup) raw shelled peanuts
2 stalks lemon grass, chopped
2 fresh red chillies, seeded and sliced
3 shallots, chopped
2 cloves garlic, chopped
1 teaspoon fish paste
2 teaspoons crushed palm sugar
315 ml (10 fl oz/1$\frac{1}{4}$ cups) coconut milk
juice $\frac{1}{2}$ lime

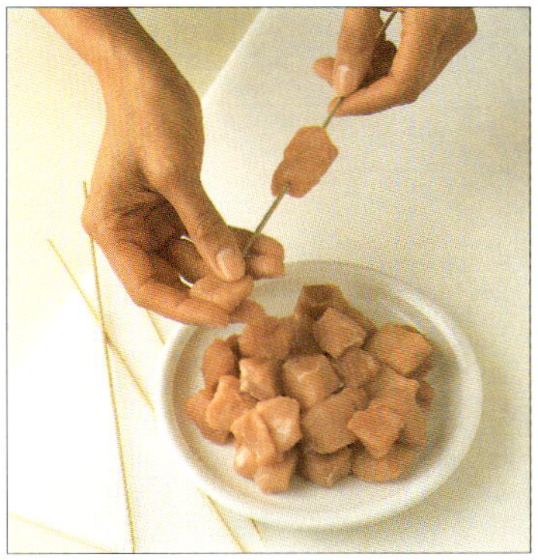

Divide pork between 4 skewers and lay them in a shallow dish. In a bowl, mix together lime juice, lemon grass, garlic and oil. Pour over pork, turn to coat, cover and set aside in a cool place for 1 hour, turning occasionally.

Preheat grill. Remove pork from dish, allowing excess liquid to drain off. Grill, turning frequently and basting, for 8-10 minutes.

Meanwhile, make sauce. Over a high heat, heat 1 tablespoon oil in a wok, add nuts and cook, stirring constantly, for 2 minutes. Using a slotted spoon, transfer to absorbent kitchen paper to drain. Using a pestle and mortar or small blender, grind to a paste. Remove and set aside.

Using a pestle and mortar or small blender, pound or mix lemon grass, chillies, shallots, garlic and fish paste to a smooth paste.

Heat remaining oil in wok, add spice mixture and cook, stirring, for 2 minutes. Stir in peanut paste, sugar and coconut milk. Bring to boil, stirring, then adjust heat so sauce simmers. Add lime juice and simmer, stirring, for 5-10 minutes until thickened. Serve in a warmed bowl to accompany pork.

Serves 4.

CARPACCIO

300 g (10 oz) piece beef fillet
85 g (3 oz) piece Parmesan, thinly sliced
225 g (8 oz) button mushrooms, thinly sliced
Leaves from 8 sprigs fresh Italian parsley
DRESSING:
115 ml (4 fl oz/½ cup) extra virgin olive oil
Juice 2 lemons
1 clove garlic, chopped
Salt and freshly ground black pepper

Put beef in freezer for 30 minutes. Using a very sharp knife, cut beef into wafer thin slices.

Lay beef slices in centre of a large serving plate and arrange Parmesan slices, mushrooms and parsley around edge.

To make dressing, whisk together all dressing ingredients in a small bowl or put in a screw-top jar and shake until thoroughly blended. Pour over beef, Parmesan, mushrooms and parsley.

Serves 6.

LAYERED COUNTRY TERRINE

8 rashers rindless, smoked streaky bacon
115 g (4 oz) chicken livers
115 g (4 oz) minced pork
115 g (4 oz) herby sausagemeat
1 clove garlic
1 onion, finely chopped
3 tablespoons chopped fresh parsley
25 g (1 oz/½ cup) fresh white breadcrumbs
55 ml (2 fl oz/¼ cup) brandy
1 small egg, beaten
¼ teaspoon freshly grated nutmeg
1 teaspoon finely grated lemon rind
salt and pepper
2 skinned and boned chicken breasts
1 bay leaf

Preheat oven to 180C (350F/Gas 4). Place the bacon on a board and stretch with the back of a knife. Use 4 rashers to line a 1.2 litre (40 fl oz/5 cup) loaf tin, reserving 4 rashers for the top. Roughly chop the chicken livers, mix them together with the pork, sausagemeat, garlic, onion and parsley. Soak the breadcrumbs in the brandy, then add to the meat mixture with the egg, nutmeg, lemon rind and seasonings.

Spread one third of the meat mixture over the bacon in the tin. Cut the chicken into very thin slices and layer half over the meat mixture. Cover with half the remaining meat mixture, then cover with the remaining chicken and the rest of the meat mixture. Lay the reserved bacon on top and add the bay leaf. Cover with foil. Stand the terrine in a baking tin three-quarters full of boiling water. Bake for 1½ hours. Allow to cool. Serve with crusty bread, salad and spiced chutney.

Serves 4-6.

FONDUTA

450 g (1 lb) fontina cheese, diced
300 ml (10 fl oz/1¼ cups) milk
55 g (2 oz) unsalted butter, melted
4 large egg yolks
Freshly ground black pepper
Fresh Italian parsley sprigs to garnish
Grissini, crusty bread or toast, for dipping

Place cheese and milk in a bowl. Leave for at least 2 hours to soften. Transfer to a double boiler or a heatproof bowl set over a pan of simmering water and heat until cheese melts and becomes stringy. Stir in butter and remove from heat.

Beat egg yolks in a small bowl then stir in a little of the hot cheese mixture. Pour back into remaining cheese mixture. Return to the heat and beat vigorously until smooth, creamy and thickened. Season with freshly ground black pepper.

Transfer to a serving dish (the dish is usually kept hot at table over a candle or spirit burner), garnish with Italian parsley sprigs and serve with grissini, crusty bread or toast for dipping.

Serves 6.

Note: If fontina cheese is not available a mixture of 225 g (8 oz) Gruyere and 225 g (8 oz) Edam is a good substitute.

MOZZARELLA FRITTERS

450 g (1 lb) mozzarella cheese
85 g (3 oz/¾ cup) plain (all-purpose) flour
1 teaspoon paprika
Salt and freshly ground black pepper
2 eggs, beaten
225 g (8 oz/2 cups) dried white breadcrumbs
Groundnut or vegetable oil for deep-frying
Fresh sage leaves to garnish

Cut mozzarella into 3.5 cm (1½ inch) cubes. Mix flour, paprika, salt and pepper in a shallow dish. Put eggs into a second dish and breadcrumbs in a third.

Coat cheese cubes lightly in the seasoned flour, dip into egg then into breadcrumbs to coat evenly. Repeat once more with egg and breadcrumbs.

Half-fill a deep-fat frying pan with oil. Preheat to 180C (350F). Deep fry a few cheese cubes at a time in the hot oil for about 2 minutes until golden. Using a slotted spoon, transfer to absorbent kitchen paper to drain. Serve hot, garnished with sage leaves.

Serves 4-6.

GOATS CHEESE TARTS

- 1-2 teaspoons extra virgin olive oil
- 25 g (1 oz) butter
- 115 g (4 oz/2 cups) soft white breadcrumbs
- 1 tablespoon sesame seeds
- 175 g (6 oz/3/4 cup) soft goats cheese
- 4 sun-dried tomatoes in oil, drained
- 4 basil fresh leaves
- 1 teaspoon finely chopped fresh mint
- Salt and freshly ground black pepper
- Mixed salad leaves to garnish, if desired

Use olive oil to grease four 7.5-10 cm (3-4 inch) tartlet tins.

Preheat oven to 200C (400F/Gas 6). Melt butter in a small saucepan and stir in breadcrumbs and sesame seeds. Divide between prepared tartlet tins, pressing firmly into base and sides. Bake in the preheated oven for 12-15 minutes until crisp and light golden. Carefully remove tartlets from tins and place on a baking sheet.

Divide goats cheese between tartlets and top each with a sun-dried tomato. Season with salt and freshly ground black pepper. Return to oven for 8-10 minutes to heat through. Serve hot or warm with a basil leaf and a sprinkling of chopped mint on each tart. Garnish with mixed salad leaves, if desired.

Serves 4.

RICOTTA MOULDS

- 350 g (12 oz/1½ cups) ricotta cheese
- 1 tablespoon finely chopped fresh Italian parsley
- 1 tablespoon chopped fresh fennel
- 1 tablespoon snipped fresh chives
- 1 tablespoon gelatine
- 150 ml (5 fl oz/2/3 cups) prepared mayonnaise
- Salt and freshly ground black pepper
- Fresh chives, fennel and Italian parsley sprigs to garnish

PEPPER (CAPSICUM) SAUCE

- 2 large red peppers (capsicums), grilled, deseeded and chopped, see page 42
- 3 tablespoons extra virgin olive oil
- Few drops balsamic vinegar
- Salt and freshly ground black pepper

In a bowl, mix together ricotta and herbs. Oil six 115-150 ml (4-5 fl oz/½ cup) moulds. In a small bowl, soak gelatine in 3 tablespoons cold water for 2 minutes. Place bowl over a saucepan of simmering water, stirring until dissolved. Cool slightly, then stir into cheese mixture with mayonnaise and salt and freshly ground black pepper. Divide between moulds and chill until set.

To make sauce, put peppers (capsicums) and oil in a food processor or blender and process until smooth. Add a few drops of balsamic vinegar and season with salt and freshly ground black pepper. Chill until required. To serve, turn out moulds onto individual plates; spoon the pepper (capsicum) sauce around the moulds and garnish with fresh herbs.

Serves 6.

MOZZARELLA TOASTS

12 thick slices French stick or slim Italian loaf
70 ml (2½ fl oz/⅓ cup) extra virgin olive oil
1 teaspoon finely chopped fresh Italian parsley
14 anchovy fillets canned in oil, drained
450 g (1 lb) mozzarella cheese, cut into 12 slices
Freshly ground black pepper
Fresh Italian parsley sprigs to garnish

Preheat grill. Arrange bread in one layer on a baking sheet. Toast both sides until golden.

Meanwhile put oil, parsley and two of the anchovy fillets in a small saucepan. Heat gently to warm, stirring with a fork to break up anchovies. Trickle oil mixture over toasted bread and top each piece with a slice of mozzarella. Season with freshly ground black pepper.

Garnish toasts with remaining anchovy fillets and return to grill for 2-3 minutes until cheese is hot and bubbling. Serve at once garnished with Italian parsley sprigs.

Serves 6.

ASPARAGUS & EGG SALAD

1 kg (2 lb) asparagus
7 eggs, hard-boiled
6 tablespoons olive oil
2 tablespoons white wine vinegar
2 small pickled gherkins, finely chopped
Salt and freshly ground black pepper
Chopped fresh Italian parsley and sprigs to garnish

Snap off and discard woody ends of asparagus stems. Using a small, sharp knife, scrape stems, rinse then tie into small bundles using string.

Stand bundles upright in a deep pan of boiling salted water so tips are above water. Cover, making a dome of foil, if necessary. Boil for 15 minutes until tips are just tender. Drain, refresh under cold running water, drain, untie bundles and leave to cool.

Finely chop four hard-boiled eggs and place in a bowl. Using a wooden spoon stir in oil, vinegar and gherkins. Season with salt and ground black pepper. Set aside. Quarter remaining eggs and arrange with asparagus around edge of a serving plate. Pour egg sauce into centre and sprinkle with chopped Italian parsley. Garnish with Italian parsley sprigs.

Serves 4-6.

BAGNA CAUDA

2 × 50 g (1¾ oz) cans anchovy fillets, drained and roughly chopped
300 ml (10 fl oz/1¼ cups) whipping cream
3 cloves garlic, crushed
55 g (2 oz) unsalted butter, diced
Fresh Italian parsley sprigs to garnish
TO SERVE:
Cubes crusty bread
Grissini
Vegetables for dipping, such as fennel, celery, peppers (capsicum), radishes, chicory, broccoli

Put anchovies in a small saucepan with cream and garlic. Bring to the boil then lower the heat and simmer gently, uncovered and stirring occasionally, for 12-15 minutes until smooth and thickened.

Stir in butter. Transfer to a serving dish and garnish with parsley. Serve with cubes of bread, grissini and vegetables for dipping.

Serves 4.

Note: Traditionally, the serving dish is kept hot at the table like a fondue, over a candle or spirit burner.

CANNELINI BEAN PASTE

225 g (8 oz) dried cannelini beans, soaked overnight and drained
½ teaspoon hot red pepper flakes
2 teaspoons tomato purée (paste)
2 sprigs fresh rosemary
25 g (1 oz) butter
2 tablespoons extra virgin olive oil
1 clove garlic, finely chopped
1 tablespoon finely chopped fresh oregano
175-225 ml (6-8 fl oz/¾ cup - 1 cup) hot chicken stock
Juice 1 lemon
Salt and freshly ground black pepper
Toasted crusty bread, vegetable sticks or warmed crusty bread to serve
Fresh rosemary sprigs to garnish

Put beans in a saucepan with 900 ml (32 fl oz/4 cups) water, the red pepper flakes, tomato purée (paste) and rosemary sprigs. Bring to the boil then lower the heat, cover and simmer gently for 2 hours until most of the water has been absorbed and beans are very tender. Discard rosemary. In a food processor or blender, purée beans and remaining liquid until very smooth.

Heat butter and oil in a medium saucepan. Add garlic and oregano. Cook for 2 minutes. Stir in bean purée and hot stock and cook gently for 10-12 minutes, stirring frequently, until mixture is very thick. Remove from heat, stir in lemon juice and season with salt and freshly ground black pepper. Serve either hot spread on toasted crusty bread or cold with fresh vegetable sticks or warmed crusty bread. Garnish with rosemary sprigs.

Serves 6.

SALADS

GRILLED PEPPER SALAD

1 large red pepper (capsicum)
1 large green pepper (capsicum)
1 large yellow pepper (capsicum)
1 small red onion, sliced
16 black olives
2 teaspoons chopped fresh basil
2 teaspoons chopped fresh thyme
DRESSING:
3 tablespoons extra virgin olive oil
1 tablespoon red wine vinegar
1 clove garlic, finely chopped
Pinch granulated sugar
Salt and freshly ground black pepper

To make dressing, mix all ingredients together in a small bowl, or shake together in a screw-top jar. Set aside. Preheat grill. Place whole peppers (capsicum) under hot grill for about 10 minutes, turning occasionally, until skins are evenly blistered and charred. Transfer peppers to a plastic bag for a few minutes, then peel away and discard skins.

Cut peppers in half, discard seeds and cut into strips. Place in salad bowl with onions and olives. Shake dressing and pour over salad. Toss gently to mix and sprinkle over herbs.

Serves 4.

COURGETTE SALAD

2 tablespoons pine nuts
450 g (1 lb) courgettes (zucchini)
2 tablespoons olive oil
1 clove garlic, crushed
2 tablespoons currants
2 teaspoons chopped fresh mint
juice ½ lemon
salt and pepper
2 spring onions

Put pine nuts in a large frying pan and cook, stirring, until just beginning to brown. Remove pine nuts and reserve. Top and tail courgettes (zucchini) and slice thinly.

Heat oil in frying pan, add courgettes (zucchini), garlic, currants and pine nuts. Cook, stirring, until courgettes (zucchini) are just beginning to soften and brown slightly.

Stir in mint, lemon juice, salt and pepper. Transfer to a serving dish and leave until cold. Slice the spring onions and scatter them over the top.

Serves 4.

BEAN & ONION SALAD

350 g (12 oz) French beans, topped and tailed
1 onion, thinly sliced
2 tablespoons capers in vinegar, drained
6 tablespoon extra virgin olive oil
Juice 1 lemon
½ teaspoon hot red pepper flakes
Pinch granulated sugar
Salt and freshly ground black pepper
2 teaspoons chopped fresh Italian parsley
1 teaspoon chopped fresh mint

Cook beans in boiling salted water for 3-4 minutes so they remain crisp. Drain and refresh under cold running water. Drain well. Place in a bowl with onion and capers.

Put olive oil, lemon juice and red pepper flakes, sugar, salt and ground black pepper, in a small bowl or screw-top jar. Beat or shake together to mix well.

Add dressing and herbs to salad, mix well.

Serves 4-6.

MUNG BEANSPROUT SALAD

185 g (6 oz/1 cup) mung beans
2 green chillies, seeded and chopped
2.5 cm (1 in) piece fresh root ginger, grated
30 g (1 oz/⅔ cup) fresh coconut, shredded
½ cucumber, diced
juice of 1 lemon
salt and pepper
1 mango
2 tablespoons vegetable oil
½ teaspoon mustard seeds
coriander leaves and shreds of lemon peel, to garnish, if desired

Wash beans, put in a bowl and cover with cold water.

Soak beans in the water for 30 minutes. Drain, then place in a sprouting tray or wrap in a damp tea-towel and leave for about 2 days, rinsing thoroughly every 12 hours, until the beans germinate. Rinse well and drain. Place sprouts in a bowl and stir in chillies, ginger, coconut, cucumber and lemon juice. Season with salt and pepper.

Peel and stone mango, then dice flesh and stir into salad. Heat oil in a small pan and add mustard seeds and fry for 1 minute, until they begin to pop. Pour contents of pan over the salad and toss well to combine. Chill for at least 30 minutes. Serve garnished with coriander leaves and lemon peel, if desired.

Serves 4-6.

Variations: Try sprouting chick-peas, whole wheat, aduki beans or alfalfa seeds for this salad.

THREE BEAN SALAD

85 g (3 oz) dried flageolet beans
85 g (3 oz) dried red kidney beans
2 sprigs thyme
450 g (1 lb) fresh broad beans, podded
1 small onion, finely chopped
red pepper (capsicum) rings, to garnish
DRESSING:
115 ml (4 fl oz/½ cup) olive oil
juice 1 lemon
1 tablespoon chopped fresh mint
1 tablespoon chopped fresh parsley
salt and pepper

Put the flageolet and the kidney beans in 2 separate bowls.

Cover with water to come well above top of beans. Leave to soak for at least 6 hours. Drain. Put flageolet and kidney beans in 2 separate saucepans each with a sprig of thyme. Cover with water. Bring to the boil and boil briskly for 10 minutes. Cover pans and simmer for 1-1½ hours until beans are tender. In a pan of boiling water, cook broad beans for 5-10 minutes until tender. Drain all the beans and put into a bowl.

To make the dressing, in a bowl, mix together oil, lemon juice, mint, parsley, salt and pepper. Pour dressing over warm beans. Add chopped onion and mix well. Leave until cold, then transfer to a serving dish. Serve the salad garnished with rings of red pepper (capsicum).

Serves 6.

TOMATO SALAD

225 g (8 oz) small tomatoes
½ small red onion
10-12 black olives
DRESSING:
4 tablespoons olive oil
1 tablespoon lemon juice
1 teaspoon chopped fresh mint
2 teaspoons chopped fresh chives
1 teaspoon clear honey
salt and pepper

To make dressing, in a bowl, mix together olive oil, lemon juice, mint, chives, honey and salt and pepper.

Cut tomatoes into slices. Slice onion thinly. Place in a serving bowl with olives.

Stir dressing and pour over tomatoes. Toss together to coat tomatoes with dressing. Serve with Greek bread.

Serves 4.

Variation: Cubes of feta cheese may be added to this salad.

TOMATO & RED ONION SALAD

4 beefsteak tomatoes, sliced
4 sun-dried tomatoes packed in oil, drained and chopped
1 red onion, chopped
Salt and freshly ground black pepper
3 tablespoons extra virgin olive oil
2 tablespoons oil from the sun-dried tomatoes
2 tablespoons red wine vinegar
Pinch granulated sugar
4 tablespoons chopped mixed fresh herbs, such as basil, oregano, parsley, chives, dill and coriander
Fresh herb sprigs to garnish

Layer tomatoes, sun-dried tomatoes and onion in a shallow serving dish. Season with salt and freshly ground black pepper.

Mix together remaining ingredients, except garnish, in a small bowl then pour over the salad. Serve garnished with fresh herb sprigs.

Serves 4-6.

COUNTRY SALAD

2 Little Gem lettuces
6 tomatoes
½ cucumber
1 bunch spring onions
2 tablespoons chopped fresh mint
2 teaspoons chopped fresh oregano
55 ml (2 fl oz/¼ cup) olive oil
6 teaspoons lemon juice
salt and pepper
175 g (6 oz) feta cheese
12 black olives

Wash and dry lettuces. Roll up the leaves and slice across to make shreds. Scatter them over a serving dish.

Cut tomatoes into quarters and arrange on lettuce. Score down side of cucumber with a fork or knife to make grooves, then slice cucumber and arrange on lettuce. Chop spring onions and scatter then over the salad with mint and oregano.

In a bowl, mix together oil, lemon juice, salt and pepper. Pour over salad. Cut feta cheese into cubes and arrange on the salad with olives. Serve immediately.

Serves 6.

TRICOLOR SALAD

1 avocado
1 tablespoon lemon juice
2 large beefsteak tomatoes
175 g (6 oz) mozzarella cheese
Salt and freshly ground black pepper
Few drops balsamic vinegar
4 tablespoons extra virgin olive oil
6 basil leaves, shredded
Fresh basil sprigs to garnish

Stone and peel avocado, slice thinly and brush with lemon juice.

Arrange tomatoes, mozzarella and avocado on a large serving plate. Sprinkle over salt and freshly ground black pepper.

Sprinkle balsamic vinegar, oil and basil over salad. Serve garnished with fresh basil sprigs.

Serves 4-6.

LENTIL SALAD

225 g (8 oz/1 ¼ cups) green lentils
55 ml (2 fl oz/¼ cup) olive oil
1 onion, finely chopped
3 tomatoes, peeled and chopped
salt and pepper
1 tablespoon chopped fresh parsley
2 tablespoons lemon juice
onion rings, chopped fresh parsley and lemon slices, to garnish

Put lentils in a bowl, cover with cold water and leave to soak for 3-4 hours. Drain well.

In a large saucepan, heat half the oil, add onion and cook until soft. Add tomatoes, cook for 1 minute, then add lentils. Cover with water, cover pan and simmer gently for 30 minutes, adding water if necessary, until lentils are tender and all water has been absorbed. The lentils should still be holding their shape.

Add salt, pepper, parsley, lemon juice and remaining oil to lentils. Mix carefully, then transfer to a serving dish and leave to cool. Serve garnished with onion rings, chopped parsley and lemon slices.

Serves 4-6.

SPANISH VEGETABLE SALAD

2 Spanish onions, unpeeled
450 g (1 lb) small aubergines (eggplants)
2 red peppers (capsicums)
3 firm but ripe beefsteak tomatoes
8 cloves garlic
10 g (1/3 oz) cumin seeds
juice 1 lemon
4 tablespoons virgin olive oil
3 tablespoons white wine vinegar
salt
2 tablespoons finely chopped fresh parsley (optional)

Preheat oven to 180C (350F/Gas 4). Place onions on a baking sheet and bake for 10 minutes. Add aubergines (eggplants).

Bake for another 10 minutes, then add peppers (capsicums). Bake for 10 minutes before adding tomatoes and 6 of the garlic cloves and cooking for a further 15 minutes, until all vegetables tender. If necessary, remove any cooked vegetables from oven. When vegetables are cool enough to handle, peel them with your fingers.

Cut core and seeds from peppers (capsicums) then cut flesh into strips. Halve tomatoes, discard seeds then slice flesh. Slice aubergines (eggplants) into strips, onions into rings. Arrange in a serving dish. Using a pestle and mortar, pound to a paste the roasted and the raw garlic and the cumin seeds. Beat in lemon juice, oil and vinegar. Add salt to taste. Pour over vegetables and sprinkle with parsley, if desired. Serve warm or cold.

Serves 4.

OLIVE & TOMATO SALAD

700 g (1½ lb) mixed yellow and green courgettes (zucchini)
1 tablespoon olive oil
115 g (4 oz/¾ cup) cherry tomatoes, halved
55 g (2 oz/⅓ cup) stoned black olives, chopped
1 small oak leaf lettuce
15 g (½ oz/3 teaspoons) pine nuts, toasted
DRESSING:
3 tablespoons olive oil
1 teaspoon balsamic vinegar
½ clove garlic, crushed
½ teaspoon chopped fresh thyme
salt and pepper

Preheat oven to 220C (425F/Gas 7). Wash and trim the courgettes (zucchini) and cut into 2.5 cm (1 in) thick slices. Place in a roasting tin, toss with the oil and bake at the top of the oven for 20 minutes until tender.

Place the tomatoes and olives in a large bowl and stir in the cooked courgettes (zucchini). Blend the dressing ingredients together, add to the bowl and stir well. Leave until the courgettes (zucchini) are cold. Wash and trim the lettuce, discarding the tough outer leaves, and tear into bite-sized pieces. Arrange the lettuce on 4 serving plates. Spoon over the salad with all the juices and sprinkle over the pine nuts. Serve at once.

Serves 4.

MEDITERRANEAN POTATO SALAD

450 g (1 lb) new potatoes
115 g (4 oz) French beans, trimmed
115 g (4 oz) trimmed fennel
25 g (1 oz/¼ cup) stoned olives
2 tablespoons capers, drained
2 tablespoons chopped fresh chives
2 teaspoons chopped fresh tarragon
55 ml (2 fl oz/¼ cup) virgin olive oil
juice ½ lemon
2 eggs
400 g (14 oz) can artichoke hearts, drained and halved

Cook the potatoes in a pan of lightly salted boiling water for 10-12 minutes until just cooked. Drain and place in a large bowl. Blanch the beans in boiling water for 1-2 minutes until just tender, drain and refresh under cold water; pat dry. Very thinly slice the fennel and halve the olives. Add to the potatoes with the beans, capers and herbs. Stir in the oil and lemon juice and set aside until potatoes are cold.

Hard-boil the eggs, plunge into cold water and peel. Roughly chop and add to the salad with the artichoke hearts. Toss well and serve at once.

Serves 4-6.

ORIENTAL CARROT SALAD

350 g (12 oz) carrots, scrubbed
3 tablespoons peanut oil
½ teaspoon sesame oil
1 teaspoon grated fresh root ginger
1 small clove garlic, sliced
1 dried red chilli, seeded and crushed
2 tablespoons lemon juice
1 teaspoon sugar
55 g (2 oz/⅓ cup) raw peanuts, toasted and chopped
salt and pepper
coriander leaves, to garnish

Finely grate the carrots and place in a large bowl.

Heat 1 tablespoon peanut oil with the sesame oil and fry the ginger, garlic and chilli until just turning golden. Whisk in the remaining oil, lemon juice and sugar and remove from the heat.

Pour the dressing over the carrots, add the nuts and toss well until evenly combined. Cover and leave to marinate for 30 minutes. Stir again, season to taste and serve garnished with coriander leaves.

Serves 4.

PEA TABBOULEH

225 g (8 oz/1¼ cups) bulgar wheat
150 ml (5 fl oz/⅔ cup) olive oil
1 clove garlic, crushed
1 tablespoon red wine vinegar
1 tablespoon chopped fresh coriander
1 tablespoon chopped fresh mint
1 teaspoon ground coriander
½ teaspoon ground cumin
115 g (4 oz) sugar snap peas, trimmed
115 g (4 oz/1 cup) frozen peas, thawed
1 large ripe peach, stoned and chopped
1 red onion, finely chopped
salt and pepper

Cover the bulgar wheat with plenty of cold water and leave to soak for 30 minutes. Drain well and squeeze out excess liquid. Mix together the oil, garlic, vinegar, herbs and spices and pour over the bulgar, stir well, cover and set aside for 30 minutes.

Cook the sugar snap peas in boiling water for 2 minutes and the peas for 1 minute. Drain both and refresh under cold water. Pat all the peas dry. Stir into the bulgar wheat with the peaches, onion and seasonings.

Serves 4-6.

VEGETABLE SALAD

450 g (1 lb) potatoes, unpeeled
1 large carrot, peeled and halved or quartered
55 g (2 oz) peas
115 g (4 oz) green beans
2 tablespoons chopped Spanish onion
1 small red pepper (capsicum), peeled, seeded and chopped
4 small pickled gherkins, chopped
1½ tablespoons capers
8-12 black or anchovy-stuffed olives
150 ml (5 fl oz/⅔ cup) mayonnaise
1 hard-boiled egg, sliced
chopped fresh parsley, to garnish

Boil potatoes in their skins until tender. Cool, peel, then cut into dice. Boil carrot, peas and beans. Dice carrot and cut beans into short lengths.

Put potatoes, carrot, peas and beans into a bowl and stir in onion, pepper (capsicum), gherkins, capers, olives and mayonnaise while vegetables are still warm. Leave to cool. Arrange hard-boiled egg and chopped parsley on top before serving.

Serves 4.

WILD & BROWN RICE SALAD

115 g (4 oz/1 cup) wild rice
salt
175 g (6 oz/1¼ cups) brown rice
55 g (2 oz/⅔ cup) pecan nuts
6 spring onions, trimmed
55 g (2 oz/⅓ cup) dried cherries, cranberries or raisins
2 tablespoons chopped fresh coriander
1 tablespoon chopped fresh parsley
DRESSING:
100 ml (3½ fl oz/⅓ cup) olive oil
2 teaspoons raspberry vinegar
¼ teaspoon clear honey or sugar
salt and pepper

Cook the wild rice in a pan of lightly salted boiling water for 35-40 minutes until just tender. Cook the brown rice in a pan of lightly salted boiling water for 25 minutes or until just tender. Drain well and place both rices in a large bowl. Meanwhile, preheat oven to 220C (400F/Gas 6).

Roast the nuts in the oven for 5-6 minutes until browned; cool and coarsely chop. Set aside. Chop the spring onions and add to the rice with the dried fruit and herbs and stir well. Blend the dressing ingredients well together and pour over the salad, stir once, cover and leave rice to cool. Just before serving, toss in the roasted nuts and season to taste.

Serves 4-6.

EIGHT-TREASURE SALAD

350 g (12 oz) lean cooked skinless turkey
1 red, 1 green and 1 yellow pepper (capsicum)
115 g (4 oz) mange tout (snow peas)
50 g (2 oz) oyster mushrooms
115 g (4 oz) spring onions
2 teaspoons sesame oil
1 tablespoon white rice vinegar
1 teaspoon clear honey
freshly ground black pepper
25 g (1 oz/¼ cup) salted cashew nuts, crushed to garnish

Cut the turkey into 0.5 cm (¼ in) slices and arrange in the centre of 4 serving plates.

Halve and seed peppers (capsicum). Cut into thin slices and arrange around turkey. Diagonally slice mange tout (snow peas). Shred oyster mushrooms and spring onions. Arrange on the serving plates.

Mix together the oil, vinegar, honey and pepper. Pour over each salad, garnish with cashew nuts and serve.

Serves 4.

SUMMER NOODLE SALAD

175 g (6 oz) egg noodles
1 teaspoon sesame oil
2 tablespoons crunchy peanut butter
2 tablespoons light soy sauce
2 teaspoons caster sugar
pinch of chilli powder
450 g (1 lb) tomatoes, thinly sliced
115 g (4 oz) spring onions, finely chopped
115 g (4 oz) bean sprouts
115 g (4 oz) grated carrot
50 g (2 oz) stoned dates, finely chopped

Cook the noodles in a pan of boiling water for 4-5 minutes. Drain well and rinse in cold water. Leave in cold water until required.

Mix together the oil, peanut butter, soy sauce, sugar and chilli powder. Drain noodles well, place in a large bowl and mix in the peanut sauce. Arrange the tomato slices on a serving plate.

Using chopsticks or 2 forks, toss the spring onions, bean sprouts, grated carrot and dates into the noodles and mix well. Pile on top of the sliced tomato and serve.

Serves 4.

TUNA SALAD

3 small carrots, thickly sliced
225 g (8 oz) potato, diced
200 g (7 oz) can tuna in olive oil, drained and chopped
50 g (1¾ oz) can anchovy fillets in oil, drained and chopped
About 12 stoned black olives, halved
2 tablespoons capers in wine vinegar, drained
2 eggs, hard-boiled, quartered
4 tablespoons extra virgin olive oil
Juice 1 small lemon
1 clove garlic, crushed
Salt and freshly ground black pepper
1 tablespoon chopped fresh Italian parsley and Italian parsley sprigs to garnish

Cook carrots in a saucepan of boiling salted water for 4 minutes until tender. Cook potato in a separate pan of boiling salted water for about 7 minutes until tender. Drain and refresh both vegetables under cold running water. Drain and allow to cool completely.

Put carrots and potatoes with tuna, anchovies, olives, capers and eggs into a large serving dish. Mix olive oil, lemon juice, garlic and salt and pepper together in a small bowl or put in a screw-top jar and shake until blended. Pour over salad and toss lightly to mix then garnish with chopped Italian parsley and Italian parsley sprigs.

Serves 4.

SESAME PRAWN SALAD

225 g (8 oz) mange tout (snow peas)
50 g (2 oz) oyster mushrooms, thinly sliced
115 g (4 oz) canned water chestnuts, rinsed and sliced
225 g (8 oz) cooked, peeled prawns, thawed and dried, if frozen
2 tablespoons sesame seeds
DRESSING:
1 tablespoon sesame oil
1 tablespoon light soy sauce
2 teaspoons white rice vinegar
1 teaspoon brown sugar
salt and freshly ground black pepper

Top and tail the mange tout (snow peas) and string if necessary. Bring a saucepan of water to the boil and cook for 2 minutes until just softened. Drain and rinse under cold water. Drain and leave to cool completely.

Mix together the sliced mushrooms, water chestnuts, prawns and sesame seeds. Stir in the cooled mange tout (snow peas). Mix together the dressing ingredients and pour over the salad just before serving.

Serves 4.

MINTED SEAFOOD SALAD

150 ml (5 fl oz/2/3 cup) dry white wine
1 shallot, chopped
5 whole black peppercorns
400 g (1 lb) shelled scallops, fresh or frozen and thawed
450 g (1 lb) cooked large prawns
4 sticks celery
2 medium carrots
About 16 whole fresh mint leaves
1/2 teaspoon finely grated lemon peel
DRESSING:
Juice 2 lemons
115 ml (4 fl oz/1/2 cup) extra virgin olive oil
1 tablespoon white wine vinegar
2 tablespoons chopped fresh Italian parsley
Salt and freshly ground black pepper

Put white wine, shallot, peppercorns and 70 ml (2½ fl oz/1/3 cup) water in a shallow saucepan. Heat until boiling then add scallops. Lower the heat and poach for 5-6 minutes, until scallops are just firm and opaque. Using a slotted spoon transfer scallops to absorbent kitchen paper to drain and cool. Discard cooking liquid. Slice scallops in half horizontally. Put in a serving dish. Peel prawns and add to dish.

Cut celery and carrots into thin matchsticks and add to seafood with mint leaves and lemon peel. Toss lightly to mix. To make dressing mix ingredients together in a small bowl until evenly blended or put in a screw-top jar and shake until blended. Pour over salad and toss. Cover and refrigerate for 30 minutes before serving.

Serves 4-6.

WARM CHICKEN LIVER SALAD

- 175 g (6 oz) young spinach leaves, cleaned
- 1 small radicchio, cleaned
- 2 oranges, peeled and cut into segments
- 1 red onion, sliced into rings
- 25 g (1 oz/6 teaspoons) butter
- 3 teaspoons hazelnut oil
- 450 g (1 lb) chicken livers, cores removed and livers halved
- 1 clove garlic, crushed
- 1 tablespoon sherry vinegar
- 1 heaped teaspoon wholegrain mustard
- 3 tablespoons dry sherry
- 1 teaspoon clear honey
- salt and pepper
- 15 g (½ oz/3 teaspoons) roughly chopped toasted hazelnuts, to garnish

Arrange the spinach and radicchio leaves on 4 plates and scatter over the orange segments and onion rings.

In a heavy-based frying pan, heat the butter and oil, add the chicken livers and cook, stirring, over a high heat until well browned. Push the livers to the side of the pan, then add the garlic, vinegar, mustard, sherry, honey and seasonings, bring to the boil and reduce slightly. Add the livers to the sauce and coat well, then spoon onto the salad. Sprinkle with the chopped toasted hazelnuts.

Serves 4.

CHICKEN & GRAPE SALAD

- 450 g (1 lb) cold cooked chicken
- 115 g (4 oz/1¼ cups) walnut halves
- 115 g (4 oz) green seedless grapes, halved
- 16 stuffed green olives, sliced
- 3 spring onions (scallions), sliced
- Salt and freshly ground black pepper

DRESSING:

- 150 ml (5 fl oz/⅔ cup) prepared mayonnaise
- 1 clove garlic, crushed
- 1 teaspoon paprika
- 2 tablespoons chopped fresh Italian parsley
- Few drops hot pepper sauce
- 2 tablespoons milk
- 1 head lettuce, separated into leaves

Cut chicken into thin strips and place in a bowl with walnuts, grapes, olives and spring onions (scallions). Season with salt and freshly ground black pepper.

To make dressing mix ingredients together in a small bowl until evenly blended. Pour over salad and toss gently to mix. Arrange lettuce on a serving plate. Pile chicken salad in centre and serve at once.

Serves 4-6.

CORONATION CHICKEN

1 tablespoon olive oil
1 small onion, diced
2 teaspoons mild curry paste
200 g (7 oz) can chopped tomatoes
55 ml (2 fl oz/¼ cup) white wine
2 tablespoons hot mango chutney, chopped if necessary
2 teaspoons apricot jam
2 teaspoons lemon juice
150 ml (5 fl oz/⅔ cup) mayonnaise
150 ml (5 fl oz/⅔ cup) Greek yogurt
450 g (1 lb) cooked chicken
350 g (12 oz/2 cups) cooked, long-grain rice
1 red pepper (capsicum), diced
2 tablespoons chopped fresh mint
3 tablespoons prepared vinaigrette

In a small saucepan, heat the oil and fry the onion gently without browning until the onion is soft. Stir in the curry paste, tomatoes and wine, bring to the boil and simmer gently for 15 minutes. Add the chutney, jam and lemon juice and cook for a further 5 minutes until thick and syrupy.

Remove from the heat and strain into a small bowl; set aside to cool. When completely cold, stir in the mayonnaise and yogurt and mix well. Cut the chicken into large pieces and stir into the sauce. Combine the rice, pepper (capsicum), mint and vinaigrette and spoon onto a large serving dish and pile the chicken in the centre.

Serves 4.

WALDORF SALAD

4 tablespoons mayonnaise
2 tablespoons crème fraîche
1 tablespoons honey
a few drops of lemon juice
salt and pepper
2 teaspoons chopped fresh chives
450 g (1 lb) cooked chicken
175 g (6 oz) seedless muscat grapes
2 eating apples
2 sticks celery
175 g (6 oz/1¾ cups) walnut halves
mixed salad leaves
FOR THE VINAIGRETTE:
4 tablespoons olive oil
1 tablespoon lemon juice

In a bowl, mix together the mayonnaise, crème fraîche and honey. Add the lemon juice, season with salt and pepper and stir in the chopped chives. Remove the skin from the cooked chicken and cut into thin strips. Halve the grapes; core and slice the apples and chop the celery. Add these ingredients to the mayonnaise with the walnuts, then mix gently.

Make the vinaigrette. In a jug, whisk together the oil, lemon juice and salt and pepper; pour over the salad leaves and toss until coated in the dressing. Arrange the salad leaves on a plate and spoon over the chicken mixture.

Serves 4.

FISH & SHELLFISH

SCALLOPS WITH CASHEWS

- 55 ml (2 fl oz/¼ cup) dry sherry or rice wine
- 3 tablespoons tomato ketchup (sauce)
- 1 tablespoon oyster sauce
- 1 tablespoon wine vinegar
- 1 tablespoon sesame oil
- 1 teaspoon Chinese chilli sauce (or to taste)
- 1 tablespoon grated orange zest and 1 tablespoon orange juice
- 1 teaspoon cornflour
- 1 tablespoon vegetable oil
- 700 g (1½ lb) queen scallops
- 2 cloves garlic, finely chopped
- 4 spring onions, thinly sliced
- 175 g (6 oz) fresh asparagus, cut into 2.5 cm (1 in) pieces
- 150 g (5 oz) cashew nuts, lightly rinsed

In a medium bowl, combine dry sherry or rice wine, tomato ketchup (sauce), oyster sauce, wine vinegar, sesame oil, chilli sauce, orange zest and juice and cornflour. Heat the wok until hot, add oil and swirl to coat wok. Add scallops and stir-fry for 1-2 minutes until they begin to turn opaque. Remove to a bowl.

Add garlic, spring onions and asparagus and stir-fry for 2-3 minutes, until asparagus is bright green and tender but still crisp. Stir sauce ingredients and pour into the wok. Bring to simmering point. Return scallops to the wok and add the cashews. Stir-fry for 1 minute until scallops are heated through, tossing to coat all ingredients. Serve with rice garnished with strips of orange rind.

Serves 4.

SQUID WITH RED WINE

- 700 g (1½ lb) squid
- 55 ml (2 fl oz/¼ cup) olive oil
- 1 large onion, chopped
- 2 cloves garlic, crushed
- 450 g (1 lb) tomatoes, peeled and roughly chopped
- 150 ml (5 fl oz/⅔ cup) red wine
- salt and pepper
- ½ teaspoon sugar
- 2.5 cm (1 in) cinnamon stick
- 3 teaspoons chopped fresh parsley
- 6 slices bread, crusts removed, and 9 teaspoons olive oil, to serve

Clean squid, see page 34. Cut into rings. Dry thoroughly with absorbent paper. In a large saucepan, heat oil. Add onion and garlic and cook until soft. Add squid and fry until lightly browned. Add tomatoes, wine, salt, pepper, sugar and cinnamon. Simmer, uncovered, for 30 minutes or until squid is tender. Stir in parsley.

Sauce should be thick and rich. If not, transfer squid to a hot dish and boil sauce to reduce. Cut bread into triangles. In a frying pan, heat oil and fry bread until golden on both sides. Serve squid in individual dishes, with fried bread tucked round the sides.

Serves 6.

PRAWN & FISH BALL CURRY

500 g (1 lb) white fish fillets, such as sole, plaice, cod, whiting or monkfish, skinned
125 g (4 oz) peeled cooked prawns
90 g (3 oz/1½ cups) fresh white breadcrumbs
2 eggs, beaten separately
2 tablespoons chopped fresh coriander
2 teaspoons lemon juice
salt and pepper
2 tablespoons vegetable oil plus extra for frying
1 large onion, finely chopped
2 fresh green chillies, seeded and chopped
4 cloves garlic, crushed
½ teaspoon turmeric
155 ml (5 fl oz/⅔ cup) Coconut Milk
440 g (14 oz) can chopped tomatoes

Wash fish and remove any bones. Mince fish and prawns, then transfer to a large bowl. Stir in 60 g (2 oz/1 cup) breadcrumbs, 1 egg, coriander and lemon juice and season with salt and pepper. Mix well and form into 24 balls. Roll balls in remaining egg, then in remaining breadcrumbs to coat completely. Chill for 30 minutes. Meanwhile, heat 2 tablespoons oil in a heavy-based pan, add onion and cook, stirring, for 5 minutes until soft.

Add chillies, garlic and turmeric and fry for 2 minutes more. Stir in coconut milk and tomatoes and cook, uncovered, for 20 minutes, stirring occasionally, until thickened. Half-fill a deep-fat pan or fryer with oil and heat to 190C (375F) or until a cube of day-old bread browns in 40 seconds. Fry fish balls for 3-5 minutes, until golden. Drain well and serve with the sauce.

Serves 4.

PRAWNS WITH RADICCHIO

2 tablespoons olive oil
4 cloves garlic, finely chopped
2 shallots, finely chopped
4 slices bacon, diced
700 g (1½ lb) raw medium prawns, shelled and deveined
115 ml (4 fl oz/½ cup) grappa or brandy
225 g (8 oz) radicchio, thinly shredded
250 ml (9 fl oz/1 cup) whipping cream
salt and freshly ground black pepper
3-4 tablespoons chopped fresh parsley
450 g (1 lb) linguine

Heat wok until hot. Add olive oil and swirl to coat wok. Add garlic, shallots and bacon.

Stir-fry for 1-2 minutes until bacon is crisp. Add prawns and stir-fry for 2 minutes until prawns turn pink and feel firm to the touch. With a Chinese strainer or slotted spoon, remove prawns to a bowl. Add grappa or brandy and bring to the boil, stirring frequently. Stir in shredded radicchio, cream, salt and pepper and bring to simmering point; cook for 1 minute until sauce thickens slightly. Return prawns to wok and stir to coat. Stir in half the parsley.

In a large saucepan of boiling water, cook the linguine according to packet directions. Drain and divide among 4 large bowls. Spoon prawns and sauce equally over pasta and sprinkle with remaining parsley.

Serves 4.

Variation: Cooked prawns can be substituted; but do not stir-fry. Add to thickened sauce and heat through gently for 1 minute before adding parsley.

PACIFIC PRAWNS

2 tablespoons peanut oil
450 g (1 lb) raw medium prawns, shelled and deveined
2 cloves garlic, finely chopped
2.5 cm (1 in) piece fresh root ginger, peeled and finely chopped
2 stalks celery, sliced
1 red pepper (capsicum), sliced
4 spring onions, cut into thin strips
225 g (8 oz) can unsweetened pineapple chunks, drained, juice reserved
2 teaspoons cornflour
2 teaspoons soy sauce
1 tablespoon lemon juice
dash hot pepper sauce
150 g (5oz/1 cup) macadamia nuts, rinsed lightly if salted

Heat the wok until hot. Add 1 tablespoon oil and swirl to coat wok. Add prawns and stir-fry for 2 minutes until prawns turn pink and feel firm to the touch. Remove to bowl. Add remaining oil to the wok. Add garlic and ginger and stir-fry for 30 seconds. Stir in celery, red pepper (capsicum) and spring onions and stir-fry for 3-4 minutes until vegetables are tender but still crisp. Stir in pineapple chunks.

Dissolve the cornflour in the reserved pineapple juice. Stir in the soy sauce, lemon juice and hot pepper sauce. Stir into the vegetable and pineapple mixture and bring to simmering point. Add reserved prawns and macadamia nuts and stir-fry until sauce thickens and prawns are heated through.

Serves 4.

HOT MUSSELS WITH CUMIN

1.5 kg (3 lb) mussels
2 tablespoons vegetable oil
1 large onion, finely chopped
2.5 cm (1 in) piece fresh root ginger, grated
6 cloves garlic, crushed
2 fresh green chillies, seeded and finely chopped
½ teaspoon turmeric
2 teaspoons ground cumin
90 g (3 oz/1¾ cups) shredded fresh coconut
2 tablespoons chopped fresh coriander
coriander sprigs, to garnish

Scrub mussels clean in several changes of fresh cold water and pull off beards.

Discard any mussels that are cracked or do not close tightly when tapped. Set aside. Heat oil in a large saucepan and add onion. Fry, stirring, for 5 minutes, until soft, then add ginger, garlic, chillies, turmeric and cumin. Fry 2 minutes, stirring constantly.

Add mussels, coconut and 250 ml (8 fl oz/1 cup) water and bring to the boil. Cover and cook over a high heat, shaking pan frequently, for about 5 minutes or until almost all the shells have opened. Discard any that do not open. Spoon mussels into a serving dish, pour over cooking liquid and sprinkle with chopped coriander. Garnish with coriander sprigs and serve at once.

Serves 4.

CURRIED CRAB

700 g (1½ lb) cooked large crab claws, thawed and dried, if frozen
1 tablespoon sunflower oil
2 cloves garlic, thinly sliced
1 large green pepper (capsicum), shredded
225 g (8 oz) small broccoli flowerets
5 tablespoons vegetable stock
1 tablespoon Madras curry paste
1 tablespoon light soy sauce
1 teaspoon brown sugar

Wrap the end of a rolling pin in cling film and tap the main part of the crab claws until the shell cracks, leaving pincers intact. Peel away hard shell to expose crab flesh, leaving shell on pincers. Heat oil in a non-stick or well seasoned wok and stir-fry crab and garlic for 1-2 minutes until crab is lightly browned. Drain on kitchen paper and set aside.

Mix together remaining ingredients and add to wok. Simmer gently for 5 minutes, stirring occasionally. Replace crab and garlic and cook gently for 2-3 minutes, stirring to coat crab with sauce. Serve immediately with rice, vegetables and lemon wedges.

Serves 4.

CAJUN CRABCAKES

1 small clove garlic, finely chopped
2 tablespoons finely chopped white and green parts spring onions
2 tablespoons finely chopped red pepper (capsicum)
1 egg, beaten
1½ tablespoons mayonnaise
450 g (1 lb) fresh white and brown crabmeat, chopped
1 tablespoon chopped fresh parsley
115 g (4 oz/2 cups) fresh breadcrumbs
squeeze lemon juice
salt and cayenne pepper
olive oil for shallow frying
sour cream and chopped chives and crisp green salad, to serve

Put garlic, spring onions, pepper (capsicum) and a pinch salt in a mortar or small bowl and crush together using a pestle or end of a rolling pin. Stir in egg, mayonnaise, crabmeat, parsley and about half breadcrumbs to bind together. Add lemon juice, salt and cayenne pepper to taste.

Form crab mixture into 8 cakes 2 cm (¾ in) thick and 6 cm (2½ in) round. Lightly press in remaining breadcrumbs. Chill for 1 hour. In a non-stick frying pan, heat a thin layer oil, add crabcakes in batches and fry for 3-4 minutes on each side until golden. Serve warm with sour cream and chives, and a crisp green salad.

Makes 8.

FISH & PESTO PARCELS

2 sheets filo pastry, 25 × 50 cm (10 × 20 in), total weight about 55 g (2 oz)
melted butter for brushing
2 fish fillets, such as turbot or salmon, about 150 g (5 oz) each, skinned
55 g (2 oz) cooked peeled prawns, finely chopped
55 g (2 oz) button mushrooms, chopped
5 tablespoons fromage frais or low fat soft cheese
2-3 teaspoons pesto sauce
salt and pepper
mixed salad, to serve

Preheat oven to 200C (400F/Gas 6). Butter a baking sheet. Brush one sheet of pastry with butter, place the other sheet on top and brush with butter, then cut in half. Place a fish fillet in centre of each pastry square. Top with prawns and mushrooms. Mix together fromage frais or low fat soft cheese and pesto sauce and season to taste. Spoon a quarter of the pesto mixture onto each portion of mushrooms. Reserve remaining mixture.

Bring together 2 opposite edges of pastry and fold down over fish. Fold remaining edges over and tuck ends under fish. Brush with melted butter and place on baking sheet. Bake in the oven for 15 minutes until browned. Using a fish slice, transfer fish to a warmed serving plate, split open top of pastry and spoon in remaining pesto mixture. Serve with a mixed salad.

Serves 2.

SOLE WITH CHIVE SAUCE

115 g (4 oz/½ cup) firm cottage cheese, drained and sieved
grated rind and juice 1 lemon
salt and pepper
90 g (3½ oz) cooked peeled prawns, finely chopped
8 sole or plaice fillets, skinned
225 ml (8 fl oz/1 cup) fish stock
1 small shallot, finely chopped
1 tablespoon dry white vermouth
6 tablespoons dry white wine
175 ml (6 fl oz/¾ cup) double (heavy) cream or fromage frais or soft cheese
1½ tablespoons finely chopped fresh chives
prawns and chopped fresh chives, to garnish
broccoli, to serve

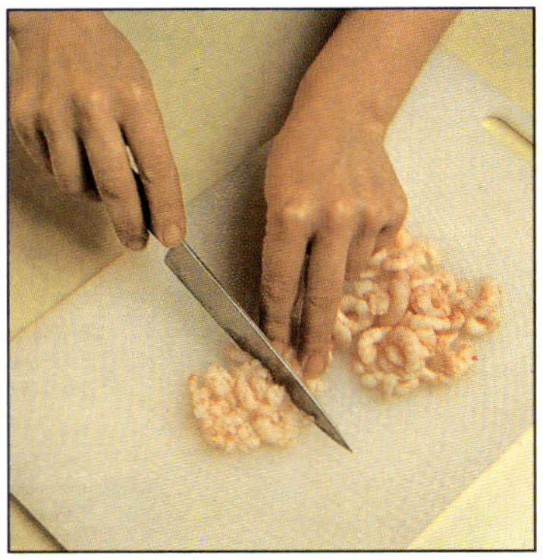

Preheat oven to 180C (350F/Gas 4). Oil a shallow baking dish. Beat together cheese, lemon rind and juice and season with salt and pepper. Mix in prawns. Spread on skinned side of fillets and roll up neatly. Secure with wooden cocktail sticks. Place fish in a single layer in dish, pour in stock to come halfway up the rolls and add chopped shallot. Cover dish and cook in the oven for about 20 minutes. Meanwhile, in a small saucepan, boil vermouth and wine until reduced by half.

Transfer sole to a warm plate and keep warm. Add stock and shallot to wines and boil hard until reduced by three quarters. Stir in cream, if using, and simmer to a light creamy consistency. If using fromage frais or soft cheese, stir in and heat without boiling. Quickly pour into a blender and mix until frothy. Add chives and season. Pour some sauce over fish and serve rest in a warm jug. Garnish rolls with prawns and chives and serve with broccoli.

Serves 4.

— SOLE WITH GREEN DRESSING —

flour for coating
salt and freshly ground black pepper
1 egg, lightly beaten
about 100 g (3½ oz/1½ cups) fresh breadcrumbs
4 fillets sole or plaice, about 175 g (6 oz) each
4 tablespoons olive oil
lemon wedges and fresh herbs, to garnish
GREEN DRESSING:
3 cloves garlic
6 canned anchovy fillets, chopped
3 tablespoons finely chopped fresh parsley
½ teaspoon chopped fresh oregano
1½ tablespoons finely chopped capers
1½ tablespoons lemon juice
150 ml (5 fl oz/⅔ cup) virgin olive oil

To make the dressing, using a pestle and mortar, crush garlic with anchovies, then mix in parsley, oregano, capers and lemon juice. Beat in oil very slowly; set aside. Put flour on a plate and season with salt and pepper. Put egg and breadcrumbs on separate plates. Coat fish in seasoned flour, then dip in egg. Allow excess to drain off, then coat fish lightly and evenly in breadcrumbs. Set aside for 5 minutes.

Heat oil in a large frying pan, add fish and cook until golden and crisp and flesh flakes easily, about 3 minutes each side. Cook fish in batches if necessary so pan is not crowded. Using a fish slice, transfer fish to absorbent kitchen paper to drain. Garnish with lemon wedges and herbs. Stir dressing and serve with hot fish.

Serves 4.

— HALIBUT WITH COURGETTES —

350 g (12 oz) small courgettes (zucchini), thinly sliced on the diagonal
4 halibut fillets, about 150-175 g (5-6 oz) each
65 g (2½ oz/5 tablespoons) unsalted butter (optional)
finely grated rind and juice 1 lemon
salt and pepper
4 sprigs chervil
lemon wedges and chervil sprigs, to garnish

Preheat the oven to 180C (350F/Gas 4). Generously butter 4 pieces of greaseproof paper large enough to loosely enclose each piece of fish.

Bring a saucepan of salted water to boil, add courgettes (zucchini) and boil for 1 minute. Drain and refresh under cold running water. Pat dry. Make a bed of courgettes (zucchini) in centre of each piece of paper. Place a piece of fish on each bed of courgettes (zucchini). Place a knob of butter, if using, on each fish, sprinkle with lemon rind and juice, season with salt and pepper and top with a chervil sprig.

Fold paper over fish and seal edges tightly. Place fish parcels on a baking sheet and bake for about 15 minutes. Either serve fish and courgettes (zucchini) in the parcels or transfer, with cooking juices, to warm plates and garnish with lemon wedges and sprigs of chervil.

Serves 4.

HALIBUT IN WHITE SAUCE

4 tablespoons olive oil
flour for coating
salt and freshly ground black pepper
1 kg (2 lb) halibut, cut into 2.5 cm (1 in) thick slices
½ Spanish onion, finely chopped
2 canned anchovy fillets, coarsely chopped
3 tablespoons chopped fresh parsley
175 ml (6 fl oz/¾ cup) dry white wine
squeeze lemon juice

Heat 3 tablespoons oil in a large frying pan. Put flour on a plate and season with salt and pepper. Coat fish evenly in the seasoned flour. Add fish slices to pan, making sure they are not crowded. Cook for 5 minutes each side.

Meanwhile, heat remaining oil in a small saucepan; add onion and cook gently for about 7 minutes until lightly coloured. Add anchovies and parsley and cook, stirring and mashing anchovies with a wooden spoon until dissolved. Stir in wine and boil until reduced by half. Add pepper and lemon juice to taste. Spoon or pour surplus oil from frying pan, then pour the anchovy sauce over the fish. Leave over moderate heat for 2 minutes, basting fish occasionally, then serve.

Serves 4.

INDONESIAN-STYLE HALIBUT

4 halibut fillets, about 175 g (6 oz) each
juice of 1 lime
2 teaspoons ground turmeric
115 ml (4 fl oz/½ cup) vegetable oil
1 clove garlic, finely chopped
1 cm (½ in) piece fresh root ginger, peeled and finely chopped
1 fresh chilli, seeded and chopped
1 onion, sliced lengthwise to form 'petals'
2 teaspoons ground coriander
150 ml (5 fl oz/⅔ cup) unsweetened coconut milk
1 teaspoon sugar
½ teaspoon salt
175 g (6 oz) mange tout (snow peas)
fresh coriander sprigs, to garnish

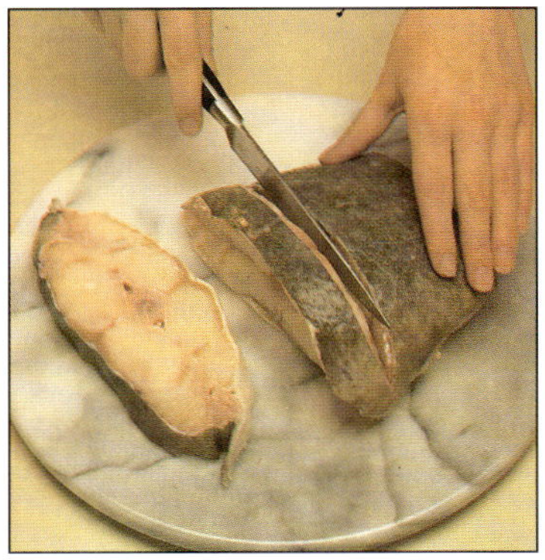

Place fish fillets in a shallow dish. Sprinkle with the lime juice and rub the turmeric into both sides of each fillet. Set aside. In a wok, heat half the oil until hot, but not smoking; swirl to coat wok. Gently slide 2 of the fish fillets into the oil and fry for 4-5 minutes, carefully turning once during cooking. Remove and drain on absorbent kitchen paper. Add remaining oil to wok and fry remaining fish fillets in the same way. Drain as before and keep fish fillets warm.

Pour off all but 1 tablespoon oil from the wok. Add garlic, ginger and chilli and stir-fry for 1 minute. Add the onion 'petals' and coriander and stir-fry for 2 minutes until onion begins to soften. Stir in coconut milk, sugar and salt and bring to the boil, adding a little more water if sauce is too thick. Stir in the mange tout (snow peas) and cook for 1 minute, until they turn bright green. Spoon sauce over fish fillets and garnish with fresh coriander. Serve immediately.

Serves 4.

ROAST COD WITH LENTILS

3 tablespoons olive oil
3 shallots, finely chopped
2 cloves garlic, finely crushed
175 g (6 oz) green or brown lentils
3½ teaspoons crushed coriander seeds
300 ml (10 fl oz/1¼ cups) fish stock
300 ml (10 fl oz/1¼ cups) dry white wine
2 tablespoons chopped fresh coriander
700 g (1½ lb) cod fillet, cut into 4 pieces
pinch saffron threads, toasted and crushed
4 tomatoes, peeled, seeded and chopped
salt and pepper
coriander sprigs, to garnish

In a saucepan, heat 1½ tablespoons oil, add 2 shallots and the garlic and cook gently until softened. Stir in lentils and 3 teaspoons coriander seeds. Cook for 2 minutes, stirring, then add stock and wine. Bring to the boil and simmer for 25-45 minutes until lentils are tender. Stir in the chopped coriander. Meanwhile, preheat oven to 230C (450F/Gas 8). Heat 1 tablespoon oil in a non-stick roasting tin and fry cod, skin side down, for 2 minutes. Transfer to oven for 8 minutes.

Heat remaining oil in a saucepan, add remaining shallot and coriander seeds and the saffron and cook gently until softened. Add tomatoes, a little liquid from the lentils and season with salt and pepper. Cook gently for 5 minutes. Drain lentils and season. Serve cod on lentils, garnished with sprigs of coriander and accompanied by the tomato relish.

Serves 4.

PLAICE WITH PROSCIUTTO

2½ large slices prosciutto ham
8 small plaice fillets
8 small sage leaves
2 tablespoons lemon juice, plus extra for seasoning
salt and pepper
1½-2 tablespoons light olive oil
15 g (½ oz/1 tablespoon) unsalted butter, diced
pasta, to serve
lemon rind shreds, to garnish

Cut ham into 8 strips lengthways. Lay a plaice fillet on each piece of ham.

Put a sage leaf at one end of each fillet, season with lemon juice and pepper, then roll up each fillet. Secure with a wooden cocktail stick.

In a non-stick frying pan, heat oil, add plaice rolls, seam side down, then cook until lightly browned all over. Transfer the fish rolls to a warm serving plate. Stir the 2 tablespoons lemon juice into pan and bring to boil. Remove pan from heat and swirl in butter. Season with salt and pepper, then pour over rolls. Serve on a bed of pasta, garnished with lemon rind.

Serves 4.

FISH FRITTERS WITH SKORDALIA

1 kg (2.2 lb) fish fillets, such as cod or John Dory
flour seasoned with salt and pepper
oil for deep frying
BATTER:
115 g (4 oz/1 cup) plain flour
1 teaspoon chopped fresh parsley
25 g (1 oz/6 teaspoons) butter, melted
1 egg white
SKORDALIA:
3 cloves garlic, crushed
5 cm (2 in) thick slice white bread
115 g (4 oz/1¼ cups) ground almonds
115 ml (4 fl oz/½ cup) olive oil
2 teaspoons lemon juice

Make the batter. Sift flour and a pinch of salt into a large bowl. Stir in parsley. Add melted butter and gradually add 175 ml (6 fl oz/¾ cup) tepid water, beating to form a smooth thick cream. Leave to stand for 1 hour. Meanwhile, make the skordalia. Put garlic in a blender or food processor. Remove crusts from bread. Squeeze bread in a little cold water, then add to garlic with ground almonds and a little olive oil.

With the motor running, gradually add remaining oil. Stir in lemon juice and salt and pepper to taste. In a bowl, whisk egg white, then fold into batter mixture. Heat oil in a deep fryer or pan. Cut fish into 6 pieces. Dip in seasoned flour then in batter. Fry for 8-10 minutes according to thickness of fish. Drain on absorbent paper, then serve with the skordalia.

Serves 6.

CHUNKY FISH CASSEROLE

100 g (3½ oz) pasta shells
3 tablespoons olive oil
2 cloves garlic, finely crushed
85 g (3 oz) button onions, halved
115 g (4 oz) button mushrooms, halved
450 g (1 lb) firm, white fish, such as cod or monkfish
225 g (8 oz) trout fillets
3 tablespoons well-seasoned plain flour
225 g (8 oz) broad beans
115 ml (4 fl oz/½ cup) dry white wine
300 ml (10 fl oz/1¼ cups) fish stock
large bouquet garni
grated rind and juice 1 lemon
150 g (5 oz) cooked peeled prawns or cooked shelled mussels or clams
chopped fresh herbs, to garnish

Preheat oven to 180C (350F/Gas 4). Cook pasta in plenty of boiling salted water for three quarters of time recommended on packet. Drain and rinse under cold running water; set aside. In a large frying pan, heat half the oil, add garlic, onions and mushrooms and cook for 3-4 minutes. Using a slotted spoon, transfer to a large, deep baking dish. Meanwhile, skin fish and cut into 2.5 cm (1 in) chunks, then toss in seasoned flour.

Add remaining oil to pan, heat and then add fish, in batches if necessary. Fry for 2-3 minutes, turning pieces carefully. Transfer to dish and add pasta and beans. Stir wine, stock, bouquet garni and lemon rind and juice into pan and bring to the boil. Simmer for a few minutes, then pour into dish. Cover and cook in oven for about 30 minutes. Add prawns, mussels or clams, cover again and cook for about 5 minutes. Garnish with plenty of chopped herbs.

Serves 4.

COD WITH A PARSLEY CRUST

750 g (1½ lb) cod, haddock or hake fillets, skinned
salt and freshly ground black pepper
2 cloves garlic, crushed
85 ml (3 fl oz/⅓ cup) olive oil
55 g (2 oz/1 cup) fresh breadcrumbs
2 tablespoons chopped fresh parsley
4 tablespoons lemon juice
parsley and lime wedges, to garnish

Season fish with salt and pepper and put in a shallow baking dish.

Mix together garlic and 4 tablespoons oil and pour over fish. Leave in a cool place for 1 hour. Preheat oven to 180C (350F/Gas 4).

Mix together breadcrumbs, parsley and lemon juice. Sprinkle evenly over fish, then trickle over remaining olive oil. Bake for about 15 minutes until fish flakes when tested with point of a sharp knife. Serve garnished with parsley and lime wedges.

Serves 4.

FISH IN GREEN SAUCE

3 tablespoons olive oil
4 hake or cod steaks, about 175 g (6 oz) each
½ Spanish onion, finely chopped
3 cloves garlic, chopped
115 ml (4 fl oz/½ cup) fish stock
2 tablespoons chopped fresh parsley
85 g (3 oz/¾ cup) slivered, roasted almonds
salt and freshly ground black pepper
dill sprigs, to garnish

Heat oil in a frying pan, add fish and cook for 2 minutes on each side.

Using a fish slice, transfer fish to a warmed plate, cover and keep warm. Add onion to oil remaining in pan and fry for 3 minutes. Stir in garlic and fry for 3 minutes, then stir in stock, parsley and almonds. Simmer for about 3 minutes until lightly thickened.

Transfer almond mixture to a blender or food processor and process until smooth. Season with salt and pepper. Return fish to pan, pour the sauce over the top and heat through for 1-2 minutes. Serve garnished with dill.

Serves 4.

COCONUT SPICED COD

four 185-250 g (6-8 oz) cod steaks
salt and pepper
2 tablespoons vegetable oil
1 onion, chopped
125 g (4 oz/1⅓ cups) desiccated coconut
5 cm (2 in) piece fresh root ginger, grated
2 cloves garlic, crushed
2 green chillies, seeded and chopped
½ teaspoon chilli powder
grated peel and juice of 1 lemon
2 tablespoons chopped fresh coriander
2 tomatoes, skinned, seeded and diced
oregano leaves, to garnish

Wash cod steaks and pat dry with absorbent kitchen paper. Place in a greased ovenproof dish and sprinkle with salt and pepper. Heat oil in a frying pan, add onion and fry, stirring, for about 5 minutes or until soft. Stir in coconut, ginger, garlic, chillies and chilli powder and fry, stirring, for 3-5 minutes, until golden brown.

Stir in lemon peel and juice and simmer, covered, for 10 minutes to soften coconut. Preheat oven to 160C (325F/Gas 3). Stir coriander and tomatoes into coconut mixture and spoon over cod steaks. Cook for 20-25 minutes, until fish flakes easily. Serve hot, garnished with oregano leaves.

Serves 4.

Note: Cover with foil during cooking if coconut begins to brown too much.

FISH GRATINS

½ teaspoon Dijon mustard
1 tablespoon lemon juice
1 tablespoon olive oil
pinch freshly grated nutmeg
salt and pepper
4 cod or haddock steaks, about 150 g (5 oz) each
85 g (3 oz) sharp Cheshire cheese, finely crumbled, or mature Cheddar cheese, thinly sliced
45 g (1½ oz) freshly grated Parmesan cheese
2 tablespoons fine fresh breadcrumbs
paprika
pattypan squash, to serve
basil sprigs, to garnish

Preheat grill. In a small bowl, whisk together mustard and lemon juice using a fork, then gradually whisk in oil. Add nutmeg and season with salt and pepper. Brush one side of fish with mustard mixture, then grill, coated side up, for 2 minutes. Turn fish over, brush top with mustard mixture and grill for 2 minutes.

Cover fish with crumbled or sliced cheese. Mix together Parmesan cheese and breadcrumbs, sprinkle evenly onto fish, then season generously with pepper. Grill until the top is golden and bubbling. Lightly sprinkle with paprika and serve with pattypan squash, garnished with sprigs of basil.

Serves 4.

FISH CAKES

450 g (1 lb) potatoes, boiled
450 g (1 lb) cooked mixed white and smoked fish, such as haddock or cod, flaked
25 g (1 oz/2 tablespoons) butter, diced
3 tablespoons chopped fresh parsley
1 egg, separated
salt and pepper
1 egg, beaten
about 55 g (2 oz/1 cup) breadcrumbs made with stale bread
olive oil for frying
lemon wedges and onion and avocado salad, to serve
dill sprigs, to garnish

In a saucepan, gently heat potatoes for a few minutes, shaking the pan occasionally.

Remove pan from heat, mash potatoes, then beat in the fish, butter, chopped parsley and egg yolk. Season with pepper. Transfer to a large bowl and mix well together. Chill if the mixture is soft.

Divide fish mixture into 8 equal portions then, with floured hands, form each portion into a flat cake. In a bowl, beat egg white with the whole egg. Spread out breadcrumbs on a plate. Dip each fish cake in egg, then in breadcrumbs. Heat a thin layer of oil in a frying pan and fry fish cakes for about 3 minutes on each side until crisp and golden. Drain on absorbent kitchen paper and serve hot with lemon wedges and onion and avocado salad, and garnished with sprigs of dill.

Serves 4.

SEA BASS UNDER A CRUST

1 kg (2 lb) sea bass, cleaned but not scaled, fins trimmed
4-5 herb sprigs, such as tarragon, basil, fennel and parsley
5 crushed black peppercorns
2 kg (4 lb) coarse sea salt
tomato, basil, red onion and caper salad, to serve
lemon wedges and basil sprigs, to garnish

Preheat oven to 220C (425F/Gas 7). Place herb sprigs and a few peppercorns in cavity of sea bass. Spread a layer of salt about 2.5 cm (1 in) deep in a deep baking dish that the fish will fit without too much space around.

Place fish on the salt, then pack salt around it until fish is completely buried and there is a 2.5 cm (1 in) layer on top. Bake fish in the oven for about 25 minutes.

To serve, crack open salt crust and remove pieces carefully to expose whole fish. Remove skin from top of fish and serve the fish with tomato, basil, red onion and caper salad, garnished with lemon wedges and sprigs of basil.

Serves 2-3.

BASS WITH GINGER & LIME

2 shallots, finely chopped
4 cm (1½ in) piece fresh ginger, finely chopped
juice 2 limes
4 tablespoons rice wine vinegar
225 ml (8 fl oz/1 cup) olive oil
2 tablespoons Chinese sesame oil
2 tablespoons soy sauce
salt and pepper
6-8 bass fillets, about 175 g (6 oz) and 1 cm (½ in) thick each
leaves from 1 bunch coriander
toasted sesame seeds, to garnish
stir-fried baby corn and sun-dried tomatoes, to serve

In a bowl, mix together first 8 ingredients. Set aside.

Preheat grill. Brush fish lightly with ginger mixture, then grill under a high heat for 2-3 minutes on each side.

Just before serving, reserve a few coriander leaves for garnish, chop remainder and mix into ginger mixture. Spoon some onto serving plates at room temperature and place fish on top. Sprinkle with sesame seeds and garnish with reserved coriander. Serve with stir-fried baby corn and sun-dried tomatoes.

Serves 6-8.

TROUT WITH TOMATO SAUCE

65 g (2½ oz) sun-dried tomatoes
2 teaspoons capers
1 large clove garlic, crushed
8 basil leaves
leaves from 2 small sprigs rosemary
leaves from 2 sprigs oregano
55 g (2 oz/¼ cup) butter, plus extra for brushing
1 tablespoon crème fraîche or sour cream
300 ml (10 fl oz/1¼ cups) fish stock
salt and pepper
6-8 trout fillets
sugar snap peas and sun-dried tomatoes, to serve
lemon wedges and oregano sprigs, to garnish

In a blender or food processor, mix together sun-dried tomatoes, capers, garlic, herbs, butter, crème fraîche and stock until smooth. Season with pepper and just a little salt. Pour into a saucepan.

Preheat grill. Brush trout with butter, season with pepper, then grill for 3-4 minutes on each side. Meanwhile, heat sauce gently, stirring occasionally. Transfer fish to warm plates, season with salt and spoon the sauce over the fish. Serve with sugar snap peas and sun-dried tomatoes, garnished with lemon wedges and sprigs of oregano.

Serves 3-4.

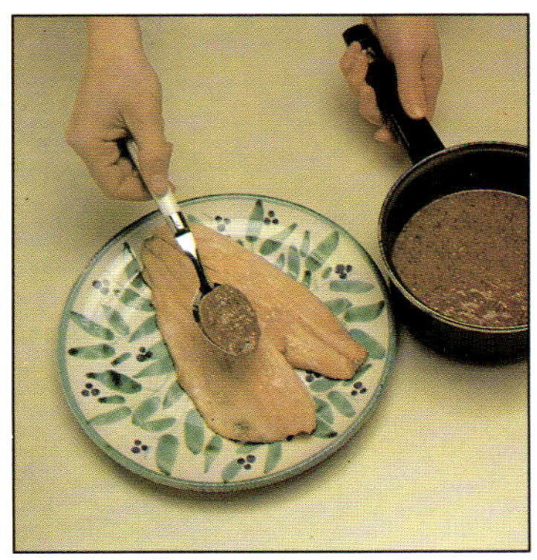

TROUT WITH PARMA HAM

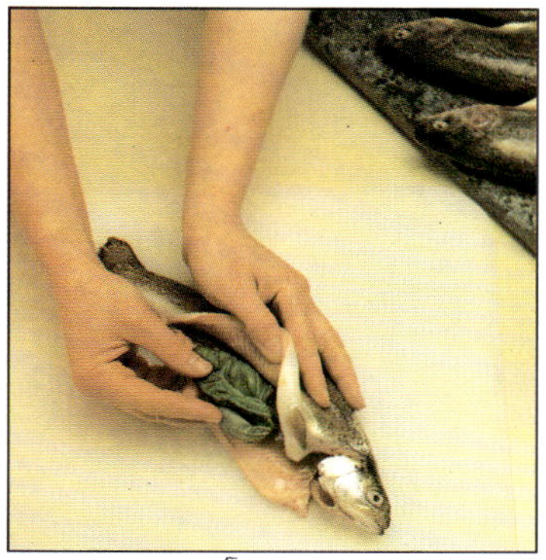

4 trout, about 300 g (10 oz) each
pepper
1 lemon, quartered
4 sprigs basil or tarragon
4 slices Parma or prosciutto ham
lemon wedges and chervil sprigs, to garnish
tomato, lime, red chicory and asparagus salad, to serve

Preheat oven to 200C (400F/Gas 6). Season trout with pepper and a squeeze of lemon juice. Place a sprig of basil or tarragon inside each fish.

Wrap a slice of ham around each fish and season with pepper. Place fish in a large, shallow baking dish with loose ends of ham underneath.

Bake fish for 15-20 minutes until cooked through and flesh flakes. Garnish with lemon wedges and sprigs of chervil and serve with tomato, lime, red chicory and asparagus salad.

Serves 4.

SALT & SOUR BAKED TROUT

2 x 300 g (10 oz) trout, cleaned
salt and freshly ground black pepper
2 spring onions, finely shredded
1 tablespoon chopped fresh coriander
strips of fresh red chilli, to garnish
SAUCE:
1 clove garlic, finely chopped
1 cm (½ in) piece fresh root ginger, peeled and finely chopped
2 tablespoons white rice vinegar
2 tablespoons light soy sauce
2 tablespoons dry sherry
1 teaspoon salt
1 teaspoon chilli powder
2 teaspoons caster sugar

Preheat oven to 180C (350F/Gas 4). Wash trout and pat dry with kitchen paper. Season trout inside and out with salt and pepper. Fill the cavities with spring onion and coriander. Using a sharp knife, score the flesh lightly in diagonal lines. Place trout in a non-stick roasting tin.

Mix together sauce ingredients and pour over trout. Cover loosely with oiled foil and bake for 20 minutes, basting halfway through. Remove foil, baste, and bake, uncovered, for 10 minutes. Skin the trout and remove flesh from bones to give 4 fillets. Brush with cooking juices, garnish with strips of chilli and serve with noodles and vegetables.

Serves 4.

SALMON WITH AVOCADO SALSA

4 salmon fillets with skin, about 175 g (6 oz) each
2½ tablespoons olive oil
sea salt and pepper
lime wedges and coriander leaves, to garnish
SALSA:
1 ripe but firm avocado
2 large ripe tomatoes, peeled, seeded and finely chopped
½ small red onion, finely chopped
½-1 fresh red chilli, seeded and thinly sliced
1 clove garlic, finely chopped
2 tablespoons lime juice
2 tablespoons chopped fresh coriander
salt and pepper

To make salsa, halve avocado, discard stone, quarter each half and remove skin. Dice avocado flesh and mix with remaining salsa ingredients. Cover and chill in refrigerator for about 1 hour.

Dry fish well, then brush skin with some of olive oil. In a heavy frying pan, heat remaining oil until hot. Add salmon, skin side down, and cook for 10-15 minutes depending on thickness of fillets, until skin is quite crisp, sides are opaque and top is slightly soft as it should be 'rare'. Season salmon with sea salt and pepper, garnish with lime wedges and coriander leaves and serve with salsa.

Serves 4.

SALMON STIR-FRY

450 g (1 lb) medium slim asparagus, trimmed
2 tablespoons groundnut oil
300 g (10 oz) salmon, skinned, boned and cut into thin strips 2.5 cm (1 in) long
squeeze lemon juice
1 tablespoon light soy sauce
2 teaspoons sesame oil
salt and pepper
lightly toasted sesame seeds, to garnish
Chinese egg noodles, to serve

Slice asparagus diagonally into 1 cm (½ in) pieces. Bring a saucepan of salted water to boil, add asparagus and cook for 1½ minutes. Drain and rinse.

In a wok or large frying pan, heat groundnut oil, add asparagus and stir-fry for 1½ minutes.

Add salmon, lemon juice, soy sauce and sesame oil to pan and stir-fry for 2 minutes. Add black pepper and a little salt. Serve immediately sprinkled with sesame seeds, accompanied by Chinese egg noodles.

Serves 4.

GRAVAD LAX

3 tablespoons sea salt
2-3 teaspoons light brown sugar
2 teaspoons crushed black peppercorns
6 tablespoons lime juice
large bunch dill
1.4-1.8 kg (3-4 lb) salmon, filleted, with skin
lime slices and dill sprigs, to garnish
DILL AND MUSTARD SAUCE:
3 tablespoons Dijon mustard
2 tablespoons white wine vinegar
1 tablespoon sugar
150 ml (5 fl oz/⅔ cup) grapeseed oil
2 tablespoons finely chopped fresh dill
salt and pepper

In a small bowl, mix together salt, sugar, peppercorns and lime juice. Spread some dill in a shallow non-metallic dish and add a quarter of salt mixture. Lay one salmon fillet, skin side down, in dish. Cover with plenty of dill and spoon over half remaining salt mixture. Place remaining salmon on top, skin-side uppermost. Cover salmon with remaining dill and pour over remaining salt mixture. Cover with greaseproof paper then plastic wrap.

Place a 900 g (2 lb) weight on top and leave in a cool place for 2 days, or bottom of refrigerator for 3 days, turning occasionally and spooning liquid back between fillets occasionally. To make sauce, mix together mustard, vinegar and sugar, then gradually whisk in oil. Add chopped dill and seasoning. Drain salmon well, pat dry and trim off any hard edges. Very thinly slice salmon on bias, discarding skin. Garnish with lime slices and sprigs of dill and serve with sauce.

Serves 8.

CHINESE SALAD WITH SALMON

350 g (12 oz) Chinese noodles
1 tablespoon salted black beans, coarsely chopped
85 g (3 oz) beansprouts
1 tablespoon groundnut oil
450 g (1 lb) salmon fillets, cut into
2.5 cm (1 in) cubes
2 teaspoons grated fresh ginger
2 tablespoons rice wine or medium sherry
2 teaspoons sesame oil
85 g (3 oz) watercress leaves and fine stalks
½ red pepper (capsicum), seeded and chopped

Cook noodles according to packet directions, drain and rinse well with cold water. Drain again, then put into a serving bowl, cover and refrigerate while preparing remaining ingredients. Soak black beans in 1-2 tablespoons hot water. Bring a pan of water to the boil, add beansprouts and boil for 1 minute. Drain, rinse under cold running water, then set aside. Heat groundnut oil in a frying pan, add salmon, in batches if necessary, and fry until just cooked and pale gold. Drain on absorbent kitchen paper.

Stir ginger, rice wine or sherry, sesame oil and half the watercress into pan. Boil for a few seconds, then add black beans and remove from heat. Add beansprouts, pepper (capsicum) and salmon to noodles, pour over warm dressing and garnish with remaining watercress.

Serves 4.

TUNA & GINGER VINAIGRETTE

2.5 cm (1 in) piece fresh ginger, finely chopped
2 large spring onions, white and some green parts, thinly sliced
225 ml (8 fl oz/1 cup) olive oil
juice 2 limes
2 tablespoons soy sauce
2 tablespoons sesame oil
1 bunch coriander, finely chopped
pepper
6 tuna steaks, about 150-175 g (5-6 oz) each
leek and red pepper (capsicum) stir-fry with sesame seeds
coriander sprigs, to garnish

Preheat grill. To make vinaigrette, stir together ginger, spring onions, olive oil, lime juice and soy sauce, then whisk in sesame oil. Add chopped coriander and season with pepper; set aside.

Grill tuna under a high heat for 3½-4 minutes each side, or a little longer for well-done fish. Spoon some dressing onto 6 plates and add the fish. Serve with leek and red pepper (capsicum) stir-fry, garnished with sprigs of coriander. Serve any remaining dressing separately.

Serves 6.

TUNA WITH SPICY SALSA

2 tablespoons sesame oil
1 tablespoon light soy sauce
1 clove garlic, finely chopped
700 g (1½ lb) tuna steaks, 2.5 cm (1 in) thick, cut into chunks
2 tablespoons vegetable oil
225 g (8 oz) daikon (mooli), peeled and diced
225 g (8 oz) cucumber, peeled, seeded and diced
1 red pepper (capsicum), diced
1 red onion, coarsely chopped
1 fresh chilli, seeded and finely chopped
2 tablespoons lime juice
1 teaspoon sugar
1 tablespoon sesame seeds, toasted
lime wedges and fresh coriander sprigs, to garnish

In a shallow dish, combine 1 tablespoon sesame oil with soy sauce and garlic. Add tuna chunks and toss gently to coat. Allow to stand for 15 minutes. Heat the wok until very hot; add 1 tablespoon of the vegetable oil and swirl to coat. Add daikon, cucumber, red pepper (capsicum), red onion and fresh chilli and stir-fry for 2-3 minutes until vegetables begin to soften and turn a bright colour. Stir in lime juice, sugar and remaining sesame oil and cook for 30 seconds until sugar dissolves. Remove to a bowl.

Add remaining vegetable oil to wok and, working in batches, if necessary, add the fish chunks and stir-fry gently for 2-3 minutes, until firm. Arrange fish on 4 dinner plates and sprinkle with the sesame seeds. Spoon some of the warm relish onto each plate and garnish with lime wedges and fresh coriander sprigs. Serve with noodles.

Serves 4.

LAYERED FISH TERRINE

450 g (1 lb) salmon, skinned and boned
salt and white pepper
150 ml (5 fl oz/⅔ cup) medium-bodied dry white wine
2 small bunches watercress, trimmed
15 g (½ oz/1 tablespoon) butter
1 shallot, finely chopped
450 g (1 lb) firm white fish, such as hake, monkfish or cod, skinned, boned and cubed
2 egg whites
210 ml (7½ fl oz/scant 1 cup) double (heavy) cream, chilled
lime slices and mint sprigs, to garnish

Cut salmon into long strips, put in a dish, season lightly and pour the wine over it. Cover and leave for about 1 hour.

Meanwhile, boil a saucepan of lightly salted water, add watercress and blanch for 1 minute. Drain watercress, rinse under cold running water, drain again, then dry on absorbent kitchen paper; set aside.

In a small saucepan, heat butter. Add shallot and cook gently until softened but not browned. Purée shallot with cubed white fish in a food processor. Add egg whites and season with salt and pepper. Mix for 1 minute, then slowly pour in cream. Remove and reserve two thirds of fish mixture. Add watercress to food processor and purée briefly. Chill both mixtures for 30 minutes.

Preheat oven to 180C (350F/Gas 4). Lightly oil a 25 × 9 cm (10 × 3½ in) terrine. Spread half the plain fish mixture in the terrine, then half the salmon strips followed by all the green mixture. Cover this with remaining salmon strips, then remaining white mixture.

Cover terrine with foil, place in a roasting tin and pour in enough boiling water to come halfway up sides of terrine. Bake in oven for about 40 minutes until a skewer inserted in centre comes out clean. Transfer terrine to a wire rack to cool, then refrigerate. Serve cut into slices, garnished with lime slices and sprigs of mint.

Serves 4-6.

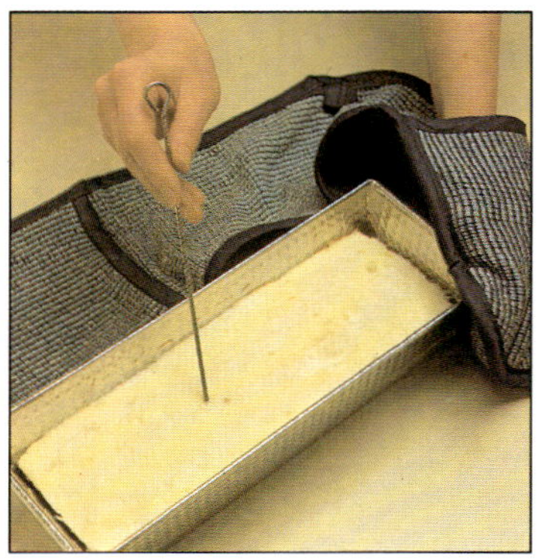

ESCABECHE

6-8 red snapper, red sea bream or catfish fillets, cleaned and scaled
3 tablespoons seasoned flour
3 tablespoons olive oil
2-3 tablespoons chopped fresh coriander
MARINADE:
large pinch saffron threads, toasted
2 tablespoons olive oil
2 red onions, thinly sliced
2 red peppers (capsicums), seeded and sliced
½ teaspoon dried chilli flakes
1½ teaspoons cumin seeds, lightly crushed
finely grated rind and juice 1 orange
2-3 tablespoons rice vinegar
pinch caster sugar
salt and pepper

To make marinade, crush saffron, then soak in warm water for 10 minutes. In a frying pan, heat oil and gently cook onions for 2 minutes. Add peppers (capsicums), chilli flakes and cumin and fry until vegetables are soft. Stir in saffron and liquid, orange rind and juice, vinegar, sugar and salt and pepper. Bubble for a few minutes, then leave to cool.

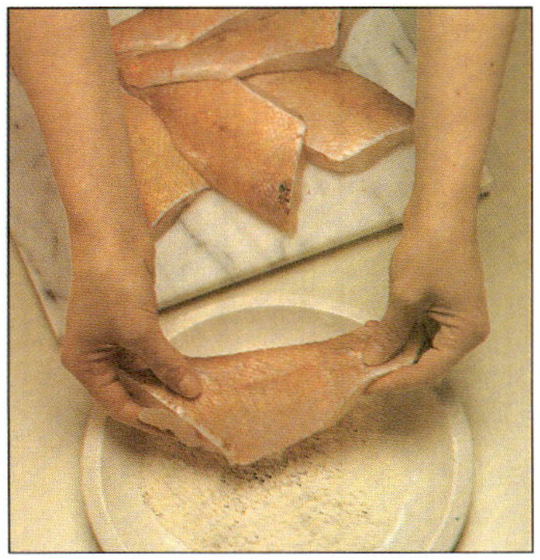

Toss fish in flour. In a frying pan, heat the 3 tablespoons oil, add fish and fry for 2-3 minutes on each side until just cooked and browned. Place the fish in a single layer in a shallow, non-metallic dish and pour marinade over it. Cover and refrigerate for 4-12 hours. Return to room temperature 15 minutes before serving. Stir in coriander.

Serves 6-8 as first course.

Note: Garnish with orange slices and sprigs of coriander, if wished.

SKATE WITH ANCHOVY SAUCE

4 small skate wings
1 tablespoon olive oil
15 g (½ oz/1 tablespoon) unsalted butter
salt and pepper
sugar snap peas and new potatoes, to serve
basil sprigs, to garnish
SAUCE:
1 large clove garlic
6 anchovy fillets, chopped
2½ tablespoons capers
2½ teaspoons wholegrain mustard
1½ tablespoons chopped fresh basil
3 tablespoons chopped fresh parsley
6 teaspoons lime juice
3 tablespoons virgin olive oil
black pepper

To make sauce, crush garlic with anchovies in a small bowl. Mix in capers, mustard, basil, parsley and lime juice, then gradually whisk in oil. Season with black pepper and set aside.

Season skate wings. In a large non-stick frying pan, heat oil and butter. Add 2 skate wings and fry for about 4 minutes on each side until lightly browned. Transfer skate to absorbent kitchen paper and fry remaining skate in same way. Return skate to pan, pour in sauce and heat briefly until warmed through. Serve with sugar snap peas and new potatoes, garnished with sprigs of basil.

Serves 4.

FISH PLAKI

about 1.15 kg (2½ lb) fish, such as bream, bass, grey mullet, red snapper or pompano, scaled
juice ½ lemon
2 tablespoons olive oil
1 onion, chopped
1 carrot, finely chopped
1 stick celery, chopped
2 cloves garlic, chopped
1 teaspoon coriander seeds, crushed
450 g (1 lb) tomatoes, peeled, seeded and chopped
3 halves sun-dried tomato, finely chopped
85 ml (3 fl oz/⅓ cup) dry white wine
leaves from bunch parsley, finely chopped
salt and pepper
parsley sprigs, to garnish

Preheat oven to 190C (375F/Gas 5). Put fish into a baking dish and squeeze over lemon juice. Heat oil in a saucepan, add onion, carrot and celery and cook, stirring occasionally, until onion has softened but not coloured. Stir in garlic and cook for about 3 minutes. Stir coriander seeds, tomatoes, sun-dried tomatoes, wine and parsley into pan, season with salt and pepper and simmer for a few minutes until well blended.

Using a fish slice, lift fish and pour about a quarter of the tomato mixture underneath. Lay fish down again and pour over remaining tomato mixture. Cover dish and bake in the oven for about 40 minutes. Serve garnished with parsley sprigs.

Serves 4.

SEAFOOD GUMBO

2 tablespoons olive oil
2 onions, chopped, and 2 cloves garlic, crushed
1 green pepper (capsicum), seeded and chopped
1 stick celery, chopped
2 tablespoons seasoned flour
685 ml (24 fl oz/3 cups) fish stock
400 g (14 oz) can chopped tomatoes
85 g (3 oz) cooked ham, chopped
bouquet garni
225 g (8 oz) fresh okra, sliced
225 g (8 oz) each white crabmeat and cooked peeled prawns
400 g (14 oz) redfish fillets or other firm white fish fillets, cut into chunks
lemon juice and dash Tabasco sauce
450 g (1 lb) boiled long-grain rice, to serve

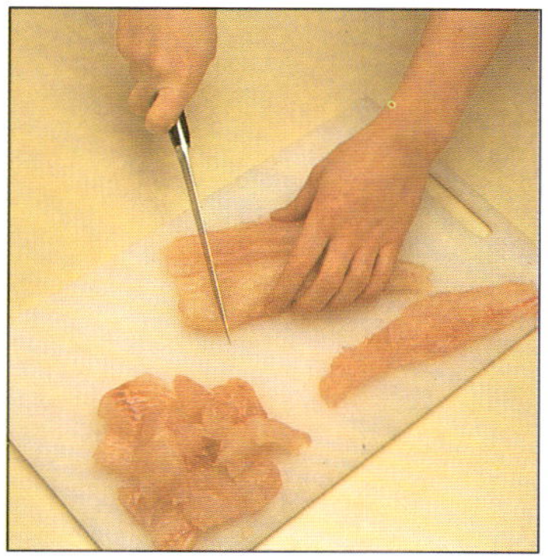

In a heavy flameproof casserole, heat oil. Add onions and cook until softened. Add garlic, pepper (capsicum) and celery and cook, stirring frequently, for 5 minutes. Sprinkle over flour and stir for 1 minute. Stir stock, tomatoes, ham and bouquet garni into casserole, partially cover and simmer for 30 minutes. Add okra and simmer, covered, for 30 minutes.

Chop crabmeat and set aside. Add fish to casserole and cook for about 7 minutes. Add crabmeat and prawns and cook for about 2½ minutes until prawns are hot. Add lemon juice and Tabasco sauce to taste. Spoon rice into warm serving bowls and ladle gumbo over it.

Serves 4-6.

Note: Sprinkle chopped fresh parsley over the top, if wished.

SMOKED SALMON SCRAMBLE

115 g (4 oz) smoked salmon trimmings, chopped
2 tablespoons single (light) cream
45 g (1½ oz/3 tablespoons) unsalted butter
4 large eggs, beaten
black pepper
chopped fresh chives and lime slices, to garnish
buttered toasted bagels, muffins or crumpets, to serve

In a small bowl, mix smoked salmon and cream together. Leave to stand for 10-15 minutes.

In a saucepan, melt half the butter, then stir in eggs. Cook over a low heat, stirring with a wooden spoon, until beginning to set. Add salmon and cream and season with pepper. Continue to stir until eggs are almost set.

Remove pan from heat and immediately stir in remaining butter. Garnish with chopped chives and lime slices and serve with buttered toasted bagels, muffins or crumpets.

Serves 2.

KEDGEREE

575 g (1¼ lb) smoked haddock (finnan haddie) or salmon
115 g (4 oz/generous ½ cup) long grain rice
2 tablespoons lemon juice
150 ml (5 fl oz/⅔ cup) single (light) or sour cream
pinch of freshly grated nutmeg
cayenne pepper
2 hard-boiled eggs, peeled and chopped
55 g (2 oz/4 tablespoons) butter, diced
2 tablespoons chopped fresh parsley
parsley sprigs and sliced hard-boiled eggs, to garnish

Poach fish just covered by water for about 10 minutes. Lift fish from cooking liquid, discard bones and skin and flake flesh. Measure fish cooking liquid to twice volume of rice; top up with water if necessary. Bring to the boil, add rice, stir, then cover and simmer for about 15 minutes until rice is tender and liquid absorbed. Meanwhile, preheat oven to 180C (350F/Gas 4) and butter a baking dish.

Remove rice from heat and stir in lemon juice, cream, fish, nutmeg and a pinch of cayenne. Gently fold in eggs. Turn into dish, dot with butter and bake for about 25 minutes. Stir chopped parsley into kedgeree and garnish with parsley sprigs and sliced hard-boiled egg. Sprinkle a little cayenne pepper over the top, if wished.

Serves 4.

POULTRY & GAME

CHICKEN & HAM CROQUETTES

55 g (2 oz/¼ cup) butter
1 onion, finely chopped
55 g (2 oz/½ cup) plain flour
300 ml (10 fl oz/1¼ cups) milk
300 g (10 oz) cooked chicken, finely chopped
55 g (2 oz) ham, finely chopped
2 tablespoons chopped fresh parsley
1 teaspoon Dijon mustard
salt and pepper
85 g (3 oz/1½ cups) fresh white breadcrumbs
vegetable oil for frying
lemon wedges and green salad, to serve

Melt the butter, add the onion and fry gently for 3-4 minutes until soft but not browned.

Add the flour and cook for 1 minute. Gradually blend in the milk and bring to the boil, stirring all the time. Reduce heat and simmer for 2 minutes until sauce forms a thick paste. Add the chopped chicken, ham, parsley, mustard and season with a little salt and pepper. Mix well and put to one side to cool. Place the breadcrumbs on a board and drop tablespoonsful of the mixture onto the breadcrumbs.

Roll mixture in crumbs to give an even coating. Chill for 30 minutes. Heat 5 cm (2 in) oil in a frying pan. Fry the croquettes until golden brown all over. Drain on kitchen paper. Serve with wedges of lemon and a salad.

Makes 12-14.

Note: To make a sauce to serve with the croquettes, mix 2 teaspoons chopped capers with 3 tablespoons crème fraîche and a squeeze of lemon.

CHICKEN BURGERS

85 g (3 oz) packet country stuffing mix
225 g (8 oz) raw chicken meat, minced
1 small egg, beaten
1 eating apple, peeled, cored and grated
salt and pepper
1-2 tablespoons oil
4 sesame seed baps
iceberg lettuce, shredded
2 tomatoes, sliced
4 squares processed Cheddar cheese slices
mayonnaise and relish, to serve

Make up the stuffing mix according to the packet instructions and set aside to cool.

In a bowl, mix together the chicken, stuffing, egg, apple and seasonings and shape into 4 burgers. In a frying pan, heat the oil and fry the burgers for 6-7 minutes on each side until cooked.

Split the buns in half and cover the bases with the shredded lettuce and tomato slices. Place the burgers over the lettuce and tomato, then cover each burger with a slice of cheese. Spoon on mayonnaise or relish and place the bap top in position.

Serves 4.

CHICKEN KIEV

115 g (4 oz/½ cup) unsalted butter, softened
3 cloves garlic, crushed
finely grated rind of ½ lemon
1 tablespoon chopped fresh parsley
salt and pepper
4 skinned and boned chicken breasts
2 eggs, beaten
175 g (6 oz/3 cups) fresh white breadcrumbs
oil for deep frying

Beat together the softened butter, crushed garlic, grated lemon rind, parsley and salt and pepper. Transfer to a piping bag fitted with a plain 0.5 cm (¼ in) nozzle.

Lay the chicken breasts on a board and insert a sharp knife into the breast to form a pocket. Take the piping bag and pipe the butter into the pocket (do not over-fill or the butter will burst through the flesh). Leave to refrigerate for 25 minutes.

Dip a filled chicken breast into the beaten eggs, then roll in the breadcrumbs. Repeat once more so chicken is well coated. Repeat with the remaining chicken. Half-fill a deep fat pan or fryer with oil and heat to 190C (375F). Lower in the chicken breasts, 2 at a time, and fry for 8-10 minutes or until cooked through and golden brown. Drain on absorbent kitchen paper and serve immediately with a squeeze of lemon.

Serves 4.

HONEY CHICKEN DRUMSTICKS

8 chicken drumsticks
4 tablespoons clear honey
2 teaspoons Dijon mustard
2 teaspoons wholegrain mustard
1 teaspoon soy sauce
1 teaspoon dried rosemary

Cut 3 diagonal slashes in the flesh on both sides of the drumsticks and place in a shallow, ovenproof dish or roasting tin.

Mix together the honey, mustards and soy sauce and pour over the drumsticks. Cover and leave to marinate for 1 hour, turning from time to time.

Preheat the oven to 200C (400F/Gas 6). Sprinkle the rosemary over the drumsticks and cook on the top shelf of the oven for 25 minutes. Increase the heat to 230C (450F/Gas 8) and cook for a further 10 minutes, basting and turning the drumsticks several times. Any leftover marinade from the pan can be added to 4 tablespoons mayonnaise with a squeeze of lemon to serve with the drumsticks.

Serves 4.

LEMON CHICKEN

1 egg white
350 g (12 oz) chicken breast, sliced
3 teaspoons cornflour
finely grated rind and juice of 1 lemon
2 tablespoons dry sherry
1 teaspoon soy sauce
2 teaspoon clear honey
3 tablespoons vegetable oil
4 spring onions, sliced
55 g (2 oz) mange tout (snow peas), topped and tailed
½ red pepper (capsicum), finely sliced
55 g (2 oz) beansprouts

Whisk egg white until frothy. Stir in chicken, 2 teaspoons cornflour and lemon rind.

In another bowl, mix together the remaining cornflour, sherry, lemon juice, soy sauce and honey. Put to one side. Heat the oil in a wok or large frying pan, add the chicken pieces a few at a time to prevent them sticking together. Stir-fry for 2 minutes or until the chicken is cooked through.

Add the spring onions, mange tout (snow peas), red pepper (capsicum) and beansprouts and continue to stir-fry for a further 1 minute. Add the lemon juice and cornflour mixture and cook for 1-2 minutes, stirring until the sauce thickens and coats the chicken and vegetables.

Serves 4.

CHICKEN IN CAPER SAUCE

1 onion, quartered
1 carrot, peeled and quartered
1 teaspoon finely grated orange rind
1 orange, peeled and sliced
bay leaves
55 ml (2 oz/¼ cup) dry white wine
225 ml (8 fl oz/1 cup) chicken stock
4 skinned and boned chicken breasts
25 g (1 oz/6 teaspoons) butter
25 g (1 oz/¼ cup) plain flour
150 ml (5 fl oz/⅔ cup) single (light) cream
1 tablespoon chopped fresh parsley
2 teaspoons capers, drained

Place the first 5 ingredients in a frying pan.

Add the wine and stock and bring to the boil. Add the chicken breasts, reduce the heat until barely simmering, then cover and poach for 20 minutes or until cooked. Remove the cooked breasts, drain well on absorbent kitchen paper and keep warm. Strain and reserve the poaching liquor.

In a pan, melt the butter, add the flour and cook for 1 minutes, remove from the heat and slowly add the poaching liquor, stirring well between each addition. Return to the heat and bring to the boil, stirring continuously, until thickened. Stir in the cream, parsley and capers and season to taste. Spoon over the chicken breasts and serve with cardamom-scented rice.

Serves 4.

TANDOORI CHICKEN

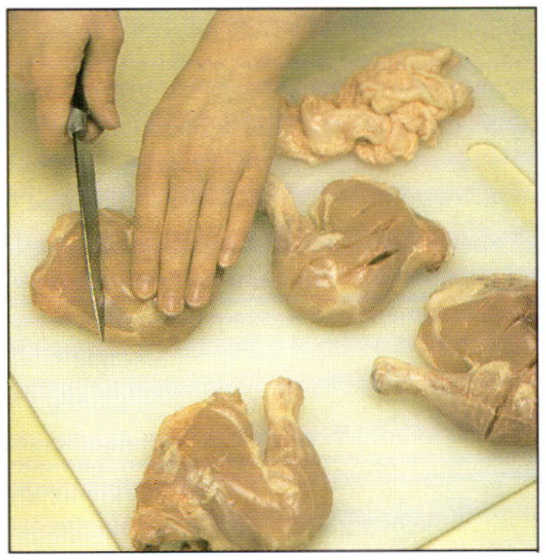

4 chicken leg quarters, skinned
juice of 1 lemon
salt
2 teaspoons ground turmeric
2 teaspoons paprika
1 teaspoon garam masala
1 teaspoon ground cardamom
½ teaspoon chilli powder
pinch saffron powder
2 cloves garlic, crushed
2 teaspoons chopped fresh root ginger
1 tablespoon olive oil
200 ml (7 fl oz/¾ cup) natural yogurt

Cut deep diagonal cuts in the chicken flesh.

Sprinkle with lemon juice and a little salt. Mix together all the remaining ingredients and use to coat the chicken quarters, cover and leave in a cool place to marinate for 4 hours or overnight.

Preheat grill and cook chicken for 25 minutes, brushing with any excess marinade and turning frequently until the chicken is tender and juices run clear when chicken leg is pierced with a knife. A slight blackening of the chicken gives an authentic look. Serve with wedges of lemon, boiled rice and an onion salad.

Serves 4.

SOUTHERN-FRIED CHICKEN

4 chicken breasts
salt and pepper
3 tablespoons paprika
2 tablespoons ground coriander
1 tablespoon ground cumin
finely grated rind and juice of 1 lemon
3 tablespoons dark soy sauce
2 tablespoons chopped fresh coriander
1 teaspoon chopped fresh thyme
1 onion, finely choppd
2 cloves garlic, crushed
1 red chilli pepper, deseeded and chopped
vegetable oil for frying
85 g (3 oz/¾ cup) plain flour
lemon wedges and coriander sprigs, to garnish

Remove the skin from the chicken breasts. Place the chicken in a shallow dish. Make several incisions in the chicken portions and season well with salt and pepper. In a small bowl, mix together 2 tablespoons paprika, 1 tablespoon ground coriander and 2 teaspoons ground cumin and sprinkle over the chicken. Mix the rind and juice of the lemon with the soy sauce, then add the coriander, thyme, onion, garlic and chilli. Pour over the chicken – making sure it is well covered by the mixture. Cover the dish with cling film and leave to marinate for at least 3 hours or overnight.

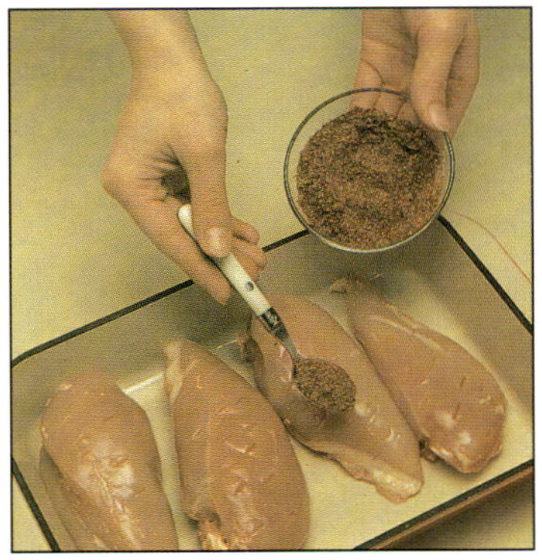

Half-fill a deep fat pan or fryer with the oil and heat to 190C (375F). Put the flour on a plate and season with salt and pepper. Add the remaining paprika, cumin, coriander and mix well. Dip the chicken pieces in the flour to thoroughly coat. Deep fry the chicken, 4 pieces at a time, for approximately 15 minutes or until chicken is golden brown and cooked through. Serve garnished with lemon wedges and coriander sprigs.

Serves 4.

JAMBALAYA

1 tablespoon olive oil
15 g (½ oz/3 teaspoons) butter
350 g (12 oz) skinned and boned chicken meat
175 g (6 oz) chorizo sausage
1 onion, thinly sliced
2 cloves garlic, sliced
1 red pepper (capsicum). sliced
1 yellow pepper (capsicum), sliced
1 green pepper (capsicum), sliced
115 g (4 oz) mushrooms, sliced
150 g (5 oz/1 cup) long-grain rice
½ teaspoon ground allspice
300 ml (10 fl oz/1¼ cups) chicken stock
150 ml (5 fl oz/⅔ cup) white wine
115 g (4 oz) large cooked peeled prawns
lime wedges and whole prawns, to garnish

In a large frying pan or paella pan, heat the oil and butter. Cut the chicken into thick strips and fry until well browned, then remove from the pan and set aside. Cut the chorizo into chunks and fry for 1 minute, stirring well, then using a slotted spoon, remove from the pan and add to the chicken. Fry the onion and garlic until slightly softened, add the peppers (capsicums), mushrooms, rice and allspice and cook for a further 1 minute.

Pour in the stock and wine and bring to the boil, return the chicken and chorizo to the pan and simmer, uncovered, for 15-20 minutes until the liquid is absorbed and the rice tender. Stir in the prawns, cook for a further 5 minutes, then season to taste. Serve garnished with wedges of lime and whole prawns.

Serves 4.

CHICKEN FAJITAS

55 ml (2 fl oz/¼ cup) dry white wine
finely grated rind and juice of 2 limes
1 tablespoon Worcestershire sauce
2 teaspoons brown sugar
½ teaspoon dried basil
½ teaspoon dried oregano
1 clove garlic, crushed
4 skinned and boned chicken breasts
6 teaspoons vegetable oil
8 spring onions, sliced
1 red pepper (capsicum), deseeded and sliced
1 green pepper (capsicum), deseeded and sliced
8 wheat flour tortillas, warmed gently
150 ml (5 fl oz/⅔ cup) thick sour cream
ripe avocado, peeled and chopped

Prepare the marinade for the chicken. In a bowl, mix together the wine, rind and juice of the limes, Worcestershire sauce, sugar, basil, oregano and garlic. Slice the chicken breast into thin strips and add to the marinade. Mix well and leave to marinate for 30-40 minutes, stirring from time to time. In a pan, heat 2 tablespoons oil and add the spring onions and peppers (capsicums) and fry until the onions are starting to colour, but the vegetables are still crisp. Remove from the pan and put to one side. Drain the chicken, reserving the marinade.

Heat the remaining oil, and when very hot, add the chicken and fry quickly until golden brown. Remove from the pan with a slotted spoon; set aside. Add the reserved marinade to the pan and boil until thickened and reduced. Return the chicken and peppers and mix well until all ingredients are coated in the marinade. Put tortillas on a plate, place the chicken mixture in the middle, spoon over some thick sour cream and chopped avocado. Roll up and serve.

Serves 4.

CHICKEN CHOW MEIN

3 tablespoons dark soy sauce
2 tablespoons dry sherry
1 teaspoon soft brown sugar
1 teaspoon sweet chilli sauce
225 g (8 oz) skinned and boned chicken, shredded
225 g (8 oz) egg thread noodles
1 teaspoon cornflour
6 tablespoons chicken stock or water
3 tablespoons vegetable oil
2.5 cm (1 in) piece fresh root ginger, finely chopped
1 clove garlic, finely chopped
4 spring onions, sliced
85 g (3 oz) green beans, cut into 2.5 cm (1 in) lengths
1 small carrot, cut into matchstick strips
1 red pepper (capsicum), finely sliced
175 g (6 oz) beansprouts

In a bowl, mix together soy sauce, sherry, brown sugar and chilli sauce. Add the chicken and leave to marinate for 30 minutes. Drain the chicken, reserving the marinade. Cook the noodles following the packet instructions; drain and set aside. Mix the reserved marinade with the cornflour and chicken stock or water and set aside.

In a wok or large frying pan, heat the oil, add the ginger and garlic and stir-fry for 15-20 seconds, then add the chicken and continue to stir-fry for further 2-3 minutes until the chicken is cooked. Add the spring onions, beans, carrot and pepper (capsicum) and stir-fry for 1 minute. Add the noodles and beansprouts and stir-fry for 30 seconds, then add the marinade mixture and stir-fry until the sauce thickens and coats the ingredients. Serve immediately.

Serves 4.

SWEET & SOUR CHICKEN

700 g (1½ lb) skinned and boned chicken breasts
salt
5 tablespoons cornflour
225 g (8 oz/2 cups) self-raising flour
3 large eggs, beaten
2.5 cm (1 in) piece fresh root ginger, finely chopped
1 tablespoon oil, plus extra for frying
100 ml (3½ fl oz/⅓ cup) white wine vinegar
55 ml (2 fl oz/¼ cup) dry sherry
100 ml (3½ fl oz/⅓ cup) orange juice
3 tablespoons soy sauce
4 tablespoons tomato purée (paste)
1 clove garlic, finely chopped
1 small onion, finely chopped
1 red pepper (capsicum), sliced
1 green pepper (capsicum), sliced

Cut the chicken into 2.5 cm (1 in) cubes. Sprinkle with salt and 2 tablespoons cornflour and mix thoroughly. Meanwhile, make the batter. Put the flour in a bowl, gradually add the eggs and 300 ml (10 fl oz/1¼ cups) water to make a smooth batter. Add half the ginger. Add the chicken and coat thoroughly. Half-fill a deep fat pan or fryer with oil and heat to 190C (375F). Add the chicken, in batches, and fry for 4-5 minutes until crispy. Remove with a slotted spoon, drain and transfer to a plate to keep warm.

In a jug, mix remaining 3 tablespoons cornflour with 150 ml (5 fl oz/⅔ cup) water, then add the wine vinegar, sherry, orange juice, soy sauce and tomato purée (paste). Heat 1 tablespoon oil in a wok or large frying pan, add the garlic and the rest of the ginger, stir-fry for 15 seconds. Add the onion and peppers (capsicums) and stir-fry for 1½-2 minutes, then pour over the sauce, stirring until it thickens. Put the chicken on a warm serving dish and pour over the sauce.

Serves 4-6.

CHICKEN BIRYANI

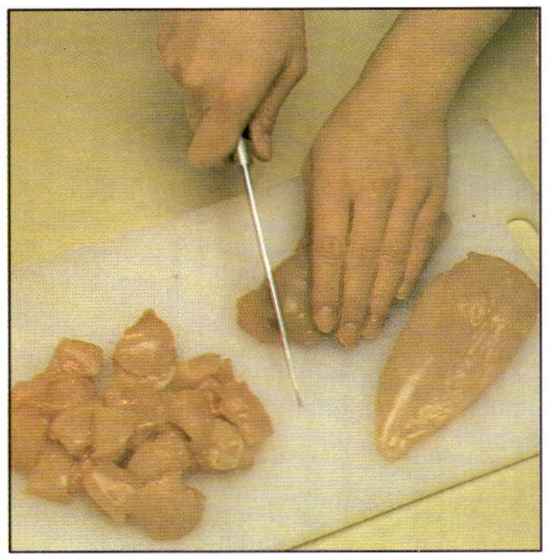

8 tablespoons vegetable oil
1 stick cinnamon
8 cloves
6 cardamom pods, bruised
2.5 cm (1 in) piece fresh root ginger, finely chopped
700 g (1½ lb) skinned and boned chicken, cubed
2 cloves garlic, crushed
1 teaspoon chilli powder
300 ml (10 fl oz/1¼ cups) natural yogurt
150 ml (5 fl oz/⅔ cup) chicken stock
pinch of saffron strands
4 tablespoons boiling water
350 g (12 oz/2¼ cups) basmati rice
4 tablespoons sultanas
4 tablespoons flaked almonds
1 onion, sliced

Preheat oven to 190C (375F/Gas 5). In a flameproof casserole, heat 4 tablespoons oil and add the spices and fry for 15 seconds. Add the chicken, garlic and chilli and fry for 4 minutes. Add the yogurt, 1 tablespoon at a time, stirring between each addition until yogurt is absorbed by the spices. Add the stock and simmer for 20-25 minutes. Transfer to a bowl. Soak the saffron in the boiling water and put to one side. Wash the rice under cold running water until the water runs clear, then cook in boiling, salted water for 3 minutes and drain.

Put 2 tablespoons oil in the casserole, spoon in a layer of rice, sprinkle with a little of the saffron water and cover with a layer of chicken. Repeat, ending with a layer of rice. Add any cooking juices left from the chicken, cover tightly and cook in the oven for 25-30 minutes. In a pan, heat the remaining oil and fry the sultanas and almonds until golden; remove. Fry the onions until crisp and golden. Sprinkle the biryani with the almonds, onions and sultanas.

Serves 4.

TIKKA KEBABS

150 ml (5 fl oz/⅔ cup) natural yogurt
1 tablespoon grated fresh root ginger
2 cloves garlic, crushed
1 teaspoon chilli powder
1 teaspoon ground cumin
1 teaspoon tumeric
1 tablespoon coriander seeds
juice of 1 lemon
½ teaspoon salt
2 tablespoons chopped fresh coriander
350 g (12 oz) chicken meat, cubed
RAITA:
150 ml (5 fl oz/⅔ cup) natural yogurt
2 teaspoons mint jelly
85 g (3 oz) finely chopped cucumber
2 spring onions, finely chopped

Blend the first 10 ingredients in a blender or food processor until smooth. Pour into a bowl. Stir in the cubed chicken, cover and allow to stand overnight in the refrigerator.

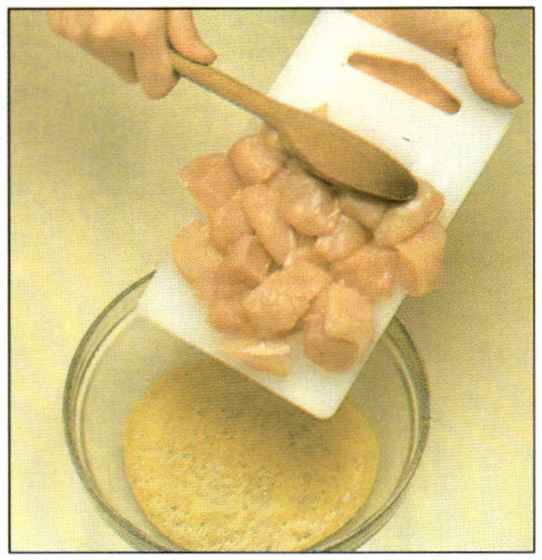

Preheat grill. Thread chicken onto skewers and cook under the hot grill for 15-20 minutes, turning frequently and brushing with any remaining marinade. In a bowl, mix together the raita ingredients. Serve the kebabs on a bed of pilau rice, garnished with sprigs of coriander and lemon wedges. Hand the raita separately.

Serves 4.

FAMILY CHICKEN PIE

700 g (1½ lb) chicken pieces
1 large onion, thickly sliced
85 ml (3 fl oz/⅓ cup) dry white wine
200 ml (7 fl oz/¾ cup) chicken stock
1 bouquet garni and salt and pepper
25 g (1 oz/6 teaspoons) butter
175 g (6 oz) button mushrooms, halved
25 g (1 oz/¼ cup) plain flour
225 g (8 oz) can sweetcorn kernels
2 tablespoons chopped fresh parsley
1 teaspoon lemon juice
4 tablespoons double (thick) cream
1 kg (2 lb) potatoes
115 ml (4 fl oz/½ cup) hot milk
85 g (3 oz/¾ cup) grated Cheddar cheese
25 g (1 oz) salted potato crisps, crushed

Place the chicken, onion, wine, stock and bouquet garni in a large pan and bring to the boil. Reduce the heat and simmer for 25-30 minutes until the chicken is tender. Drain the liquid and reserve for the sauce. Discard the bouquet garni and remove skin and bones from the chicken; coarsely chop the flesh. Melt the butter in a pan and gently fry the mushrooms, then stir in the flour and cook for 1 minute. Add the reserved poaching liquor and onion.

Return to the heat and bring to the boil, stirring continuously. Stir in the chicken, sweetcorn, parsley, lemon juice and cream and season to taste with salt and pepper. Cook the potatoes and mash with the milk and 55 g (2 oz/½ cup) of the cheese and season to taste. Preheat grill. Spoon the chicken mixture into a flameproof dish and cover with creamed potato. Mix the crisps with the remaining cheese. Sprinkle over the potato crisps and grill until golden.

Serves 4.

CHICKEN & HAM PIE

25 g (1 oz/6 teaspoons) butter
225 g (8 oz) sweetcure ham, cut into 2.5 cm (1 in) cubes
350 g (12 oz) skinned and boned chicken, cut into 2.5 cm (1 in) cubes
1 onion, chopped
225 g (8 oz) leeks, trimmed and sliced
175 g (6 oz) button mushrooms, sliced
25 g (1 oz/¼ cup) plain flour
300 ml (10 fl oz/1¼ cups) chicken stock
150 ml (5 fl oz/⅔ cup) single (light) cream
finely grated rind of ½ lemon
salt and pepper
225 g (8 oz) shortcrust pastry
2 tablespoons grated Parmesan cheese
milk for glazing

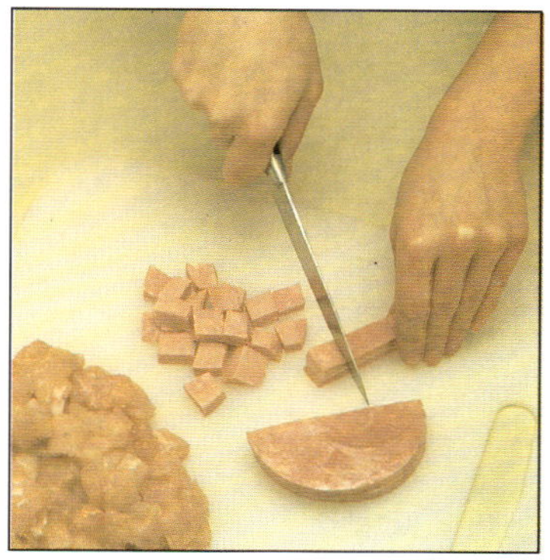

Preheat oven to 200C (400F/Gas 6). In a pan, melt the butter, add the ham and chicken and cook for 2-3 minutes. Remove from the pan and reserve. Add the vegetables and cook for 2-3 minutes until starting to soften. Return the ham and chicken to the pan, stir in the flour and cook for 1-2 minutes until vegetables are starting to soften. Remove from the heat and gradually add the chicken stock and the cream. Return to the heat and, stirring, cook for 2 minutes until thickened. Add the lemon rind and season with salt and pepper.

Transfer the chicken and ham mixture to a 1 litre (35 fl oz/4½ cup) pie dish. Mix the pastry with the Parmesan, then roll out on a floured surface 2.5 cm (1 in) larger than the pie dish. Cut off a 2.5 cm (1 in) strip to fit the edge of the dish. Brush the edge with a little water, then cover with the pastry lid. Pinch the edges together to seal and brush the pie with milk to glaze. Bake in the oven for 25-30 minutes or until the pastry is golden brown.

Serves 4.

CIDER APPLE CHICKEN

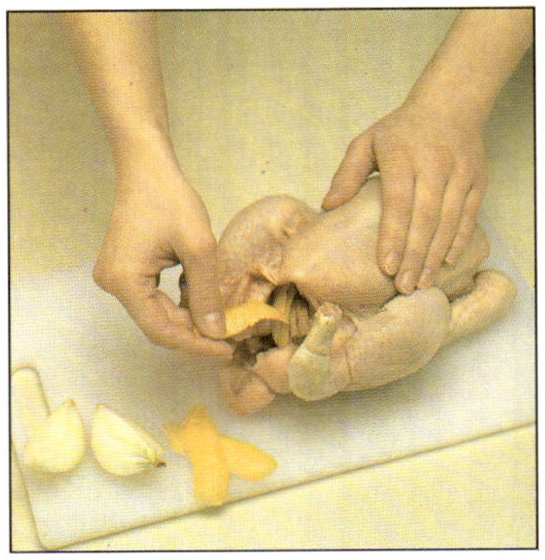

pared rind of 1 lemon plus 1 teaspoon juice
½ cinnamon stick
1 onion, quartered
1.5 kg (3¼-3½ lb) chicken
salt and pepper
85 g (3 oz/⅓ cup) butter
1 tablespoon oil
3 tablespoons brandy
450 g (1 lb) eating apples, peeled and cored
150 ml (5 fl oz/⅔ cup) cider
300 ml (10 fl oz/1¼ cups) crème fraîche
1 tablespoon each chopped fresh chives and parsley

Place rind, cinnamon stick and onion in the chicken. Season well.

Preheat oven to 180C (350F/Gas 4). Heat 55 g (2 oz/¼ cup) butter and the oil in a flameproof casserole and brown the chicken on all sides. Pour over the brandy and ignite. Thinly slice one of the apples and add to the casserole once the flames have died down. Add the cider to the casserole, bring to the boil, cover and cook in the oven for 1¼ hours.

Melt the remaining butter in a pan, cut the remaining apples into thick slices and sauté until just cooked. Remove the chicken from the casserole and place on a warmed serving platter and surround with the sautéed apples. Add the crème fraîche and lemon juice to the casserole, stir well and boil to reduce slightly. Season well and pour over the chicken. Sprinkle with the chopped herbs and serve at once.

Serves 4-6.

CHICKEN PROVENÇALE

25 g (1 oz/6 teaspoons) butter
1 tablespoon oil
6 cloves garlic, unpeeled
4 chicken joints, cut in half
115 ml (4 fl oz/½ cup) medium sherry
400 g (14 oz) can chopped tomatoes
2 tablespoons tomato purée (paste)
2 tablespoons chopped fresh herbs
salt and pepper

In a large pan, heat the butter and oil, add the garlic and the chicken, skin-sides down, and cook for 15 minutes on one side until the chicken is half cooked.

Add the sherry to the pan and boil rapidly until reduced by half. Turn the chicken pieces over and continue to boil until the sherry is reduced to a syrup.

Add the tomatoes and tomato purée (paste) and continue cooking for a further 15 minutes until the chicken is tender and the sauce has reduced to a glaze. Add the chopped herbs and season with a little salt and pepper. Serve with saffron rice and French beans.

Serves 4.

CHICKEN WITH WALNUT SAUCE

6 chicken breasts
salt and freshly ground black pepper
juice 1 orange
115 g (4 oz/1¼ cups) walnut halves
2 cloves garlic, chopped
85 ml (3 fl oz/⅓ cup) walnut oil
85 ml (3 fl oz/⅓ cup) olive oil
squeeze lemon juice
chopped fresh parsley or chives and lemon slices, to garnish

Preheat oven to 200C (400F/Gas 6). Season chicken breasts and pour the orange juice over them; set aside.

Spread walnuts on a baking sheet and place in oven until lightly browned, about 5-10 minutes. Transfer to a food processor or blender with garlic, 2 tablespoons water and a pinch of salt. Mix to a paste. With motor running, slowly pour in walnut and olive oils to make a smooth, mayonnaise-like sauce. Add lemon juice and pepper to taste; set aside.

Preheat grill. Grill chicken for 5-7 minutes each side until juices run clear when thickest part is pierced with a sharp knife. Garnish with chopped parsley or chives and lemon slices, then serve with the sauce.

Serves 6.

CHICKEN WITH SHERRY

4 tablespoons raisins
225 ml (8 fl oz / 1 cup) oloroso sherry
3 tablespoons olive oil
1.75 kg (3½ lb) chicken, cut into 8 pieces
1 Spanish onion, finely chopped
1 clove garlic, finely chopped
225 ml (8 fl oz / 1 cup) chicken stock
salt and freshly ground black pepper
4 tablespoons pine nuts

In a small bowl, soak raisins in sherry for 30 minutes.

In a flameproof casserole, heat 2 tablespoons oil, add chicken and cook gently until lightly and evenly browned, about 10 minutes. Transfer to absorbent kitchen paper to drain. Add onion and garlic to casserole and cook gently, stirring occasionally, until softened and lightly coloured, about 7 minutes. Strain raisins and set aside.

Stir sherry into casserole. Simmer until reduced by half. Add stock, chicken and seasoning, bring to boil, then simmer gently until chicken is cooked, about 35 minutes. In a small pan, fry nuts in remaining oil until lightly coloured. Drain on absorbent kitchen paper, then stir into casserole with raisins. Transfer chicken to a warm serving dish. Boil liquid in casserole to concentrate slightly. Pour over chicken.

Serves 4.

LEMON & CORIANDER CHICKEN

4 chicken thighs, skinned
4 chicken drumsticks, skinned
60 ml (2 fl oz/¼ cup) vegetable oil
5 cm (2 in) piece fresh root ginger, grated
4 cloves garlic, crushed
1 fresh green chilli, seeded and finely chopped
½ teaspoon turmeric
1 teaspoon ground cumin
1 teaspoon ground coriander
salt and cayenne pepper
grated peel and juice of 1 lemon
125 g (4 oz) fresh coriander leaves, chopped
coriander leaves and lemon slices, to garnish

Wash chicken joints and pat dry with absorbent kitchen paper. Heat oil in a large frying pan, add chicken, and fry, stirring frequently, until browned all over. Remove from pan with a slotted spoon and set aside. Add ginger and garlic to pan and fry for 1 minute. Stir in chilli, turmeric, cumin and ground coriander and season with salt and cayenne pepper, then cook for 1 minute more.

Return chicken to pan, add 125 ml (4 fl oz/½ cup) water and lemon peel and juice. Bring to the boil, then cover and cook over a medium heat for 25-30 minutes or until chicken is tender. Stir in chopped coriander, then serve hot, garnished with fresh coriander leaves and lemon slices.

Serves 4.

Variation: Use fresh parsley, or parsley and mint, instead of coriander, if preferred.

APRICOT & CHICKEN CURRY

1.25 kg (2½ lb) chicken joints, skinned
½ teaspoon chilli powder
3 teaspoons Garam Masala
2.5 cm (1 in) piece fresh root ginger, grated
2 cloves garlic, crushed
125 g (4 oz/1 cup) ready-to-eat dried apricots
2 tablespoons vegetable oil
2 onions, finely sliced
440 g (14 oz) can chopped tomatoes
3 teaspoons sugar
6 teaspoons white wine vinegar
salt

Wash chicken and pat dry with absorbent kitchen paper. Cut each joint into 4 pieces and put in a large bowl. Add chilli powder, garam masala, ginger and garlic and toss well to coat chicken pieces. Cover and leave in a cool place for 2-3 hours, to allow chicken to absorb flavours. In a separate bowl, put apricots and 155 ml (5 fl oz/⅔ cup) water and leave to soak for 2-3 hours.

Heat oil in a large heavy-based pan and add chicken. Fry over a high heat for 5 minutes or until browned all over. Remove from pan and set aside. Add onions to pan and cook, stirring, for about 5 minutes, until soft. Return chicken to pan with tomatoes and cook, covered, over a low heat for 20 minutes. Drain apricots, add to pan with sugar and vinegar. Season with salt. Simmer, covered, for 10-15 minutes. Serve hot.

Serves 4.

GOLDEN STEAMED CHICKEN

125 g (4 oz/¾ cup) basmati rice
1.75 kg (3½ lb) chicken
3 tablespoons vegetable oil
½ teaspoon chilli powder
60 g (2 oz/⅓ cup) raisins
60 g (2 oz/½ cup) flaked almonds
1 tablespoon chopped fresh thyme
salt and cayenne pepper
½ teaspoon ground cumin
½ teaspoon turmeric
1 teaspoon ground coriander
2 teaspoons Garam Masala
125 ml (4 fl oz/½ cup) hot water
thyme sprigs, to garnish

Wash rice thoroughly and soak in cold water for 30 minutes, then drain. Wash chicken, pat dry with absorbent kitchen paper and set aside. Heat 1 tablespoon oil in a saucepan, add rice and fry, stirring, for 2-3 minutes, until golden brown. Stir in chilli powder, raisins, almonds, thyme, 185 ml (6 fl oz/¾ cup) water and salt. Bring to the boil, then cover and simmer for 10-12 minutes, until rice has absorbed all the liquid. Leave to cool, then use to stuff chicken.

Truss chicken, then place in a steamer and steam for 1 hour. Heat remaining oil in a large pan, add cumin, turmeric, coriander and garam masala. Season with salt and cayenne pepper and fry for 1 minute. Transfer chicken to this pan and fry for 5 minutes, turning chicken until well coated. Pour hot water down side of pan, cover and cook over a low heat for 15-20 minutes, until tender. Serve hot, garnished with thyme sprigs.

Serves 4.

CHICKEN WITH LENTILS

250 g (8 oz) boneless chicken breasts (fillets)
250 g (8 oz/1¼ cups) red split lentils
½ teaspoon turmeric
60 ml (2 fl oz/¼ cup) vegetable oil
6 green cardamom pods, bruised
1 onion, finely sliced
1 cm (½ in) piece fresh root ginger, grated
salt and cayenne pepper
6 teaspoons lemon juice
1 teaspoon cumin seeds
2 cloves garlic, finely sliced

Wash chicken, pat dry and cut into cubes. Set aside.

Wash lentils, put in a large saucepan and add 940 ml (30 fl oz/3¾ cups) water and turmeric. Bring to the boil, then cover and simmer for 20-30 minutes or until tender. Drain thoroughly. Meanwhile, heat half the oil in a large saucepan, add cardamom pods and fry for 1 minute. Add onion and fry, stirring frequently, for about 8 minutes, until golden brown. Add chicken and fry for 5 minutes, until browned all over. Add ginger and fry for 1 minute more. Season with salt and cayenne pepper.

Stir in lemon juice and 155 ml (5 fl oz/⅔ cup) water and cover. Simmer for 25-30 minutes or until chicken is tender. Stir in lentil mixture and cook, stirring, for 5 minutes. Meanwhile, heat remaining oil, add cumin and garlic and fry, stirring, for 1-2 minutes, until garlic is golden. Transfer chicken and lentils to serving dish and pour garlic mixture over. Serve hot.

Serves 4.

CHICKEN & ALLIOLI

4 chicken portions
salt and freshly ground black pepper
6 tablespoons olive oil
3 tablespoons lemon juice
2 tablespoons finely chopped spring onions
2 tablespoons chopped fresh parsley
Allioli, see page 159
2 lemons, quartered

Rub chicken with salt and pepper, then place in a single layer in a non-metallic dish.

Pour the oil and lemon juice over the chicken and leave for 1 hour, turning chicken over once or twice.

Preheat grill. Place chicken on a grill rack and grill slowly for 8-10 minutes on each side, basting occasionally with the oil and lemon mixture, until crisp on the outside and tender throughout. Transfer to a warm serving plate and scatter spring onions and parsley over the top. Serve with Allioli and lemon quarters.

Serves 6.

CHICKEN IN BALSAMIC VINEGAR

mixed salad leaves for serving
2 tablespoons olive oil
1 onion, finely chopped
2 cloves garlic, finely minced or crushed
700 g (1½ lb) skinned and boned chicken breasts, cut into 2.5 cm (1 in) strips
9 teaspoons balsamic vinegar
3 teaspoons Dijon mustard
freshly ground black pepper
2 tablespoons shredded fresh basil
fresh basil leaves, to garnish

Arrange salad leaves on 4 dinner plates and set aside.

Heat the wok until hot. Add olive oil and swirl to coat wok. Add onion and garlic and stir-fry for 1-2 minutes until onion begins to soften. Add chicken strips, working in 2 batches, and stir-fry for 3-4 minutes until golden and chicken feels firm to the touch. Return all chicken to the wok.

Stir in vinegar and mustard and stir-fry for 2-3 minutes until chicken is cooked through and well coated with vinegar and mustard. Season with pepper and sprinkle with shredded basil. Spoon onto salad-lined plates and garnish with additional basil leaves. Serve with sautéed potatoes.

Serves 4.

CHICKEN & BASIL STIR-FRY

450 g (1 lb) boneless chicken thighs
1 tablespoon dark soy sauce
1 tablespoon cornflour
1 tablespoon groundnut (peanut) oil
2 cloves garlic, thinly sliced
1 fresh red chilli, seeded and thinly sliced
1 teaspoon chilli powder
1 tablespoon hoisin sauce
small bunch basil leaves, shredded
basil leaves and blanched red chilli strips, to garnish

Skin and trim the chicken. Cut into 2.5 cm (1 in) strips and place in a bowl. Stir in the soy sauce and cornflour.

Heat the oil in a non-stick or well seasoned wok and stir-fry chicken with garlic and chilli for 7-8 minutes.

Add chilli powder and hoisin sauce and cook for a further 2 minutes. Remove from heat and stir in shredded basil. Garnish with basil and chilli strips and serve on a bed of rice.

Serves 4.

BANG BANG CHICKEN

55 ml (2 fl oz/¼ cup) peanut oil
3 carrots, cut into julienne strips
1 fresh chilli, seeded and chopped
225 g (8 oz) beansprouts, trimmed
½ cucumber, seeded and cut into julienne strips
800 g (1¾ lb) skinned and boned chicken breasts, cut into shreds
2.5 cm (1 in) fresh ginger, cut in julienne strips
2 cloves garlic, finely chopped
4 spring onions, thinly sliced
9 teaspoons cider vinegar or rice vinegar
2 tablespoons dry sherry or rice wine
1 tablespoon sugar
1 teaspoon Chinese chilli sauce
150 ml (5 fl oz/⅔ cup) chicken stock
3 tablespoons each light soy sauce and tahini

Heat wok until hot. Add 2 tablespoons peanut oil and swirl to coat wok. Add carrots and chilli and stir-fry for 2-3 minutes. Remove to a bowl. Stir-fry beansprouts for 1 minute and remove to bowl. Add cucumber to bowl. Heat remaining oil in wok and add chicken. Working in 2 batches, stir-fry for 2-3 minutes until the chicken is white and the juices run clear. Remove to another bowl. Increase heat, add ginger and garlic to wok and stir-fry for 1 minute. Add spring onions and stir-fry for 1 minute. Add remaining ingredients and stir-fry until sauce is smooth and thick.

Pour half the sauce over carrot mixture and remaining sauce over chicken; toss each mixture well. Spoon chicken onto centre of a serving dish, then spoon vegetables around chicken. Serve with rice or noodles.

Serves 6.

Note: Garnish with sesame seeds or chopped peanuts and coriander, if wished.

COQ AU VIN

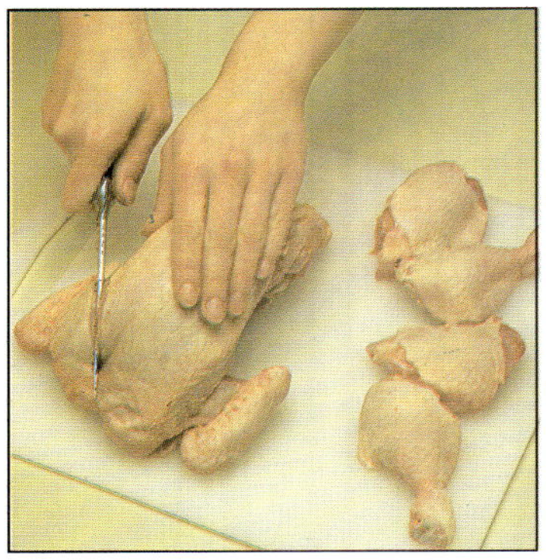

550 ml (20 fl oz/2½ cups) red wine
3 cloves garlic, sliced
1 small onion, chopped
2 tablespoons olive oil
1 teaspoon brown sugar
1 teaspoon mixed peppercorns, crushed
1 teaspoon coriander seeds, crushed
1 bouquet garni
1.5 kg (3¼-3½ lb) chicken, cut into 8 pieces
45 g (1½ oz/3 tablespoons) seasoned flour
115 g (4 oz) piece smoked bacon, derinded and diced
175 g (6 oz) button onions, peeled
175 g (6 oz) button mushrooms
425 ml (15 fl oz/2 cups) chicken stock
2 tablespoons chopped parsley
fried bread croûtons, to garnish

Mix together the wine, garlic, chopped onion, 1 tablespoon of the oil, sugar, peppercorns and coriander. Add the bouquet garni and the chicken pieces. Cover and marinate in the refrigerator for 2-3 hours, turning regularly. Remove chicken from marinade (reserving marinade) and pat dry on kitchen paper, then toss in the seasoned flour. Heat the remaining oil in a casserole and fry the bacon until browned, remove with a slotted spoon and set to one side. Add the chicken pieces to the casserole and fry until well browned, set aside with the bacon.

Add the button onions and cook until browned. Add mushrooms and any remaining flour. Cook for 1 minute. Add the stock and marinade, stirring until thick. Return chicken and bacon, cover and simmer for 40 minutes. Remove the chicken and vegetables to a serving dish using a slotted spoon; keep warm. Bring the sauce to the boil for 3-4 minutes until thick. Check the seasoning and stir in the parsley. Spoon the sauce over the chicken and garnish with bread croûtons.

Serves 4.

BOMBAY CHICKEN THIGHS

2 tablespoons vegetable oil
2.5 cm (1 in) piece fresh root ginger, peeled and finely chopped
2 cloves garlic, finely chopped
1 fresh chilli, seeded and chopped
700 g (1½ lb) skinned and boned chicken thighs, cut into pieces
1 onion, coarsely chopped
2 teaspoons curry paste
400 g (14 oz) can chopped tomatoes
1 teaspoon ground coriander
grated rind and juice of ½ lemon
2 bay leaves
freshly ground black pepper
150 ml (5 fl oz/⅔ cup) unsweetened coconut milk
fresh coriander or lemon leaves, to garnish

Heat the wok until hot. Add oil and swirl to coat wok. Add ginger, garlic and chilli and stir-fry for 1 minute until very fragrant. Add chicken pieces and stir-fry for 3-4 minutes until chicken begins to colour. Stir in onion and curry paste and stir to coat. Add tomatoes and their juice, coriander, lemon rind and juice, bay leaves and black pepper. Bring to simmering point and cook for 3-4 minutes until sauce is slightly thickened.

Stir in coconut milk and reduce heat. Simmer for 5-6 minutes until sauce is thickened and chicken pieces are tender. Remove bay leaves and garnish with coriander or lemon leaves. Serve with steamed basmati rice.

Serves 4.

SMOKED CHICKEN KEDGEREE

25 g (1 oz/6 teaspoons) butter
1 teaspoon coriander seeds, crushed
1 onion, sliced
1 teaspoon ground coriander
2 teaspoons ground cumin
85 g (3 oz/½ cup) long-grain rice
85 g (3 oz/½ cup) red lentils
550 ml (20 fl oz/2½ cups) chicken stock
350 g (12 oz) smoked chicken, coarsely chopped
juice of ½ lemon
115 ml (4 fl oz/½ cup) natural Greek yogurt
2 tablespoons chopped fresh parsley
2 hard-boiled eggs, coarsely chopped
1 lemon, sliced, to garnish
mango chutney and poppadoms, to serve

In a large pan, melt the butter, add the crushed coriander seeds and the onion and cook over a gentle heat until slightly softened, then stir in the ground coriander, cumin, rice and lentils and coat well with the butter. Pour in the stock, bring to the boil, then cover and simmer for 10 minutes.

Remove the lid, add the chicken and continue cooking for a further 10 minutes until all the liquid has been absorbed and the rice and lentils are tender. Stir in the lemon juice, yogurt, parsley and chopped hard-boiled eggs, and heat through gently. Spoon into a warmed serving dish and garnish with lemon. Serve with mango chutney and poppadoms.

Serves 4.

KLEFTIKO

1 chicken, weighing 1.35 kg (3 lb)
1 lemon, quartered
2 teaspoons dried oregano
salt and pepper
6 teaspoons olive oil
1 red onion, finely sliced
115 ml (4 fl oz/½ cup) dry white wine
lemon rind strips and oregano sprigs, to garnish

Preheat oven to 170C (325F/Gas 3). Cut chicken into 4 portions. Rub each chicken portion all over with a lemon quarter.

Mix together dried oregano, 1 teaspoon salt and pepper to taste. Rub mixture over each chicken portion. Cut 4 squares of foil large enough to wrap around a chicken portion. Brush foil with olive oil. Place a piece of chicken in the middle of each foil square. Scatter sliced onion over chicken. Pour 5-6 teaspoons wine over each piece of chicken.

Seal edges of foil to make a parcel. Place parcels on a baking sheet and bake in the oven for 1-1½ hours until chicken is well cooked and the juices run clear when the thickest part is pierced with a knife. To serve, open each parcel and slide contents onto a warmed plate. Garnish with lemon rind and sprigs of oregano.

Serves 4.

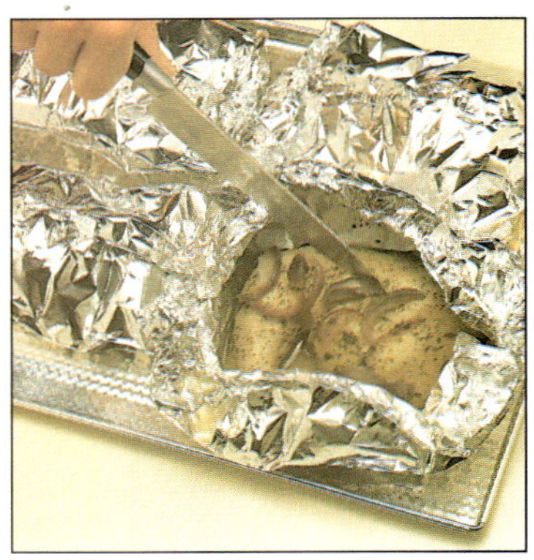

TURKEY CHILLI

700 g (1½ lb) small turkey thighs
2-3 tablespoons vegetable oil
1 onion, chopped
4 cloves garlic, finely chopped
1-2 fresh chillies, seeded and chopped
4 teaspoons chilli powder
cayenne pepper, to taste
1½ teaspoons ground cumin
400 g (14 oz) can peeled tomatoes
1½ teaspoons soft brown sugar
salt
two 425 g (15 oz) cans red kidney beans
sour cream and chopped fresh parsley, to garnish

With a small, sharp knife, remove skin from turkey and discard. Slice meat from thigh bones; cut into small pieces. Heat the wok until hot. Add 1 tablespoon oil and swirl to coat wok. Add half the turkey meat and stir-fry for 4-5 minutes until brown. Remove to a bowl; repeat with remaining turkey meat, adding a little more oil if necessary. Remove meat to bowl. Add remaining oil to wok and add onion and garlic. Stir-fry for 3-4 minutes, until onion softens. Stir in chillies, chilli powder, cayenne pepper and ground cumin.

Stir in tomatoes, with their liquid, then add the sugar and season with salt. Add turkey and kidney beans to the wok. Bring mixture to the boil and reduce heat. Simmer, covered, for 45-55 minutes. Remove cover and cook 15 minutes more until chilli is thick and well reduced. Taste and adjust seasoning, if necessary. Garnish with sour cream and chopped parsley and serve with rice.

Serves 6-8.

TURKEY WITH CHILLI RELISH

700 g (1½ lb) boneless turkey breast fillets, cut into strips
3-4 tablespoons seasoned flour
3-4 tablespoons vegetable oil
70 ml (2½ fl oz/⅓ cup) chicken stock
2 tablespoons cider vinegar
½ teaspoon chilli powder
cayenne pepper, to taste
2-3 plum tomatoes, peeled, seeded and chopped
1 red onion, finely chopped
1 fresh chilli, seeded and chopped
1 dessert apple, cored and chopped
2 tablespoons chopped fresh coriander
1 tablespoon chopped peanuts or walnuts

Dredge the turkey strips in the seasoned flour.

Heat the wok until hot. Add 2 tablespoons oil and swirl to coat wok. Add half the turkey strips and stir-fry for 1-2 minutes. Remove to serving plate; keep warm. Add 1-2 tablespoons more oil and cook remaining strips in the same way. Remove to the serving plate and keep warm.

Add stock and stir to deglaze the wok. Add cider vinegar, chilli powder, cayenne pepper to taste, tomatoes, onion, chilli and chopped apple. Cook for 1-2 minutes until sauce thickens. Return turkey strips to wok and stir them into the sauce. Sprinkle with coriander and peanuts or walnuts. Serve with pasta.

Serves 4.

TURKEY MARSALA

70 ml (2½ fl oz/⅓ cup) sweet Marsala
3 tablespoons raisins
25 g (1 oz/2 tablespoons) butter
4 leeks (pale green and white parts only), cut in half lengthwise and sliced
250 ml (9 fl oz/1 cup) chicken stock
1 bay leaf
½ teaspoon dried thyme
¼ teaspoon dried rubbed sage
575 g (1¼ lb) boneless turkey breast fillets, cut into strips
finely grated rind of 1 lemon
2 teaspoons plain flour
2 tablespoons whipping cream
fresh sage leaves and lemon slices, to garnish

In a small bowl, combine Marsala with the raisins. Leave to stand 20 minutes. Heat the wok until hot. Add 1 tablespoon butter and swirl to melt and coat wok. Add leeks and stir-fry for 1 minute. Add 70 ml (2½ fl oz/⅓ cup) chicken stock, bay leaf, thyme and sage and cook, covered, for 4-6 minutes until leeks are tender and liquid has evaporated. Discard bay leaf. Remove to a bowl and cover to keep warm. Wipe wok dry.

Add remaining butter to wok and swirl to coat. Add the turkey, in 2 batches, and stir-fry for 2 minutes. Remove to a plate. Cook lemon rind and flour for 1 minute. Slowly add remaining stock and bring to the boil. Add Marsala, raisins and cream and simmer for 2 minutes. Spoon leek mixture onto plates, top with turkey and spoon sauce over. Garnish with sage and lemon. Serve with rice.

Serves 4.

GREEN PEPPERCORN TURKEY

2 tablespoons olive oil
700 g (1½ lb) boneless turkey breast fillets
1 clove garlic, finely chopped
4 spring onions, thinly sliced
1 tablespoon green peppercorns
55 ml (2 fl oz/¼ cup) brandy or white wine
115 ml (4 fl oz/½ cup) whipping cream
½ teaspoon salt
1 pear or apple, cut in half lengthwise, cored and cut lengthwise into thin slices
toasted slivered almonds and fresh chives, to garnish

Heat the wok until hot. Add oil and swirl to coat wok. Arrange turkey in wok in a single layer, working in 2 batches, if necessary.

Cook for 3-5 minutes, turning halfway through cooking. Remove to serving plate and keep warm. Add garlic, spring onions and green peppercorns to wok and stir-fry for 1 minute until onions begin to soften. Add brandy or wine and stir to deglaze. Cook for 1-2 minutes to reduce slightly.

Stir in whipping cream and salt and bring to the boil. Reduce heat and add pear or apple slices. Cook, covered, for 1-2 minutes until fruit slices are heated through, then arrange them over turkey breast fillets. Pour sauce over and sprinkle with toasted almonds and chives. Serve with mange tout (snow peas).

Serves 4.

DUCK & COCONUT CURRY

- 4 duck portions, skinned
- 2 tablespoons vegetable oil
- 1 teaspoon mustard seeds
- 1 onion, finely chopped
- 3 cloves garlic, crushed
- 5 cm (2 in) piece fresh root ginger, grated
- 2 fresh green chillies, seeded and chopped
- 1 teaspoon ground cumin
- 3 teaspoons ground coriander
- 1 teaspoon turmeric
- 3 teaspoons white wine vinegar
- salt and cayenne pepper
- 315 ml (10 fl oz/1¼ cups) Coconut Milk
- 2 tablespoons shredded coconut, toasted, and lemon wedges, to garnish

Wash duck and pat dry with absorbent kitchen paper. Heat oil in a large frying pan, add duck and fry, stirring, over a high heat for 8-10 minutes, until browned all over, then remove from pan. Pour off all but 2 tablespoons fat from pan, add mustard seeds and fry for 1 minute or until they begin to pop.

Add onion to pan and cook, stirring, over a medium heat for 8 minutes or until soft and golden. Stir in garlic, ginger, chillies, cumin, coriander and turmeric and fry for 2 minutes. Stir in vinegar and season with salt and cayenne pepper. Return duck to pan and turn pieces to coat them in spice mixture. Stir in coconut milk and bring to the boil. Cover and cook over a low heat for about 40 minutes or until duck is tender. Garnish and serve hot.

Serves 4.

DUCK IN GINGER SAUCE

- 3 tablespoons olive oil
- 1 onion, chopped, and 5-6 cloves garlic, chopped
- 5 cm (2 in) piece of fresh root ginger, peeled and sliced
- 1 tablespoon plain flour
- 115 ml (4 fl oz/½ cup) red wine
- 250 ml (9 fl oz/1 cup) port
- 3-4 sprigs each fresh thyme and rosemary
- 2 bay leaves
- 1 tablespoon black peppercorns
- 685 ml (24 fl oz/3 cups) veal, duck or chicken stock
- 700 g (1½ lb) duckling breast fillet, skinned and excess fat removed, cut crosswise into thin strips
- 450 g (1 lb) shiitake mushrooms, sliced
- 75 g (3 oz) raisins
- 6 spring onions, cut into 5 cm (2 in) pieces
- 450 g (1 lb) pappardelle or wide egg noodles

Heat wok until hot. Add 2 tablespoons of the oil and swirl to coat wok. Add onion, garlic and ginger and stir-fry for 2-3 minutes until onion is softened. Stir in flour until completely blended. Slowly pour in wine, stirring until thickened and blended. Add port, thyme, rosemary, bay leaves, peppercorns and stock. Bring to the boil and skim any foam which comes to the surface. Simmer, stirring often, for 15-20 minutes until lightly thickened and reduced by about half. Strain into a bowl.

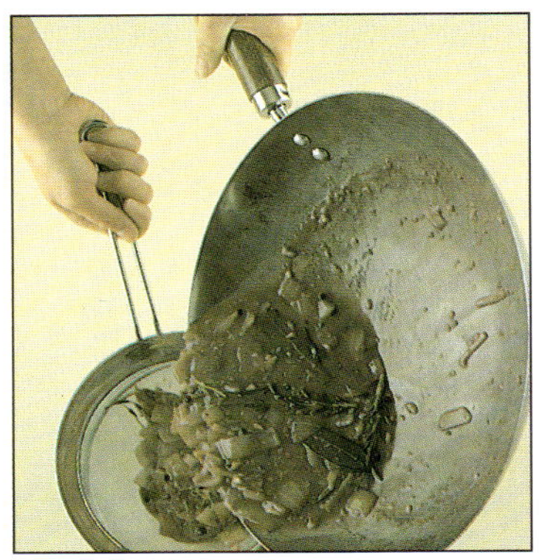

Wipe wok and heat until very hot, but not smoking. Add remaining oil and swirl to coat wok. Add duckling strips and cook for 2-3 minutes until golden. Remove to a bowl. Stir in mushrooms, raisins and spring onions and stir-fry for 2-3 minutes. Add sauce and bring to simmering point. Add duckling strips. Cook pappardelle or egg noodles according to packet directions. Drain and place in a serving dish. Toss with a little of the sauce, then pour over the remaining sauce.

Serves 4.

RABBIT STIFADO

6 teaspoons plain flour
salt and pepper
700 g-1 kg (1½-2.2 lb) rabbit joints
70 ml (2½ fl oz/⅓ cup) olive oil
450 g (1 lb) tiny pickling onions, peeled
1 clove garlic, crushed
3 teaspoons tomato purée (paste)
300 ml (10 fl oz/1¼ cups) red wine
300 ml (10 fl oz/1¼ cups) chicken stock
1 bay leaf
2 sprigs thyme
2 slices bread, crusts removed, and 2 tablespoons chopped fresh parsley, to garnish

On a plate, mix together flour, salt and pepper. Toss rabbit pieces in seasoned flour. Heat half oil in a frying pan. Fry rabbit pieces until brown on both sides. Transfer to a flameproof casserole. Add onions to frying pan; cook until they begin to brown. Add garlic and tomato purée (paste) to pan and stir in wine and stock. Add bay leaf, thyme, salt and pepper. Add to casserole, cover and cook over a low heat for 1½-2 hours until rabbit is tender.

Cut each slice of bread into 4 triangles. In a frying pan, heat remaining oil and fry bread until golden brown on both sides. Dip one edge of each triangle into chopped parsley. To serve, place rabbit on a shallow plate and arrange onions around edge. Pour the sauce over the rabbit and garnish with fried bread.

Serves 6.

SOY-ROASTED DUCKLING

2.25 kg (5 lb) duckling, giblets removed
4 tablespoons dark soy sauce
2 tablespoons brown sugar
DIP
1 tablespoon sunflower oil
4 spring onions, finely chopped
1 clove garlic, finely chopped
3 tablespoons dark soy sauce
2 teaspoons brown sugar
2 tablespoons dry sherry

Preheat oven to 190C (375F/Gas 5). Wash duckling and pat dry. Place on a wire rack in a roasting tin. Prick all over with a fork.

Sprinkle over soy sauce, brown sugar and garlic. Bake for 2 hours 15 minutes until juices run clear and skin is well browned. Make the dip. Heat the oil in a non-stick or well seasoned wok and stir-fry spring onions and garlic for 1 minute. Drain on kitchen paper and mix with remaining ingredients.

To serve, remove all skin and fat from duckling and shred flesh away from bone. Serve with the dip, soft pancakes and shredded spring onions and cucumber.

Serves 4.

Note: Soft pancakes can be bought ready-made from Chinese supermarkets.

GUINEA FOWL CASSEROLE

55 ml (2 fl oz/¼ cup) olive oil
1 guinea fowl, cut into 4 pieces
1 large onion, finely sliced
1 clove garlic, crushed
400 g (14 oz) can chopped tomatoes
1 tablespoon chopped fresh oregano
salt and pepper
450 g (1 lb) small okra
halved black olives, to garnish

In a flameproof casserole, heat oil. Add guinea fowl pieces. Cook on both sides until brown. Transfer to a plate.

Add onion and garlic to casserole and cook until soft. Add tomatoes, oregano, 300 ml (10 fl oz/1¼ cups) water, salt and pepper. Bring to the boil, then add guinea fowl and coat well with sauce. Cover pan and simmer gently for 40 minutes.

Trim ends of okra without cutting pods. Put into a bowl of cold water; rinse gently and strain. Repeat until water is clear. Spread okra over guinea fowl. Cover and simmer for a further 30 minutes until okra is tender. Scatter black olives over the top and serve.

Serves 4.

QUAIL WITH GRAPES

3 tablespoons olive oil
1 Spanish onion, finely chopped
2 small carrots, finely chopped
salt and freshly ground black pepper
8 quail
8 slices streaky bacon
4 black peppercorns
2 cloves garlic
250 g (9 oz) moscatel grapes, peeled and seeded
pinch freshly grated nutmeg
225 ml (8 fl oz/1 cup) medium-bodied dry white wine
4 tablespoons Spanish brandy

Preheat oven to 190C (375F/Gas 5). Heat oil in a heavy flameproof casserole that will hold the quail in a single layer. Add onion and carrots and cook, stirring occasionally, for 4-5 minutes. Season quail inside and out, lay a slice of bacon over each one and tie in place with string. Place on the vegetables, then cook in the oven for 30 minutes.

Meanwhile, using a pestle and mortar, crush peppercorns and garlic, then work in half the grapes, the nutmeg, wine and brandy. Pour the mixture over the quail and cook for 30 minutes, basting occasionally. Add remaining grapes, then carefully pour cooking liquid into a saucepan; keep casserole warm. Boil liquid until lightly thickened, then season to taste. Transfer quail, bacon, vegetables and grapes to a warm serving plate and pour the sauce over them.

Serves 4-6.

MEAT

MINTY LAMB PATTIES

60 g (2 oz/⅓ cup) whole brown lentils
315 ml (10 fl oz/1¼ cups) boiling water
3 onions, finely chopped
500 g (1 lb) minced lamb
6 teaspoons Garam Masala
2 dried red chillies, seeded and crushed
1 egg, beaten
60 ml (2 fl oz/¼ cup) natural yogurt
2 tablespoons chopped fresh mint
2 fresh green chillies, seeded and chopped
60 ml (2 fl oz/¼ cup) vegetable oil
fresh mint leaves, to garnish

Put lentils in a bowl, add water and leave to soak for 2 hours.

Put lentils, their soaking water, 2 onions, lamb, garam masala and red chillies in a large heavy-based pan and bring to the boil. Cook, uncovered, over a medium heat, stirring constantly, until all the liquid has evaporated and mixture is very dry. Remove from heat and leave to cool. Put mixture in a blender or food processor fitted with a metal blade and process to a smooth paste. Add egg and yogurt and blend again. Chill for 2-3 hours, then form into 16 balls.

Mix together remaining onion, mint and green chillies. Make an indentation in each lamb ball and stuff with a little minty mixture, then cover up with meat. Flatten balls into 5 cm (2in) patties. Heat oil in a frying pan and fry patties a few at a time for 4-6 minutes, turning over after half the time, until well browned. Serve, garnished with fresh mint leaves.

Serves 4.

LAMB STEAKS WITH PASTA

4 thick lamb leg steaks
salt and pepper
2 cloves garlic, sliced
400 g (14 oz) can chopped tomatoes
70 ml (2½ fl oz/⅓ cup) olive oil
3 teaspoons chopped fresh marjoram
3 teaspoons chopped fresh parsley
315 g (10 oz) orzo (rice-shaped pasta)
salad leaves, to serve

Preheat oven to 200C (400F/Gas 6). Season meat with salt and pepper. Place in a large roasting tin.

Scatter garlic over meat. Add 150 ml (5 fl oz/⅔ cup) water and tomatoes. Stir in olive oil, salt, pepper, marjoram and parsley. Cook for 40 minutes, basting from time to time and turning pieces of lamb over.

Add 300 ml (10 fl oz/1¼ cups) boiling water and the pasta. Stir in more salt and pepper. Cook for a further 40 minutes until pasta is cooked. If necessary, add more hot water. Serve with salad leaves.

Serves 6.

LAMB WITH SPINACH

3 tablespoons soy sauce
¼ teaspoon five-spice powder
2.5 cm (1 in) piece fresh root ginger, peeled and cut into julienne strips
2 cloves garlic, finely chopped
700 g (1½ lb) lamb fillet, cut crosswise into thin strips
1 tablespoon sesame oil
1 fresh red chilli, seeded and thinly sliced
8 spring onions, cut into 5 cm (2 in) pieces
1 mango, peeled and cut into 1 cm (½ in) thick pieces
175 g (6 oz) fresh baby spinach leaves, washed and dried
3 tablespoons dry sherry or rice wine
1 teaspoon cornflour dissolved in 1 tablespoon water

In a shallow baking dish, combine soy sauce, five-spice powder, ginger and garlic. Add lamb strips and toss to coat well. Leave to marinate for 1 hour, covered, stirring occasionally. Heat the wok until very hot. Add sesame oil and swirl to coat. With a slotted spoon and working in 2 batches, add lamb to wok, draining off and reserving as much marinade as possible. Stir-fry lamb for 2-3 minutes until browned on all sides. Remove to a bowl. Add chilli to oil remaining in wok and stir-fry for 1 minute.

Add spring onions and mango and stir-fry for 1 minute. Stir in spinach leaves, reserved lamb, dry sherry or rice wine and reserved marinade. Stir cornflour mixture and stir into wok. Stir-fry for 1 minute, tossing all ingredients until spinach wilts and lamb is lightly glazed with sauce. Serve with potatoes or noodles.

Serves 4.

LAMB WITH LEMON & GARLIC

3 tablespoons olive oil
1 kg (2¼ lb) lean, boneless lamb, cut into 2.5 cm (1 in) pieces
1 Spanish onion, finely chopped
3 cloves garlic, crushed
1 tablespoon paprika
3 tablespoons finely chopped fresh parsley
3 tablespoons lemon juice
salt and freshly ground black pepper
3 tablespoons dry white wine (optional)

Heat oil in a heavy flameproof casserole, add lamb and cook, stirring occasionally, until lightly browned. Do this in batches if necessary so the pieces are not crowded. Using a slotted spoon, transfer meat to a plate or bowl and reserve.

Stir onion into casserole and cook for about 5 minutes, stirring occasionally, until softened. Stir in garlic, cook for 2 minutes, then stir in paprika. When well blended, stir in lamb and any juices on plate or in bowl, the parsley, lemon juice and seasoning. Cover tightly and cook over very low heat for 1¼-1½ hours, shaking casserole occasionally, until lamb is very tender. If necessary, add wine or 3 tablespoons water.

Serves 4-6.

BRAISED LAMB & VEGETABLES

450 g (1 lb) firm, yellow-flesh potatoes, cut into 0.5 cm (¼ in) slices
2 cloves garlic, pounded to a paste
6-8 spring onions, thinly sliced
2 medium-large artichoke bottoms sliced
150 g (5 oz) chestnut mushrooms, chopped
handful parsley, finely chopped
1 tablespoon mixed herbs, chopped
salt and freshly ground black pepper
3 tablespoons olive oil
4 lamb shoulder or loin chops
175 ml (6 fl oz/¾ cup) full-bodied dry white wine

Preheat oven to 190C (375F/Gas 5). In a bowl, combine potatoes, garlic, spring onions, artichoke bottoms, mushrooms, parsley, mixed herbs and seasoning. Place half the mixture in a heavy flameproof casserole. Heat oil in a frying pan, add lamb and brown on both sides. Drain on absorbent kitchen paper, then season and place in casserole.

Over the heat, stir wine into pan to dislodge cooking juices, bring to boil and pour over lamb. Cover with remaining vegetables and add sufficient water to come almost to the level of the vegetables. Bring to the boil, cover and cook in the oven for about 30 minutes. Uncover and cook for a further 1 hour. Add a little water if it seems to be drying out.

Serves 4.

ORANGE-GLAZED LAMB

1 tablespoon vegetable oil
700 g (1½ lb) lean lamb, cut into 1 cm (½ in) strips
150 ml (5 fl oz/⅔ cup) dry white wine
150 ml (5 fl oz/⅔ cup) freshly squeezed orange juice
1 teaspoon ground coriander
½ teaspoon dry mustard powder
salt and freshly ground black pepper
3 teaspoons cornflour dissolved in 2 tablespoons water
1 large orange, zest removed and cut into julienne strips, and flesh divided into segments
fresh mint, to garnish (optional)

Heat the wok until very hot. Add vegetable oil and swirl to coat wok.

Add lamb strips and stir-fry for 4-5 minutes. Remove to a plate and keep warm. Pour off all the fat from the wok and add the white wine, stirring to deglaze. Add orange juice, coriander, mustard powder, salt and pepper and bring to the boil. Stir the cornflour mixture and slowly pour into the wok, stirring constantly until sauce thickens.

Return the lamb strips to the sauce, turning to coat each one, and cook for 1-2 minutes until sauce has glazed the lamb strips and they are heated through. Add orange julienne and segments and cook for 1 minute to heat through. Arrange lamb and orange segments on 4 dinner plates and garnish with mint, if wished. Serve with green beans.

Serves 4.

SPICED RACK OF LAMB

3 teaspoons plain flour
salt and pepper
2 racks of lamb
1 clove garlic, finely chopped
6 teaspoons olive oil
450 g (1 lb) tomatoes, roughly chopped
½ lemon, chopped
1 stick cinnamon
3 cloves
1 small red chilli, seeded and chopped
115 ml (4 fl oz/½ cup) dry white wine
6 teaspoons tomato purée (paste)
lemon slices, to garnish

Preheat oven to 180C (350F/Gas 4). Mix together flour, salt and pepper. Rub over lamb. Press garlic into gaps between bones. In a roasting tin, heat oil. Put lamb, skin side down, in oil to brown. Remove lamb. Add tomatoes, lemon, cinnamon, cloves and chilli to roasting tin. Return lamb, skin side up, to tin.

In a bowl, mix together wine, 115 ml (4 fl oz/½ cup) water and tomato purée (paste). Pour over lamb. Cover tin loosely with foil. Cook in the oven for 1 hour. Remove foil and cook for a further 30 minutes until lamb is cooked. Cut lamb into individual chops and keep warm. Place roasting tin on heat and boil liquid to reduce to a thick sauce. Pour over meat. Garnish with lemon slices.

Serves 6.

LAMB CHILINDRON

4 tablespoons olive oil
750 g (1½ lb) lean lamb, cubed
salt and freshly ground black pepper
1 Spanish onion, chopped
2 cloves garlic, chopped
3 large red peppers (capsicums), peeled, seeded and cut into strips
4 beefsteak tomatoes, peeled, seeded and chopped
1 dried red chilli, chopped
chopped fresh herbs, to garnish

Heat oil in a flameproof casserole. Season lamb and add to casserole.

Cook, stirring, until evenly browned, then using a slotted spoon, transfer to a bowl. Add onion to casserole and cook for about 4 minutes, stirring occasionally, until softened but not coloured. Stir in garlic, cook for 1-2 minutes, then stir in peppers (capsicums), tomatoes and chilli. Simmer for 5 minutes.

Return lamb, and any juices that have collected in bowl, to casserole. Cover tightly and cook gently for about 1½ hours until lamb is tender. Season if necessary. Serve garnished with chopped herbs.

Serves 6.

PORK & BAMBOO SHOOTS

2 tablespoons vegetable oil
4 cloves garlic, very finely chopped
350 g (12 oz) lean pork, very finely chopped
115 g (4 oz) canned bamboo shoots, chopped or sliced
4 tablespoons peanuts, coarsely chopped
2 teaspoons fish sauce
freshly ground black pepper
4 large spring onions (scallions), thinly sliced
Thai holy basil sprig, to garnish

In a wok, heat oil, add garlic and fry, stirring occasionally, for about 3 minutes until lightly coloured.

Add pork and stir-fry for 2 minutes. Add bamboo shoots and continue to stir for a further minute.

Stir in peanuts, fish sauce, plenty of black pepper and half of spring onions (scallions). Transfer to a warmed serving plate and sprinkle over remaining spring onions (scallions) and basil sprig.

Serves 4.

PORK WITH PEARS

6 teaspoons olive oil
2 onions, chopped
1 kg (2.2 lb) boned lean pork, cut into cubes
250 ml (9 fl oz/1 cup) red wine
grated rind ½ orange
½ cinnamon stick
salt and pepper
2 pears
2 teaspoons clear honey
chopped fresh coriander leaves, orange rind strips and pitta bread, to garnish

In a flameproof casserole, heat oil. Add onions; cook until soft. Push to side of pan, turn up heat and brown meat in batches.

Add wine, orange rind, cinnamon stick, salt, pepper and 300 ml (10 fl oz/1¼ cups) water. Bring to simmering point, then cover casserole and cook for 1 hour.

Peel, core and slice pears and place on top of meat. Drizzle honey over pears. Cover pan and simmer gently for 30-40 minutes until meat is tender. Garnish with chopped coriander leaves, strips of orange rind and pieces of pitta bread.

Serves 6.

Note: This recipe is traditionally made with quinces. If quinces are available, use them instead of pears.

PORK WITH HERB SAUCE

25 g (1 oz/½ cup) fresh white breadcrumbs
2 tablespoons white wine vinegar
2 cloves garlic
2 canned anchovy fillets, drained
15 g (½ oz/¼ cup) chopped fresh parsley
2 teaspoons capers
1 hard-boiled egg yolk
225 ml (8 fl oz/1 cup) extra virgin olive oil
salt and freshly ground black pepper
4 loin chops, about 2.5 cm (1 in) thick

In a small bowl, soak the breadcrumbs in the white wine vinegar.

Meanwhile, using a pestle and mortar, crush garlic with anchovy fillets, parsley, capers and egg yolk. Squeeze vinegar from breadcrumbs, then mix breadcrumbs into mortar. Stir in oil in a slow trickle to make a creamy sauce. Add black pepper, and salt if necessary Set aside.

Preheat grill. Grill chops for about 12 minutes each side until lightly browned on both sides and cooked through but still juicy in centre. Season chops and spoon on some of sauce. Serve remaining sauce separately.

Serves 4.

PORK KEBABS

450 g (1 lb) lean pork
1 onion
1 green pepper (capsicum)
8 cherry tomatoes
shredded lettuce, orange slices and thyme sprigs, to garnish
MARINADE:
juice ½ orange
2 tablespoons olive oil
1 clove garlic, crushed
1 teaspoon chopped fresh thyme
1 teaspoon coriander seeds, crushed
salt and pepper

To make the marinade, in a bowl, mix together orange juice, olive oil, garlic, thyme, coriander seeds, salt and pepper. Cut pork into 2 cm (¾ in) cubes and add to marinade. Mix thoroughly, cover and leave in a cool place for 2 hours. Cut onion into quarters and separate the layers. Cut pepper (capsicum) into small squares, removing seeds.

Thread pork, onion, pepper (capsicum) and tomatoes onto 8 bamboo satay skewers. Grill on a barbecue or under a grill, turning from time to time, for 10-15 minutes until pork is cooked through. Serve on a bed of shredded lettuce, garnished with orange slices and thyme.

Makes 8.

STIR-FRIED PORK & BEANS

2 tablespoons vegetable oil
6 cloves garlic, chopped
350 g (12 oz) lean pork, finely chopped
350 g (12 oz) long beans or slim green beans
12 water chestnuts
115 g (4 oz) cooked peeled prawns
1 tablespoon fish sauce
½ teaspoon crushed palm sugar
freshly ground black pepper

In a wok, heat oil, add garlic and fry, stirring occasionally, until golden.

Add pork and beans and stir-fry for 2 minutes, then add water chestnuts. Stir for 1 minute.

Add prawns, fish sauce, sugar, plenty of black pepper and about 3 tablespoons water. Bubble for a minute or two, then transfer to a warmed serving plate.

Serves 4.

MIXED VEGETABLES & PORK

225 g (8 oz) lean pork, finely chopped
freshly ground black pepper
2 tablespoons vegetable oil
3 cloves garlic, finely chopped
450 g (1 lb) prepared mixed vegetables, such as mange tout (snow peas), broccoli flowerets, red pepper (capsicum) and courgettes (zucchini)
1 tablespoon fish sauce
½ teaspoon crushed palm sugar
3 spring onions (scallions), finely chopped

In a bowl, mix together pork and plenty of black pepper. Set aside for 30 minutes.

In a wok or frying pan, heat oil, add garlic and cook, stirring occasionally, for 2-3 minutes, then stir in pork.

Stir briefly until pork changes colour. Stir in mixed vegetables, then fish sauce, sugar and 125 ml (4 fl oz/½ cup) water. Stir for 3-4 minutes until mange tout (snow peas) are bright green and vegetables still crisp. Stir in spring onions (scallions).

Serves 4.

PORK & PRUNE MEDLEY

450 g (1 lb) pork fillet, cut into thin slices
2 tablespoons soy sauce
6 teaspoons balsamic or cider vinegar
2 tablespoons olive oil
2 courgettes (zucchini), sliced
1 onion, cut lengthwise into 'petals'
1 red pepper (capsicum), cut into thin strips
115 g (4 oz) mushrooms, sliced
115 g (4 oz) mange tout (snow peas)
115 g (4 oz) asparagus, cut into 5 cm (2 in) pieces
55 g (2 oz/½ cup) walnut halves
175 g (6 oz) ready-to-eat prunes, stoned
salt and freshly ground black pepper

In a shallow baking dish, sprinkle pork slices with soy sauce and balsamic or cider vinegar and toss to coat well. Allow to stand for 30 minutes. Heat the wok until hot. Add olive oil and swirl to coat wok. Add pork slices and stir-fry for 3-5 minutes, until golden on all sides. With a slotted spoon, remove to a bowl.

Add courgettes (zucchini), onion, red pepper (capsicum), mushrooms, mange tout (snow peas), asparagus, walnut halves and prunes and stir-fry for 2-3 minutes until well coated with oil. Add 2 tablespoons water to wok and cover wok quickly. Steam for 1-2 minutes until vegetables just begin to soften. Uncover wok, return pork to wok and toss to mix. Season with salt and pepper. Stir-fry for a further 1-2 minutes until pork is heated through.

Serves 4.

COCONUT PORK WITH LIME

6 pork escalopes, about 115 g (4 oz) each
1 cm (½ in) piece fresh root ginger, peeled and grated
2 teaspoons ground cumin
1 teaspoon ground coriander
1 teaspoon chilli powder (to taste)
1 teaspoon paprika
½ teaspoon salt
2-3 tablespoons vegetable oil
1 onion, cut lengthwise in half and thinly sliced
3-4 cloves garlic, finely chopped
300 ml (10 fl oz/1¼ cups) unsweetened coconut milk
grated rind and juice of 1 large lime
1 small Chinese cabbage, shredded
lime slices and coriander leaves, to garnish

Place escalopes between 2 sheets of greaseproof paper. Pound to a 0.5 cm (¼ in) thickness. Cut into strips. In a large, shallow dish, combine ginger, cumin, coriander, chilli powder, paprika and salt. Stir in pork strips and leave to stand for 15 minutes. Heat wok until very hot. Add half the oil and swirl to coat wok. Add half the pork and stir-fry for 2-3 minutes. Remove to a plate and keep warm. Cook remaining strips using remaining oil. Keep warm. Pour off all but 1 tablespoon oil from the wok.

Add onion and garlic to wok; stir-fry for 2-3 minutes until onion is softened. Slowly add coconut milk. Bring to simmering point but do not boil. Stir in lime rind and juice and shredded cabbage. Simmer gently for 5-7 minutes, stirring frequently, until cabbage is tender and sauce slightly thickened. Add pork and cook, covered, for 1-2 minutes until heated through. Arrange pork and cabbage on plates and garnish with lime slices and coriander.
Serve with noodles.

Serves 6.

RATATOUILLE-STYLE PORK

1 tablespoon olive oil
4 boneless loin pork chops, about 575 g (1¼ lb) and 2.5 cm (1 in) thick, trimmed of fat
1 onion, coarsely chopped
2 cloves garlic, chopped
1 small aubergine (eggplant), cut into 2.5 cm (1 in) cubes
1 red or green pepper (capsicum), diced
2 courgettes (zucchini), thickly sliced
225 g (8 oz) can chopped tomatoes
1 teaspoon chopped fresh oregano or basil leaves or ½ teaspoon dried oregano or basil
½ teaspoon dried thyme leaves
salt and freshly ground black pepper
fresh parsley or coriander sprigs, to garnish

Heat the wok until very hot. Add olive oil and swirl to coat. Arrange pork chops on bottom and side of wok, if necessary, in a single layer. Fry for 4-5 minutes until well browned on both sides, turning once and rotating during cooking. Remove to a plate. Add onion and garlic to remaining oil in wok and stir-fry for 1 minute until onion begins to soften. Add the aubergine (eggplant) cubes and diced pepper (capsicum) and stir-fry for 3-5 minutes to brown and soften.

Add courgettes (zucchini), chopped tomatoes and their juice, the fresh or dried oregano or basil, thyme and season with salt and pepper. Stir well and return pork chops to wok, covering them with the ratatouille mixture. Lower the heat and cook, covered, for 6-8 minutes, shaking wok occasionally to prevent sticking. Uncover and cook for 2-3 minutes more to allow sauce to thicken slightly. Garnish with parsley or coriander. Serve with fresh pasta.

Serves 4.

PORK WITH WALNUTS

450 g (1 lb) lean pork fillet
1 tablespoon rice wine
1 tablespoon light soy sauce
1 teaspoon cornflour
1 bunch spring onions
2 teaspoons sunflower oil
1 teaspoon caster sugar
salt and freshly ground black pepper
25 g (1 oz/¼ cup) walnut pieces

Trim any fat and silver skin from pork and cut into 0.5 cm (¼ in) strips. Place in a bowl and add rice wine, soy sauce and cornflour. Mix well, cover and chill for 30 minutes.

Trim the spring onions, discarding any damaged outer leaves. Cut the spring onions into 5 cm (2 in) pieces.

Heat oil in a non-stick or well seasoned wok and stir-fry pork mixture for 2-3 minutes until browned. Add spring onions, sugar and seasoning and stir-fry for 3 minutes. Sprinkle with walnut pieces and serve with noodles.

Serves 4.

PORK ESCALOPES NORMAND

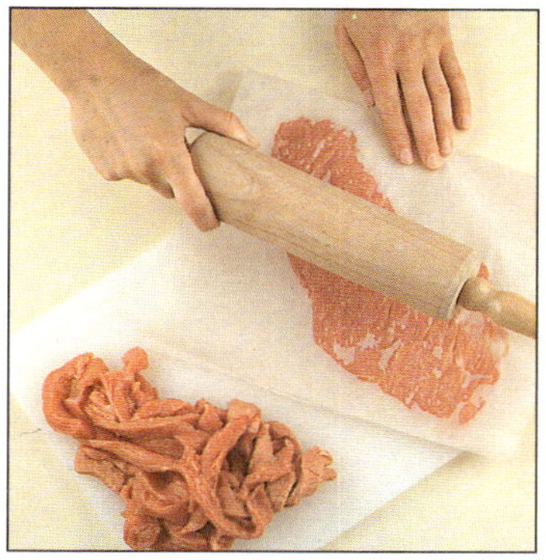

4 pork escalopes about 575 g (1¼ lb), 1 cm (½ in) thick
2 tablespoons vegetable oil
25 g (1 oz/2 tablespoons) butter
1 clove garlic, chopped
2 dessert apples, halved lengthwise, cored and thinly sliced
½ teaspoon dried thyme
3 tablespoons Calvados or brandy
115 ml (4 fl oz/½ cup) double or whipping cream
salt and freshly ground black pepper
apple slices and parsley sprigs, to garnish

Place pork escalopes between 2 sheets of greaseproof paper and pound to a 0.5 cm (¼ in) thickness. Cut into thin strips.

Heat the wok until very hot. Add oil and swirl to coat wok. Add half the pork strips and stir-fry for 2-3 minutes until golden on all sides. Remove to a plate, keep warm, and cook the remaining strips in the same way. Pour off any oil from the wok. Add butter to the wok and allow to melt. Add garlic, apple slices and thyme and stir-fry for 1-2 minutes until apple slices are golden.

Add Calvados or brandy to the wok and stir to deglaze. Add cream and bring to the boil. Add salt and pepper to taste. Cook for 1 minute, stirring constantly, until sauce thickens slightly and apples are tender. Arrange pork strips on 4 dinner plates and spoon over apples and sauce. Garnish with apple slices and parsley sprigs. Serve with buttered egg noodles or sautéed potatoes.

Serves 4.

PORK WITH CHILLI & PEAS

450 g (1 lb) pork fillet, cut crosswise into thin slices
1½ tablespoons soy sauce
6 teaspoons cider vinegar
1 tablespoon vegetable oil
2.5 cm (1 in) piece fresh root ginger, peeled and finely chopped
2 cloves garlic, finely chopped
1 fresh red chilli, seeded and thinly sliced
225 g (8 oz) fresh or frozen green peas or sugar snap peas
85 g (3 oz) red cabbage or radicchio, thinly shredded

In a small baking dish, sprinkle pork slices with soy sauce and vinegar. Toss to coat well. Leave to stand for 15-20 minutes.

Heat the wok until hot. Add oil and swirl to coat wok. Add pork slices and stir-fry for 2 minutes. Push to one side and add ginger, garlic and chilli; stir-fry for 1 minute to mix.

Add peas or sugar snap peas and red cabbage or radicchio and stir-fry for 2-3 minutes until vegetables are tender but still crisp. Serve with rice and wild rice.

Serves 4.

SPICED PORK LOIN

1 tablespoon paprika
3 cloves garlic, finely crushed
1 teaspoon chopped fresh oregano
½ teaspoon finely crushed cumin seeds
1 bay leaf, crushed
salt
3 tablespoons virgin olive oil
750 g (1½ lb) boned and rolled loin of pork
olive oil for frying
4 tablespoons full-bodied dry white wine
stoned green olives, to serve

In a small bowl, mix together paprika, garlic, oregano, cumin seeds, bay leaf and salt, then stir in olive oil.

Place pork in a non-metallic dish, spoon the marinade mixture over the top, cover and leave in refrigerator for 2-3 days. Return pork to room temperature 30 minutes before cooking.

Cut pork into 4 slices. Heat oil in a frying pan over fairly high heat. Add pork, brown quickly on both sides, then cook more gently for 4-5 minutes a side until cooked through. Transfer slices to a warm serving plate. Stir wine into cooking juices, boil for 2-3 minutes, then pour over pork. Scatter green olives over the top.

Serves 4.

PORK WITH BASIL

250 g (9 oz) thin egg noodles
55 ml (2 fl oz/¼ cup) olive oil
575 g (1¼ lb) pork fillet, cut into shreds
1 red onion, cut lengthwise in half, and thinly sliced
4 tablespoons shredded fresh basil leaves
6 teaspoons balsamic vinegar
3 tablespoons toasted pine nuts
salt and freshly ground black pepper
fresh basil leaves, to garnish

In a large saucepan of boiling water, cook the egg noodles according to the packet directions. Drain and rinse. Turn into a large bowl and toss with 2 tablespoons olive oil. Keep warm.

Heat the wok until very hot. Add remaining olive oil and swirl to coat wok. Add shredded pork and stir-fry for 2-3 minutes until pork is golden. Add red onion and toss with the pork, then stir-fry for 1 minute.

Stir in shredded basil, the balsamic vinegar and pine nuts and toss to mix well. Add noodles to the wok, season to taste and toss with pork mixture. Turn onto shallow serving dish and garnish with basil leaves.

Serves 4.

SPICED HONEY GAMMON

1.5 kg (3 lb) joint wood-smoked gammon
finely shredded peel and juice of 2 oranges
6 teaspoons clear honey
1 teaspoon ground mace
1 teaspoon grated fresh root ginger
125 g (4 oz) kumquats, sliced
6 teaspoons whole cloves
3 teaspoons cornflour

Soak gammon joint overnight in a bowl of cold water. Drain, transfer to a large saucepan and cover with fresh cold water. Bring to boil, cover and cook for 30 minutes. Drain and cool. Remove skin from gammon, leaving a layer of fat on surface of gammon.

Score fat on the surface of gammon into a lattice pattern with a sharp knife. Preheat oven to 190C (375F/Gas 5); place gammon in roasting tin. In a bowl, mix together orange peel, juice, honey, mace and ginger until evenly blended. Brush a little mixture over surface of gammon and bake in the oven for 30 minutes. Remove gammon from oven, brush surface with more orange mixture. Cover surface of gammon with kumquat slices, held in position with whole cloves.

Return to oven for a further 30-40 minutes until gammon is golden brown and tender. Remove and place on a serving dish. Keep warm. Add 185 ml (6 fl oz/¾ cup) water to roasting tin, stir to mix juices, then strain into a saucepan. Blend cornflour with remaining orange juice and honey mixture, add to pan, bring to boil and cook for 1 minute. Pour into a jug and serve with gammon. Garnish with remaining kumquat slices.

Serves 8.

HAM & PLUM STIR-FRY

2 tablespoons vegetable oil
1 red pepper (capsicum), cut lengthwise in half, thinly sliced
350 g (12 oz) plums or nectarines, stoned, thinly sliced
225 g (8 oz) oyster mushrooms, sliced
2 leeks, trimmed, washed and cut diagonally into 1 cm (½ in) pieces
6 spring onions, thinly sliced
450 g (1 lb) gammon steaks, cut into 2.5 cm (1 in) strips
250 ml (9 fl oz/1 cup) orange juice
2 tablespoons peach or apricot preserve
2 tablespoons soy sauce
6 teaspoons wine vinegar
2 teaspoons cornflour dissolved in 2 tablespoons water

Heat the wok until hot. Add oil and swirl to coat wok. Add red pepper (capsicum), plums or nectarines and stir-fry for 1-2 minutes. Add oyster mushrooms and leeks and stir-fry for 1-2 minutes until vegetables begin to soften. Push vegetables to one side and add spring onions and gammon strips. Stir-fry for 2-3 minutes, tossing ingredients to mix, until gammon is heated through.

Stir in orange juice, peach or apricot preserve, soy sauce and vinegar. Stir the cornflour mixture, then stir into wok. Bring to the boil and stir-fry for 1-2 minutes until sauce thickens and coats ingredients. Serve with rice or noodles.

Serve 4-6.

SAUSAGE & PEPPERS

2 tablespoons olive oil
700 g (1½ lb) hot, sweet or mixed Italian sausages
2 onions, halved lengthwise, then cut lengthwise into 'petals'
4-6 cloves garlic, finely chopped
1 each large red, green and yellow pepper (capsicum), cut in half lengthwise then into strips
225 g (8 oz) can peeled tomatoes
1 tablespoon fresh shredded oregano or basil or 1 teaspoon dried oregano or basil
½ teaspoon crushed chillies
½ teaspoon dried thyme
½ teaspoon rubbed sage
salt and freshly ground black pepper
fresh oregano or basil leaves, to garnish
Parmesan cheese, to serve

Heat the wok until hot. Add olive oil and swirl to coat wok. Add sausages and cook over moderate heat for 8-10 minutes until sausages are golden brown on all sides, turning and rotating sausages frequently during cooking. Remove sausages to a plate and pour off all but 2 tablespoons oil from the wok. Add onions and garlic and stir-fry for 2 minutes until golden. Add the red, green and yellow pepper (capsicum) strips and stir-fry for 1-2 minutes until just beginning to soften.

Add tomatoes and their liquid, fresh or dried oregano or basil, crushed chillies, thyme, sage, salt and pepper. Stir to break up the tomatoes and mix well. Return sausages to wok and cover with the vegetable mixture. Simmer for 15-20 minutes until vegetables are tender and sauce is thickened. Garnish with fresh oregano or basil leaves and sprinkle with shaved or grated Parmesan cheese. Serve with saffron rice or spaghetti.

Serves 6.

SPICY BRAISED BEEF

1.35 kg (3 lb) beef topside joint
2 cloves garlic, crushed
½ teaspoon ground cinnamon
¼ teaspoon ground cloves
salt and pepper
9 teaspoons olive oil
4 onions, thinly sliced
115 ml (4 fl oz/½ cup) red wine
6 teaspoons tomato purée (paste)
450 g (1 lb) spaghetti
3 teaspoons balsamic vinegar
fresh herbs, to garnish

With a sharp knife, make slits in the beef.

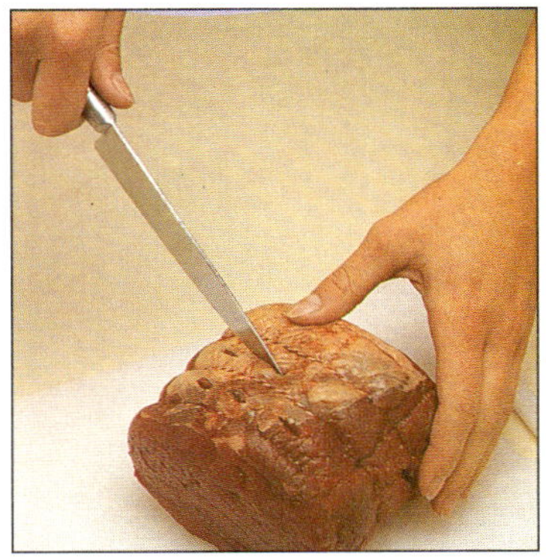

In a bowl, mix garlic, cinnamon, cloves, salt and pepper, press mixture into slits and leave beef in a cool place for 1 hour. Heat oil in a flameproof casserole into which meat will just fit. Turn meat in hot oil until brown all over. Remove from casserole. Add onions and cook gently until soft and lightly browned. Replace meat. Add the wine and enough hot water to barely cover it. Mix tomato purée (paste) with a little water; stir into casserole. Season.

Cover casserole and cook over a gentle heat for about 1½ hours, turning meat frequently, until it is tender. Bring a large pan of salted water to the boil and cook spaghetti until *al dente*. Remove meat and keep hot. Add vinegar to sauce. Boil briskly until reduced to a smooth glossy sauce. Slice beef. Garnish with herbs and serve with some sauce poured over beef and remainder stirred into spaghetti.

Serves 6.

BEEF-STUFFED CABBAGE

2 onions
5 tablespoons vegetable oil
3 cloves garlic, crushed
2 fresh green chillies, seeded and chopped
7.5 cm (3 in) piece fresh root ginger, grated
500 g (1 lb) lean minced beef
¼ teaspoon turmeric
2 teaspoons Garam Masala
1 savoy cabbage
440 g (14 oz) can chopped tomatoes
6 teaspoons lemon juice
salt and pepper
lemon or lime slices, to garnish

Chop 1 onion and slice the other.

Heat 2 tablespoons oil in a heavy-based pan, add chopped onion and cook over a medium heat, stirring, for about 8 minutes, until soft and golden brown. Add garlic, chillies and one-third of the ginger and cook for 1 minute, then remove with a slotted spoon and set aside.

Add beef to pan and cook, stirring, until browned and well broken up. Stir in turmeric and garam masala and cook for 1 minute, then add onion mixture.

Cook, covered, for 20-30 minutes, stirring occasionally, until cooking liquid is absorbed. Leave to cool. Remove core from cabbage with a sharp knife. Cook whole cabbage in boiling salted water for 8 minutes, then drain and rinse in cold water. Leave until cool enough to handle, then carefully peel off 12-16 outside leaves, keeping them whole. Finely shred remaining cabbage.

To make sauce, heat remaining oil in a heavy-based pan, add sliced onion and cook, stirring frequently, for 5 minutes or until soft but not brown. Add shredded cabbage, tomatoes, remaining ginger, lemon juice and 155ml (5 fl oz/⅔ cup) water. Season with salt and pepper. Bring to the boil, then simmer, uncovered, for 5 minutes.

Preheat oven to 190C (375F/Gas 5). Put about 2 tablespoons mince mixture on each cabbage leaf, fold sides in and roll up neatly. Pour a little sauce into base of an ovenproof casserole, add cabbage rolls and pour over remaining sauce. Cover and cook for 40-50 minutes, until cabbage is tender. Serve hot, garnished with lemon or lime slices.

Serves 4.

BEEF WITH TOMATO SAUCE

2 cloves garlic, thinly sliced
1 tablespoon finely chopped fresh thyme
1 tablespoon finely chopped fresh marjoram
750 g (1½ lb) piece chuck steak
2 tablespoons olive oil
SAUCE:
2 tablespoons olive oil
8 cloves garlic, chopped
1 sprig thyme
2 sprigs marjoram
3 sprigs parsley
400 g (14 oz) can chopped tomatoes
8 canned anchovy fillets, chopped
175 ml (6 fl oz/¾ cup) dry white wine
24 small black olives, stoned
salt and freshly ground black pepper

To make the sauce, heat oil in a saucepan, add garlic and herbs and cook gently for 5 minutes. Add tomatoes with their juice, then stir in anchovies, wine and olives. Simmer for 15 minutes. Taste and adjust seasoning.

Meanwhile, mix sliced garlic with chopped herbs. Using the point of a sharp knife, cut small slits in beef and push the herb-covered slices of garlic deep into slits. Heat oil in a flameproof casserole, add beef and cook until evenly browned, 10 minutes. Pour over sauce, cover tightly and cook gently for about 1½ hours turning beef occasionally, until it is tender.

Serves 4.

GARLIC BEEF

2 tablespoons olive oil
115 g (4 oz) piece green (unsmoked) bacon, cut into 5 cm (2 in) cubes
1 kg (2 lb) chuck steak, cut into 4 cm (1½ in) cubes
1 Spanish onion, chopped
1 head garlic, divide into cloves
225 ml (8 fl oz/1 cup) red wine
2 cloves
bouquet garni of 1 sprig marjoram, 1 sprig thyme, 2 sprigs parsley and 1 bay leaf
salt and freshly ground black pepper

In a heavy flameproof casserole, heat oil, add bacon and cook over a low heat until bacon gives off its fat. Increase heat, add beef and cook for about 5 minutes, stirring occasionally, until browned all over. Using a slotted spoon, transfer beef and bacon to a bowl.

Stir onion and garlic into casserole and cook gently for 6 minutes, stirring occasionally. Stir in wine, cloves, bouquet garni and salt and pepper. Return meat to casserole, cover tightly and cook gently for 2 hours, stirring occasionally, until meat is very tender. Check from time to time to ensure casserole is not drying out.

Serves 6.

TERIYAKI STEAKS

55 ml (2 fl oz/¼ cup) mirin or dry sherry sweetened with 1 teaspoon sugar
55 ml (2 fl oz/¼ cup) light soy sauce
1 cm (½ in) piece fresh root ginger, peeled and minced
1 clove garlic, finely chopped
1 teaspoon sugar
½ teaspoon red pepper sauce (or to taste)
4 sirloin or fillet steaks, cut into strips
2 tablespoons sesame oil
4 spring onions, thinly sliced
fresh coriander leaves, to garnish

In a shallow baking dish, combine mirin or sweetened dry sherry, soy sauce, ginger, garlic, sugar and red pepper sauce to taste.

Add the steak strips and turn to coat well. Leave to stand for 1 hour, turning strips once or twice.

Heat the wok until very hot. Add sesame oil and swirl to coat. Drain meat, reserving marinade, and add to wok. Stir-fry for 2-3 minutes until browned on all sides. Pour over marinade and add spring onions. Cook for 3-5 minutes until steaks are cooked to desired doneness and most of marinade has evaporated, glazing the meat. Garnish with coriander leaves and serve with marinated cucumber or daikon (mooli) salad and rice.

Serves 4.

SPICY SESAME BEEF

1 tablespoon cornflour
3 tablespoons light soy sauce
450 g (1 lb) rump, sirloin or fillet steak, cut crosswise into thin strips
350 g (12 oz) broccoli
2 tablespoons sesame oil
2.5 cm (1 in) piece fresh root ginger, peeled and cut into julienne strips
2 cloves garlic, finely chopped
1 fresh chilli, seeded and thinly sliced
1 red pepper (capsicum), thinly sliced
400 g (14 oz) baby corn
115 ml (4 fl oz/½ cup) beef or chicken stock, or water
4-6 spring onions, cut into 5 cm (2 in) pieces
toasted sesame seeds, to garnish

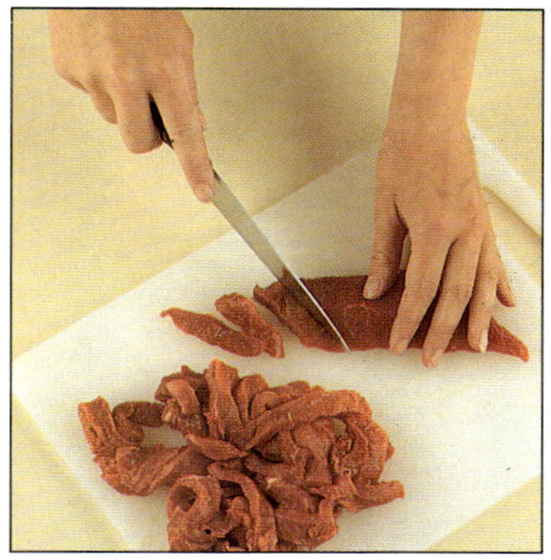

In a bowl, combine cornflour and soy sauce. Add beef strips and toss to coat well. Leave to stand for 20 minutes. Cut large flowerets from the broccoli and divide into small flowerets. With a swivel-bladed vegetable peeler, peel the stalk and cut diagonally into 2.5 cm (1 in) pieces. Heat the wok until very hot. Add sesame oil and swirl to coat. Add beef strips and marinade and stir-fry for 2-3 minutes until browned.

With a slotted spoon, remove beef strips to a bowl. Add ginger, garlic and chilli to the wok and stir-fry for 1 minute. Add broccoli, red pepper (capsicum) and baby corn and stir-fry for 2-3 minutes until broccoli is tender but still crisp. Add the stock and stir for 1 minute until sauce bubbles and thickens. Add spring onions and reserved beef strips and stir-fry for 1-2 minutes until beef strips are heated through. Sprinkle with sesame seeds and serve with rice or noodles.

Serves 4.

BEEF IN OYSTER SAUCE

3 teaspoons cornflour
1½ tablespoons soy sauce
1½ tablespoons rice wine or dry sherry
450 g (1 lb) rump, sirloin or fillet steak, cut crosswise into thin strips
2 tablespoons sesame oil
1 cm (½ in) piece fresh root ginger, peeled and chopped
2 cloves garlic, finely chopped
4 stalks celery, sliced
1 red pepper (capsicum), sliced
115 g (4 oz) mushrooms, sliced
4 spring onions, sliced
2 tablespoons oyster sauce
115 ml (4 fl oz/½ cup) chicken stock or water

In a bowl, combine 2 teaspoons of the cornflour with soy sauce and rice wine or sherry. Add beef strips and toss to coat well. Allow to stand for 25 minutes. Heat the wok until very hot. Add oil and swirl to coat wok. Add beef strips and stir-fry for 2-3 minutes until browned. With a slotted spoon, remove to a bowl. Add ginger and garlic to oil remaining in wok and stir-fry for 1 minute. Add the celery, red pepper (capsicum), mushrooms and spring onions and stir-fry for 2-3 minutes until vegetables begin to soften.

Stir in oyster sauce and combine remaining cornflour with the stock or water, then stir into the wok and bring to the boil. Add reserved beef strips and toss beef and vegetables for 1 minute until sauce bubbles and thickens and beef is heated through. Serve with rice and wild rice.

Serves 4.

CHILLI BEEF WITH PEPPERS

1 tablespoon cornflour
55 ml (2 fl oz/¼ cup) light soy sauce
1 tablespoon honey or brown sugar
1 teaspoon Chinese chilli sauce
2 tablespoons vegetable oil
450 g (1 lb) rump or sirloin steak, cut crosswise into thin strips
1 tablespoon sesame oil
2 cloves garlic, finely chopped
1 chilli, seeded and thinly sliced
1 onion, thinly sliced
1 red pepper (capsicum), cut into thin strips
1 green pepper (capsicum), cut into thin strips
1 yellow pepper (capsicum), cut into thin strips

In a small bowl, dissolve the cornflour with 55 ml (2 fl oz/¼ cup) water. Stir in the soy sauce, honey or sugar and chilli sauce until blended. Set aside. Heat the wok until very hot. Add vegetable oil and swirl to coat wok. Add beef strips and stir-fry for 2-3 minutes until beef is browned. With a slotted spoon, remove beef to a bowl.

Add sesame oil to the wok and add garlic and chilli. Stir-fry for 1 minute until fragrant. Add onion and pepper (capsicum) strips and stir-fry for 2-3 minutes until beginning to soften. Stir cornflour mixture, then stir into wok and stir until sauce bubbles and begins to thicken. Add beef strips and any juices and stir-fry for 1 minute until beef is heated through. Serve with rice.

Serves 4.

MEXICAN BEEF WITH BEANS

450 g (1 lb) minced (ground) beef
1 onion, chopped
3-4 cloves garlic, finely chopped
1 green or red pepper (capsicum), diced
115 g (4 oz) can chopped green chillies, drained
425 g (15 oz) can red kidney beans, drained
320 g (11½ oz) can whole-kernel sweetcorn, drained
6 teaspoons chilli powder (or to taste)
2 teaspoons ground cumin
1 teaspoon dried oregano
800 g (28 oz) can peeled tomatoes
salt and freshly ground black pepper
3 tablespoons chopped fresh parsley
115 g (4 oz/1 cup) grated mature Cheddar cheese
chopped fresh parsley, to garnish

In the wok, place minced beef and heat until it begins to release juices. Increase heat and stir to break up meat and stir-fry for 5-6 minutes until meat is browned. Add onion, garlic, green or red pepper (capsicum), chopped chillies, kidney beans and sweetcorn and bring to the boil.

Stir in chilli powder, cumin, oregano and peeled tomatoes with their juice. Stir to break up tomatoes. Season with salt and pepper, lower heat and cook, covered, for 20-30 minutes until slightly thickened. Remove from heat, stir in the parsley and half the cheese. Sprinkle with remaining cheese and garnish with chopped parsley.

Serves 6-8.

BEEF STROGANOFF

2 tablespoons groundnut oil
800 g (1¾ lb) fillet or boneless sirloin steak, cut crosswise into 1 cm (½ in) strips
25 g (1 oz/2 tablespoons) butter
1 onion, thinly sliced
225 g (8 oz) mushrooms, thinly sliced
salt and freshly ground black pepper
1 tablespoon flour
115 ml (4 fl oz/½ cup) beef or veal stock
1 tablespoon Dijon mustard (optional)
250 ml (9 oz/1 cup) sour cream
pinch of cayenne pepper
dill sprigs, to garnish

Heat the wok until very hot. Add oil and swirl to coat wok. Add half the beef strips.

Stir-fry for 1 minute until just browned and still rare. With a slotted spoon, remove beef to a bowl. Allow wok to reheat and add remaining beef strips. Stir-fry for 1 minute and turn beef and any juices into bowl. Add butter to wok, then add onion. Reduce heat to moderate and stir-fry onion for 3-4 minutes until softened and beginning to colour. Add mushrooms and increase heat; stir-fry for 2 minutes until mushrooms and onions are softened and golden. Add salt and pepper and stir in flour until well blended.

Add beef stock and bring to the boil, then simmer for 1 minute until sauce thickens. Stir in mustard, if using, and gradually add the sour cream. (Do not allow sour cream to boil.) Return beef strips and any juices to sauce and cook gently for 1 minute until beef is heated through. Sprinkle a little cayenne pepper over and garnish with dill sprigs. Serve with rice.

Serves 6.

STEAK AU POIVRE

1½ teaspoons green peppercorns
1 teaspoon black peppercorns
1 teaspoon white peppercorns
4 rump steaks, each weighing about 185 g (6 oz)
45 g (1½ oz/9 teaspoons) unsalted butter
few drops Tabasco sauce
few drops Worcestershire sauce
2 tablespoons brandy
3 tablespoons double (thick) cream
salt
sauté or jacket baked potatoes and green salad, to serve

Coarsely crush all peppercorns in a pestle and mortar.

Sprinkle crushed pepper over both sides of steaks, pressing in well with palm of hand. Set aside for 30 minutes. Melt 15 g (½ oz/3 teaspoons) butter in a large frying pan and heat until foaming. Add steaks and cook for 2-3 minutes, then turn and cook other sides for 2-3 minutes. (This timing gives medium-rare steaks, so adjust cooking time to suit personal preference). Turn steaks once again and top each one with 7 g (¼ oz/1½ teaspoons) butter and sprinkle with a few drops Tabasco sauce and Worcestershire sauce.

Pour over brandy and allow to heat through for a few seconds. Set it alight and remove from heat. When flames subside, lift steaks from pan and arrange on a warmed serving plate and keep warm. Add cream to pan, stir well and heat through for 1 minute, scraping up sediment from pan. Season with salt and spoon mixture over steaks. Serve at once with sauté or jacket baked potatoes and a green salad.

Serves 4.

DRY-FRIED BEEF STRIPS

2 tablespoons sesame oil
450 g (1 lb) rump or sirloin steak, cut crosswise into julienne strips
2 tablespoons rice wine or dry sherry
1 tablespoon light soy sauce
2 cloves garlic, finely chopped
1 cm (½ in) piece fresh root ginger, peeled and finely chopped
1 tablespoon Chinese chilli bean paste (sauce)
2 teaspoons sugar
1 carrot, peeled and cut into julienne strips
2 stalks celery, cut into julienne strips
2-3 spring onions, thinly sliced
¼ teaspoon ground Szechuan pepper
cucumber matchsticks, to garnish

Heat the wok until very hot. Add the oil and swirl to coat wok. Add beef and stir-fry for 15 seconds to quickly seal meat. Add 1 tablespoon rice wine or sherry and stir-fry for 1-2 minutes until beef is browned. Pour off and reserve any excess liquid and continue stir-frying until beef is dry.

Stir in soy sauce, garlic, ginger, chilli bean paste, sugar, remaining rice wine or sherry and any reserved cooking juices and stir to blend well. Add carrot, celery, spring onions and ground Szechuan pepper and stir-fry until the vegetables begin to soften and all the liquid is absorbed. Garnish with cucumber matchsticks and serve with rice and wild rice.

Serves 4.

GINGER BEEF WITH PINEAPPLE

450 g (1 lb) lean rump or sirloin steak
salt and freshly ground black pepper
1 tablespoon ginger wine
2.5 cm (1 in) piece fresh root ginger, peeled and finely chopped
1 clove garlic, finely chopped
1 teaspoon cornflour
225g (8 oz) fresh pineapple
1 tablespoon sunflower oil
2 red peppers (capsicum), thinly sliced
4 spring onions, chopped
2 tablespoons light soy sauce
1 piece stem ginger in syrup, drained and thinly sliced

Trim any visible fat from the beef and cut into 0.5 cm (¼ in) strips. Place in a bowl and season. Add the ginger wine, chopped ginger, chopped garlic and the cornflour and mix well. Cover and chill for 30 minutes. Meanwhile, peel and core the pineapple and cut into 2.5 cm (1 in) cubes.

Heat oil in a non-stick or well seasoned wok, add beef mixture and stir-fry for 1-2 minutes until beef is browned all over. Add peppers (capsicum) and stir-fry for a further minute. Add spring onions, pineapple and soy sauce and simmer gently for 2-3 minutes, to heat through. Sprinkle with stem ginger and serve on a bed of noodles.

Serves 4.

BEEF IN SPINACH SAUCE

2 tablespoons olive oil
750 g (1½ lb) chuck steak, cut into 4 cm (1½ in) cubes
8 button onions
1 tablespoon red wine vinegar
225 g (8 oz) fresh spinach, trimmed
1 tablespoon breadcrumbs
3 cloves garlic
425 ml (15 fl oz/scant 2 cups) veal stock, or water
salt and freshly ground black pepper
1 tablespoon black olive paste

In a large, flameproof casserole, heat oil, add beef and brown on all sides. Remove and set aside. Add onions to casserole and cook, stirring frequently, until evenly browned. Stir in vinegar and boil for 1 minute.

Put spinach, breadcrumbs, garlic and half the stock or water in a blender or food processor and mix until smooth. Return beef to casserole, pour over spinach mixture with remaining stock or water. Season. Heat to simmering point, then cover and simmer very gently for 1½-2 hours until beef is tender. Stir in black olive paste and serve.

Serves 4-6.

CALVES LIVER WITH BACON

4 rashers bacon, cut into strips
1 onion, thinly sliced lengthwise into 'petals'
1 green dessert apple, cored and thinly sliced
salt and freshly ground black pepper
1 tablespoon vegetable oil
350 g (12 oz) calves liver, cut into thin strips
6 teaspoons cider vinegar
55 ml (2 fl oz/¼ cup) dry white wine or apple juice
2 teaspoons cornflour dissolved in 55 ml
(2 fl oz/¼ cup) chicken stock or water
½ teaspoon dried thyme leaves
thyme sprigs or lemon wedges, to garnish

Place bacon in cold wok and heat over moderate heat until bacon begins to cook.

Increase heat and stir-fry for 1-2 minutes until bacon is crisp. Remove to a bowl. Add onion to dripping in wok and stir-fry for 1-2 minutes until just beginning to soften. Add apple slices and stir-fry for a further 1-2 minutes until apple begins to soften. Season with salt and pepper and remove to bowl. Add oil to wok and increase heat. Add liver strips and stir-fry for 1-2 minutes until just browned. The liver should be pink inside. Remove to bowl.

Stir cider vinegar into wok to deglaze, then stir in white wine or apple juice. Stir cornflour mixture and stir into wok with the thyme. Add reserved bacon, onion, apple and liver strips and cook for 1 minute until sauce bubbles and liver is heated through. Garnish with thyme sprigs or lemon wedges and serve with mashed or sautéed potatoes.

Serves 2.

VEAL WITH ANCHOVIES

100 ml (3½ fl oz/scant ½ cup) olive oil
flour for coating
salt and freshly ground black pepper
4 veal loin chops, 2 cm (¾ in) thick
2 small cloves garlic, coarsely chopped
2 canned anchovy fillets, chopped
2 tablespoons chopped fresh parsley
1½ tablespoons coarsely chopped capers
squeeze lemon juice
parsley and lemon slices, to garnish

Heat 4 tablespoons oil in a frying pan large enough to take chops in a single layer. Season flour with salt and pepper, then dredge chops with seasoned flour.

Add chops to frying pan and cook for about 10 minutes, turning occasionally, until light brown and crisp on outside and just cooked in centre.

Meanwhile, in a small saucepan, heat remaining oil, add garlic and cook until garlic is pale gold. Stir in anchovies and parsley. Cook for 20-30 seconds, mashing and stirring anchovies with a wooden spoon. Add capers, and black pepper and lemon juice to taste. Transfer chops to a warmed plate and spoon the sauce over the top. Serve garnished with parsley and lemon slices.

Serves 4.

VEGETARIAN MAIN COURSES

BRAISED FENNEL PROVENÇAL

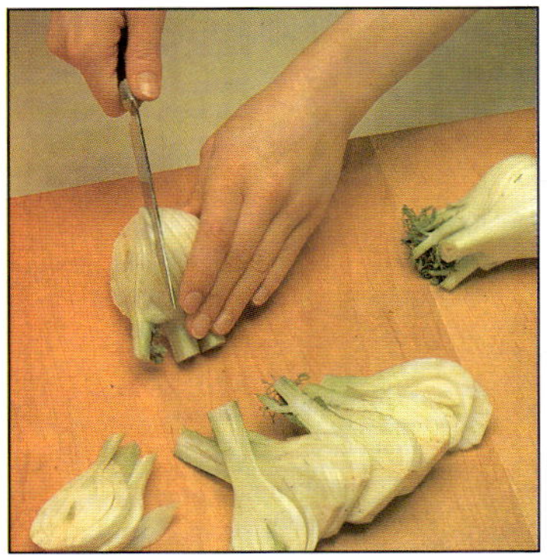

3 fennel bulbs, trimmed
3 tablespoons olive oil
4 cloves garlic, peeled
450 g (1 lb) ripe plum tomatoes, skinned, seeded and diced
150 ml (5 fl oz/2/3 cup) dry white wine
12 Niçoise olives
4 sprigs thyme
2 bay leaves
pinch of sugar
salt and pepper
thyme sprigs, to garnish

Cut the fennel bulbs lengthways into 1 cm (1/2 in) slices.

Heat the oil in a large frying pan and fry the fennel slices and garlic for 4-5 minutes on each side until golden; remove from pan with a slotted spoon and reserve.

Add the tomatoes and wine to the pan and boil rapidly for 5 minutes. Stir in the olives, herbs and sugar and arrange the fennel slices over the top, in a single layer, if possible. Cover and simmer gently for 20 minutes, season and serve hot or leave to cool and serve at room temperature, garnished with thyme.

Serves 4.

BROCCOLI CAPONATA

2 tablespoons olive oil
1 red onion, chopped
1 red pepper (capsicum), seeded and chopped
1 clove garlic, chopped
1 teaspoon chopped fresh thyme
85 ml (3 fl oz/1/3 cup) red wine
450 g (1 lb) tomatoes, skinned, seeded and chopped
150 ml (5 fl oz/2/3 cup) vegetable stock
1 tablespoon red wine vinegar
1 tablespoon brown sugar
450 g (1 lb) broccoli, trimmed and chopped
2 tablespoons tomato purée (paste)
55 g (2 oz/1/2 cup) stoned green olives
25 g (1 oz/1/4 cup) capers, drained
1 tablespoon shredded fresh basil

In a large pan, heat the oil and fry the onion, pepper (capsicum), garlic and thyme for 6-8 minutes until lightly browned. Add the wine and boil rapidly for 3 minutes. Add the tomatoes, stock, vinegar and sugar. Stir well, then cover and simmer gently for 20 minutes.

Steam the broccoli for 5 minutes until almost cooked, add to the tomato mixture with the tomato purée (paste), olives, caper and basil. Cook for a further 3-4 minutes, remove from the heat and leave to cool. Serve at room temperature.

Serves 4.

GRATIN OF VEGETABLES

115 g (4 oz/2/3 cup) long-grain rice
3 courgettes (zucchini)
1 red pepper (capsicum)
1 onion
6 ripe tomatoes
2 tablespoons olive oil
2 sprigs fresh thyme
2 sprigs fresh rosemary
2 bay leaves
1 teaspoon dried oregano
1 teaspoon fennel seeds, roasted
150 ml (5 fl oz/2/3 cup) vegetable stock
85 g (3 oz) Pecorino or vegetarian Cheddar cheese, grated

Preheat oven to 200C (400F/Gas 6). Put the rice into a small pan and cover with cold water. Bring to the boil and cook for 3 minutes, drain well and transfer to a gratin dish. Thickly slice the courgettes (zucchini), roughly chop the pepper (capsicum) and onion and skin, seed and roughly chop the tomatoes.

Place the prepared vegetables in a large bowl, add the oil and stir well until vegetables are coated. Snip in the fresh herbs, add the bay leaves, oregano and fennel seeds, stir and spoon over the rice. Pour over the stock, cover with foil and bake for 40 minutes. Remove the foil, sprinkle over the cheese and return to the oven for a further 10-15 minutes until cheese is melted and all the liquid is absorbed. Brown under a hot grill, if wished, and serve hot.

Serves 6.

TOMATO & BEAN TIAN

3 tablespoons olive oil
1 red onion, chopped
1 garlic clove, crushed
1 large red pepper (capsicum), seeded and chopped
3 teaspoons chopped fresh thyme
2 teaspoons chopped fresh rosemary
400 g (14 oz) can chopped tomatoes
432 g (15.2 oz) can cannellini beans, drained
25 g (1 oz/1/2 cup) each fresh breadcrumbs, chopped pine nuts and grated Parmesan cheese or vegetarian Cheddar cheese
2 large courgettes (zucchini), thinly sliced
2 ripe beef tomatoes, thinly sliced
rosemary sprigs, to garnish

Preheat oven to 190C (375F/Gas 5). In a saucepan, heat 2 tablespoons of the oil and fry the onion, garlic, pepper (capsicum), 2 teaspoons thyme and 1 teaspoon rosemary for 5 minutes. Add the tomatoes, cover and cook for 20 minutes. Stir in the beans and transfer to a shallow baking dish.

Mix the breadcrumbs, pine nuts and cheese together and sprinkle half over the tomato layer. Arrange courgettes (zucchini) and beef tomatoes in rows over the top and sprinkle over the remaining crumb mixture. Drizzle over the remaining oil and more herbs, if wished. Cover with kitchen foil and bake for 30 minutes. Remove foil and bake for a further 15-20 minutes until golden. Garnish with rosemary sprigs and serve hot with a crisp green salad.

Serves 4-6.

PARSNIP, PEAR & ALMOND SAUTÉ

12 baby onions
3 tablespoons olive oil
575 g (1¼ lb) baby parsnips, halved or quartered
1 clove garlic, chopped
2 teaspoons chopped fresh thyme
115 ml (4 fl oz/½ cup) dry cider
150 ml (5 fl oz/⅔ cup) vegetable stock
1 tablespoon brown sugar
2 teaspoons wholegrain mustard
2 small pears, cored and thickly sliced
55 g (2 oz/½ cup) blanched almonds, toasted
salt and pepper

Place the onions in a small pan, cover with cold water and bring to the boil. Drain, refresh under cold water, peel and cut in half. Heat 2 tablespoons of the oil in a large pan and stir-fry the onions, parsnips, garlic and thyme for 10 minutes until browned all over. Add the cider and boil rapidly for 5 minutes. Blend the stock, sugar and mustard together and stir into the pan. Cover and cook for 10-12 minutes until parsnips are tender.

Meanwhile, heat the remaining oil and fry the pear slices over a high heat for 1 minute on each side until browned, then remove pears with a slotted spoon. Pour the juices from the parsnips into the pan and boil rapidly for 2-3 minutes until thickened. Pour over the parsnips, add the pears and almonds and heat through. Season to taste and serve at once.

Serves 4.

— MUSHROOM & BEAN CHILLI —

4 tablespoons olive oil
1 large aubergine (eggplant), diced
175 g (6 oz) button mushrooms, wiped
1 large onion, chopped
1 clove garlic, chopped
1½ teaspoons paprika
½-1 teaspoon chilli powder
1 teaspoon ground coriander
½ teaspoon ground cumin
900 g (2 lb) tomatoes, skinned and chopped
150 ml (5 fl oz/⅔ cup) vegetable stock
25 g (1 oz) tortilla chips
1 tablespoon tomato purée (paste)
400 g (14 oz) can red kidney beans
1 tablespoon chopped fresh coriander
salt and pepper

In a large pan, heat 2 tablespoons oil and stir-fry the aubergine (eggplant) for 10 minutes until golden, then remove from the pan with a slotted spoon. Add 1 tablespoon oil to the pan and stir-fry the mushrooms until golden; remove with a slotted spoon. Add the remaining oil to the pan and fry the onion, garlic and spices for 5 minutes. Add the tomatoes and stock and cook, covered, for 45 minutes.

Finely crush the tortilla chips and blend with 4 tablespoons water and the tomato purée (paste). Whisk into the chilli sauce and add the mushroom and aubergine (eggplant). Drain the beans and add to the pan with the coriander. Cover and cook for a further 20 minutes. Season to taste and serve with plain boiled rice and thick sour cream, if wished.

Serves 6.

VEGETABLE & FRUIT CURRY

1½ teaspoons each coriander and cumin seeds
4 tablespoons vegetable oil
1 large onion, chopped
2 carrots, chopped
2 potatoes, diced
3 cloves garlic, crushed, or 1 tablespoon garlic purée
2 teaspoons grated fresh root ginger
1 teaspoon each curry powder and turmeric
450 g (1 lb) ripe tomatoes
450 ml (16 fl oz/2 cups) vegetable stock
115 g (4 oz/1 cup) frozen peas, thawed
1 apple, cored and chopped
1 mango, peeled, stoned and chopped
85 g (3 oz/⅔ cup) cashew nuts, toasted
25 g (1 oz) creamed coconut
1 tablespoon chopped fresh coriander

In a small pan, roast the coriander and cumin seeds until browned and grind in a blender or spice grinder. Heat half the oil in a large pan and fry the onions, carrots and potatoes for 10 minutes until browned. Heat the remaining oil in a small pan and fry the garlic, ginger, ground spices, curry powder and turmeric for 5 minutes. Skin, seed and chop the tomatoes and stir into the spice mixture. Cover and cook for 10 minutes. Stir into the carrot mixture with the stock and simmer gently for 20 minutes.

Add the peas, apple and mango and cook for a further 5 minutes. Grind half the cashew nuts and mix with the creamed coconut. Stir in enough pan juices to form a paste and carefully stir into the curry until evenly combined. Heat through and serve at once, sprinkled with the whole nuts and coriander.

Serves 4-6.

BUTTERNUT SQUASH CRUMBLE

700 g (1½ lb) peeled butternut squash (about 3 small squash)
1 small fennel bulb (about 115 g/4 oz), trimmed
1 clove garlic, crushed
1 tablespoon chopped fresh sage
400 g (14 oz) can chopped tomatoes
150 ml (5 fl oz/⅔ cup) double (thick) cream
salt and pepper
115 g (4 oz/1 cup) wholemeal flour
55 g (2 oz/¼ cup) butter, diced
55 g (2 oz/⅓ cup) macadamia nuts, chopped
25 g (1 oz/¼ cup) grated Parmesan or vegetarian Cheddar cheese

Preheat oven to 200C (400F/Gas 6). Scrape out and discard the squash seeds, cut the flesh into 1 cm (½ in) pieces and place in a large ovenproof dish. Very finely shred the fennel and scatter over the squash with the garlic and sage. Pour in the tomatoes and cream and add a little salt and pepper.

Put the flour in a bowl and rub in the butter until the mixture resembles fine breadcrumbs. Stir in the nuts and cheese and sprinkle the crumble topping over the squash. Cover with foil and bake in the oven for 40 minutes. Remove foil and bake for a further 15-20 minutes until the topping is golden and the squash is tender.

Serves 6.

LENTIL-STUFFED PEPPERS

125 g (4 oz/⅔ cup) red split lentils
60 ml (2 fl oz/¼ cup) vegetable oil
4 green or red peppers (capsicums)
1 teaspoon cumin seeds
2 onions, finely chopped
2 green chillies, seeded and chopped
2.5 cm (1 in) piece fresh root ginger, grated
3 teaspoons ground coriander
salt and pepper
2 tablespoons chopped fresh coriander
coriander leaves, to garnish

Wash lentils, then soak in cold water for 30 minutes.

Heat half the oil in a frying pan and fry peppers (capsicums) for 3-5 minutes, until golden brown on all sides. Drain on absorbent kitchen paper and leave to cool. Add remaining oil to pan, then add cumin seeds and fry until just beginning to pop. Add onions and chillies and fry, stirring, for 8 minutes, until onions are soft and golden brown. Stir in ginger and ground coriander. Drain lentils and add to pan with 315 ml (10 fl oz/1¼ cups) water and stir well.

Cook, covered, over low heat for 15-20 minutes, until tender and liquid has been absorbed. Season with salt and pepper and add fresh coriander. Preheat oven to 180C (350F/Gas 4). Cut tops from peppers (capsicums) and remove seeds. Stuff peppers (capsicums) with lentil mixture and replace tops. Stand in an ovenproof dish and cook for 15-20 minutes, until soft. Serve hot, garnished with coriander leaves.

Serves 4.

DHAL BALLS WITH YOGURT

125 g (4 oz/⅔ cup) whole green lentils
440 ml (14 fl oz/1¾ cups) natural yogurt
6 tablespoons chopped fresh coriander
¼ teaspoon chilli powder
4 tablespoons shredded fresh coconut
60 g (2 oz/1 cup) fresh breadcrumbs
2 fresh green chillies, seeded and chopped
2.5 cm (1 in) piece fresh root ginger, grated
1 egg, beaten
salt and pepper
60 g (2 oz/½ cup) wholewheat flour
vegetable oil for deep frying
coriander leaves, to garnish

Put lentils in a sieve and wash thoroughly.

Pick over lentils and remove any grit. Put in a bowl, cover with cold water and soak for 2 hours. Meanwhile, mix yogurt with 2 tablespoons coriander, and chilli powder. Cover and chill. Drain lentils, cover with fresh water and simmer for 30 minutes or until tender. Purée in a blender or food processor or mash well. Transfer to a bowl, add 2 tablespoons coconut, breadcrumbs, remaining coriander, chillies, ginger and egg. Season with salt and pepper and mix well. Chill for 30 minutes.

With damp hands, carefully roll mixture into 2.5 cm (1 in) balls, then roll balls in flour to coat completely. Half-fill a deep-fat pan or fryer with oil and heat to 190C (375F) or until a cube of day-old bread browns in 40 seconds. Fry about 6 balls at a time for 2-3 minutes, until golden. Drain well. Serve hot with yogurt sauce, sprinkled with remaining coconut and garnished with coriander leaves.

Serves 4.

TAMIL NADU VEGETABLES

125 g (4 oz/2/3 cup) red split lentils
1/2 teaspoon turmeric
1 small aubergine (eggplant)
60 ml (2 fl oz/1/4 cup) vegetable oil
30 g (1 oz/1/3 cup) desiccated coconut
1 teaspoon cumin seeds
1/2 teaspoon mustard seeds
2 dried red chillies, crushed
1 red pepper (capsicum), seeded and sliced
125 g (4 oz) courgettes (zucchini), thickly sliced
90 g (3 oz) green beans, cut into 2 cm (3/4 in) pieces
155 ml (5 fl oz/2/3 cup) vegetable stock
salt
red pepper (capsicum) strips, to garnish

Wash lentils and put in a large saucepan with turmeric and 625 ml (20 fl oz/2 1/2 cups) water. Bring to the boil, then reduce heat and simmer, covered, for 15-20 minutes, until lentils are soft. Meanwhile, cut aubergine (eggplant) into 1 cm (1/2 in) dice. Heat oil in a large shallow pan, add coconut, cumin and mustard seeds and chillies.

Fry for 1 minute, then add aubergine (eggplant), red pepper (capsicum), courgettes (zucchini), green beans, stock and salt. Bring to the boil, then simmer, covered, for 10-15 minutes, until the vegetables are just tender. Stir in lentils and any cooking liquid and cook for a further 5 minutes. Serve hot, garnished with red pepper (capsicum) strips.

Serves 4.

MIXED VEGETABLE CURRY

3 tablespoons vegetable oil
1 onion, sliced
1 teaspoon ground cumin
1 teaspoon chilli powder
2 teaspoons ground coriander
1 teaspoon turmeric
250 g (8 oz) potatoes, diced
185 g (6 oz) cauliflower flowerets
125 g (4 oz) green beans, sliced
185 g (6 oz) carrots, diced
4 tomatoes, skinned and chopped
315 ml (10 fl oz/1 1/4 cups) hot vegetable stock
onion rings, to garnish

Heat oil in a large saucepan, add onion and fry for 5 minutes, until softened. Stir in cumin, chilli powder, coriander and turmeric and cook for 2 minutes, stirring occasionally. Add potatoes, cauliflower, green beans and carrots, tossing them in the spices until coated.

Add tomatoes and stock and cover. Bring to the boil, then reduce heat and simmer for 10-12 minutes or until vegetables are just tender. Serve hot, garnished with onion rings.

Serves 4.

Variation: Use any mixture of vegetables to make a total of 750 g (1 1/2 lb) – turnips, swedes, courgettes (zucchini), aubergines (eggplant), parsnips and leeks are all suitable for this curry.

CHICKPEA & PEPPER TORTILLA

2 tablespoons olive oil
1 red onion, chopped
1 red pepper (capsicum), seeded and chopped
2 cloves garlic, crushed
175 g (6 oz/1 cup) cooked chickpeas
1 teaspoon ground turmeric
2 tablespoons chopped fresh parsley
4 large eggs
salt and pepper
parsley sprigs, to garnish

In a non-stick frying pan, heat the oil and fry the onion, pepper (capsicum) and garlic for 10 minutes until lightly golden and softened. Add the chickpeas, mashing them lightly as you go, then stir in the turmeric and parsley. Stir-fry for 2 minutes. Lightly beat the eggs with salt and pepper and stir into the pan until evenly mixed.

Cook over a medium heat for 5-6 minutes until cooked and browned underneath. Loosen around the edges with a spatula and carefully slip the tortilla out onto a plate. Invert the pan over the tortilla and flip over so that the top is now on the bottom. Cook for a further 3-4 minutes until golden underneath and turn out onto a plate. Allow to cool to room temperature. Garnish with parsley and serve with a tomato salad.

Serves 6.

FRESH HERB FRITTATA

6 eggs
2 egg whites
2 spring onions, trimmed and chopped
115 g (4 oz/½ cup) cottage cheese
25 g (1 oz/½ cup) fresh chopped mixed herbs
25 g (1oz/1 cup) rocket
salt and pepper
olive oil

Whisk the eggs and the egg whites together until thoroughly mixed and stir in the spring onions, cheese and herbs. Roughly chop the rocket and add to mixture together with the seasonings.

Preheat grill. Heat about 4 teaspoons oil in a non-stick frying pan and pour in the egg mixture, swirling to reach the edges of the pan. Cook, stirring, over a medium-low heat for about 3 minutes until eggs are beginning to set.

Place pan under the hot grill and cook for a further 2-3 minutes until set and lightly golden. Turn out onto a plate, cut into wedges and serve warm or cold with a tomato and olive salad.

Serves 2-4.

POTATO & ONION FLAN

200 g (7 oz/1¾ cup) plain flour
pinch of salt
100 g (3½ oz) unsalted butter, diced
1 egg yolk
2 tablespoons iced water
FILLING:
450 g (1 lb) waxy potatoes
25 g (1 oz/6 teaspoons) butter
2 large onions, thinly sliced
1 teaspoon chopped fresh rosemary
½ teaspoon caraway seeds
200 ml (7 fl oz/1 cup) low-fat fromage frais
25 g (1 oz/¼ cup) grated vegetarian Cheddar cheese
freshly grated nutmeg

Preheat oven to 200C (400F/Gas 6). Sift the flour and salt into a large bowl and rub in the butter until mixture resembles fine breadcrumbs. Make a well in the centre, work in the egg yolk and water to form a soft dough. Knead on a floured surface, wrap and chill for 30 minutes. Roll out thinly and use to line a deep 23 cm (9 in) fluted flan tin. Prick the base, then chill for 20 minutes. Line with foil and baking beans and bake blind for 10 minutes; remove beans and foil and bake for a further 10-12 minutes until crisp.

Increase oven temperature to 230C (450F/Gas 8). Cook the potatoes for 15 minutes until just tender. Allow to cool, carefully peel and cut into very thin slices. Melt the butter and fry the onions, rosemary and caraway seeds for 10 minutes until golden. Spread the onion mixture over pastry case and arrange the potato slices over the top. Beat the remaining ingredients together, spread over the potatoes and bake at the top of the oven for 15 minutes until golden.

Serves 6-8.

BREAD & CHEESE PUDDING

550 ml (20 fl oz/2½ cups) milk
1 bay leaf
2 cardamom pods, bruised
15 g (½ oz/3 teaspoons) butter
1 onion, thinly sliced
½ teaspoon chopped fresh thyme
55 g (2 oz/½ cup) drained sun-dried tomatoes, chopped
55 g (2 oz/¼ cup) Mascarpone cheese
225 g (8 oz) vegetarian Double Gloucester cheese, grated
350 g (12 oz) thinly sliced wholemeal bread
3 eggs
pinch of freshly grated nutmeg
salt and pepper

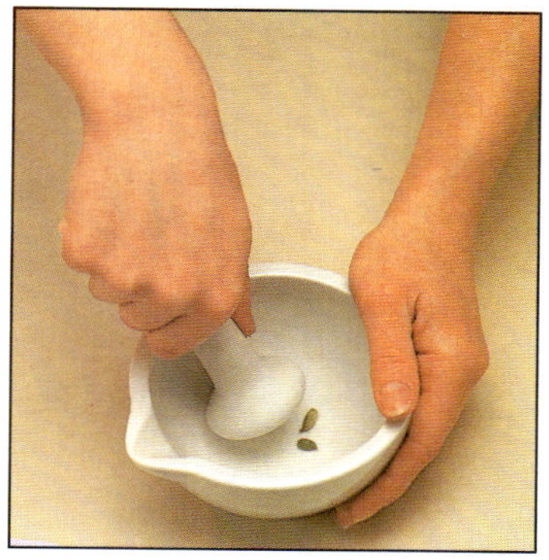

Preheat oven to 200C (400F/Gas 6) and lightly oil a 2 litre (3¾ pint/9 cup) pie dish. Put the milk, bay leaf and cardamom pods into a small pan and heat until almost boiling. Remove from the heat and leave to infuse for 10 minutes; strain into a bowl. Heat the butter and fry the onion and thyme for 10 minutes until soft. Add the tomatoes, remove from the heat, cool slightly and stir in the Mascarpone and one-quarter of the grated cheese.

Spread half the mixture over the base of the dish, top with half the bread and the remaining onion mixture. Sprinkle over half the remaining cheese, top with the rest of the bread. Whisk the eggs, nutmeg and seasonings into the milk and pour into the dish. Sprinkle over the rest of the cheese and place the dish in a roasting tin. Pour in boiling water to come two-thirds of the way up the side of the dish, cover with foil and bake for 30 minutes. Uncover and cook 20 minutes.

Serves 6-8.

BROCCOLI & OLIVE FLAN

225 g (8 oz) home-made or bought wholemeal pastry, thawed if frozen
1 yellow pepper (capsicum)
1 red pepper (capsicum)
115 g (4 oz) broccoli flowerets
55 g (2 oz/½ cup) stoned black olives, halved
2 eggs, beaten
115 ml (4 fl oz/½ cup) single (light) cream
115 g (4 oz/½ cup) soft goat cheese
2 tablespoons chopped fresh parsley
salt and pepper

Roll out the pastry on a lightly floured surface and use to line a deep 23 cm (9 in) fluted flan tin. Prick the base and chill for 20 minutes. Preheat the oven to 200C (400F/Gas 6). Quarter and seed the peppers (capsicums) and grill for 4-5 minutes on each side until lightly charred. Leave to cool slightly, then peel and thinly slice the flesh. Steam the broccoli for 3 minutes.

Line the flan case with foil and baking beans and bake blind for 10 minutes; remove beans and foil and bake for a further 10-12 minutes until pastry is crisp and golden. Cool slightly and arrange peppers (capsicums), broccoli and olives over the base. Beat the remaining ingredients together until smooth and pour into the case. Bake for 35 minutes until risen and firm in the centre. Cool and serve warm or cold.

Serves 6-8.

BAKED EGGS WITH MOZZARELLA

1 large ripe tomato
1 spring onion, trimmed and chopped
45 g (1½ oz) Mozzarella cheese, diced
4 stoned black olives, sliced
1 tablespoon chopped fresh basil
salt and pepper
85 ml (3 fl oz/⅓ cup) double (thick) cream
4 eggs
parsley sprigs, to garnish

Preheat oven to 190C (375F/Gas 5) and lightly butter 4 ramekin dishes. Skin and seed the tomato and finely dice the flesh.

Mix with the spring onion, cheese, olives, basil and seasoning. Divide between the 4 dishes.

Heat the cream in a small pan until almost boiling, pour over the tomato mixture and crack an egg into each dish. Place in a roasting tin and pour in enough boiling water to come two-thirds of the way up the sides of the ramekins. Bake for 10-15 minutes until eggs are just set. Cool slightly, garnish with parsley and serve with toasted bread fingers or Melba toast.

Serves 4.

VEGETABLE FILO PARCELS

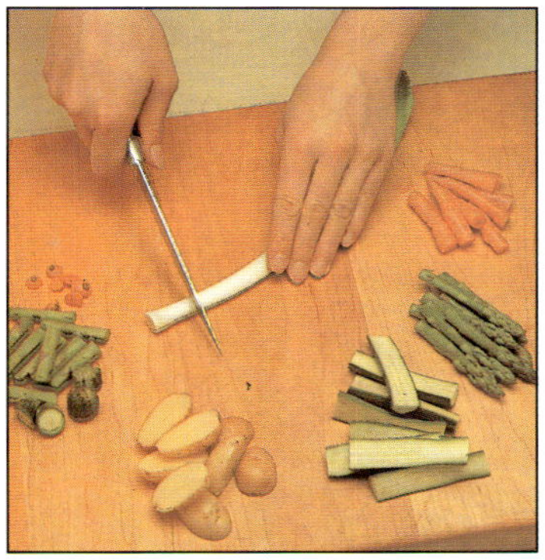

4 small new potatoes, halved
8 baby carrots, trimmed
8 baby courgettes (zucchini), halved
8 asparagus tips, trimmed
1 baby leek, trimmed and sliced into 8
55 g (2 oz/¼ cup) butter, softened
1 tablespoon chopped fresh mint
¼ teaspoon ground cumin
pinch of cayenne pepper
salt and pepper
4 large sheets filo pastry
85 ml (3 fl oz/⅓ cup) olive oil

Preheat oven to 190C (375F/Gas 5) and place a baking sheet on the middle shelf.

Cook the potatoes in boiling water for 6-8 minutes until almost cooked. Blanch the remaining vegetables for 2-3 minutes, depending on the size, until almost tender. Drain all the vegetables, plunge into cold water, allow to cool, then drain and dry thoroughly. Cream together the butter, mint, spices and salt and pepper. Take one large sheet of pastry and using a 25 cm (10 in) plate or saucepan lid as a template, carefully cut out a circle; repeat to make 4 in total. Brush liberally with oil.

Take a quarter of the vegetables and place a small pile on one side of the pastry circle. Dot with the mint butter and fold the other side of pastry over the filling, pressing the edges together well. Brush a little oil along the edge and turn over a bit at a time to ensure filling is totally enclosed. Repeat to make 4 parcels and transfer to the heated baking sheet. Carefully brush over remaining oil and bake for 12-15 minutes until pastry is golden. Serve immediately

Serves 4.

POLENTA WITH MUSHROOMS

850 ml (30 fl oz/3¾ cups) vegetable stock
½ teaspoon salt
150 g (5 oz/1 cup) polenta
1 teaspoon chopped fresh thyme
25 g (1 oz/¼ cup) freshly grated Parmesan or Cheddar cheese
25 g (1 oz/6 teaspoons) butter
15 g (½ oz/¼ cup) dried ceps (mushrooms)
85 ml (3 fl oz/⅓ cup) boiling water
55 ml (2 fl oz/¼ cup) port
3 tablespoons virgin olive oil
1 clove garlic, crushed
1 shallot, finely chopped
350 g (12 oz) mixed fresh mushrooms, sliced
1 tablespoon chopped fresh parsley

Bring 700 ml (25 fl oz/3¼ cups) of the stock and the salt to the boil in a pan and immediately whisk in the polenta. Stir, cover and simmer gently for 25 minutes, stirring frequently. Add the thyme and cook for a further 5 minutes. Stir in the cheese and butter and pour into a lightly oiled, shallow tin. Smooth the surface and leave to cool. Soak the ceps in the boiling water for 20 minutes. Strain liquid into a pan and chop the ceps. Add the port and the remaining stock to the pan and boil until reduced to about 115 ml (4 fl oz/½ cup). Set aside.

Turn out polenta and cut into 12 triangles, brush with oil and grill for 8-10 minutes on each side until golden. Meanwhile, heat the oil in a large pan and fry the garlic, shallot and ceps for 5 minutes. Add the fresh sliced mushrooms and stir-fry for 3-4 minutes until golden. Add the reduced liquid, cover and cook for 5 minutes. Add parsley and serve sauce with the grilled polenta triangles.

Serves 6.

TOFU, LEEK & MUSHROOM SATÉ

350 g (12 oz) plain tofu
3 leeks, trimmed
12 shiitake or button mushrooms, wiped
2 tablespoons dark soy sauce
1 clove garlic, crushed
½ teaspoon grated fresh root ginger
1 small red chilli, seeded and chopped
grated zest and juice 1 lime
3 tablespoons sweet sherry
2 teaspoons clear honey
55 g (2 oz/¼ cup) crunchy peanut butter
25 g (1 oz) creamed coconut
olive oil

Cut tofu into 12 cubes and leeks into 12 thick slices and place in a shallow dish with mushrooms. Mix together the soy sauce, garlic, ginger, chilli, lime zest and juice, sherry, honey and 3 tablespoons water and pour over the tofu mixture. Marinate for several hours, stirring from time to time.

Preheat grill. Thread the tofu, leeks and mushrooms onto 8 bamboo skewers and put 150 ml (5 fl oz/⅔ cup) of the marinade into a small pan. Add the peanut butter and coconut and heat gently until melted, then stir until thickened. Brush the ingredients on the skewers with oil, pour over the remaining marinade and grill for 10-12 minutes, turning and brushing with pan juices, until golden and lightly charred. Serve with the saté sauce as a dip.

Serves 4.

—OLIVE & MOZZARELLA PUFFS—

55 g (2 oz/½ cup) stoned green olives
25 g (1 oz) Mozzarella cheese
2 teaspoons chopped fresh parsley
½ teaspoon chopped fresh sage
pinch of chilli powder
225 g (8 oz) bought puff pastry, thawed if frozen
1 egg
salt

Preheat oven to 220C (425F/Gas 7) and lightly oil a baking sheet. Very finely chop the olives and cheese and mix with the herbs and chilli powder to form a paste. Set aside.

Roll out the pastry thinly and stamp out 8 rounds, using a 10 cm (4 in) fluted pastry cutter. Place a heaped teaspoon of olive mixture in the centre of each round. Lightly dampen the edges of pastry, fold in half to form semi-circles, pressing edges together well to seal. Transfer to the baking sheet.

Beat the egg with a little salt and brush over pastries. Cut 2 small slashes in each one and bake for 12-15 minutes until puffed up and golden. Serve warm or cold with a salad garnish.

Serves 8.

Note: These make ideal buffet party nibbles. Make up double quantity of the filling, cut pastry into small rounds to make bite-sized appetizers.

WINTER VEGETABLE PIE

175 g (6 oz/1 ¼ cups) self-raising flour
salt
115 g (4 oz/½ cup) hard white vegetable fat, divided into 4
2 tablespoons chopped fresh mixed herbs
4-5 tablespoons iced water
175 g (6 oz) baby onions, halved
1 clove garlic, chopped
575 g (1 ¼ lb) prepared mixed winter vegetables (carrots, turnips, parsnips, cauliflower flowerets)
115 g (4 oz) button mushrooms, wiped
2 tablespoons olive oil
150 ml (5 fl oz/⅔ cup) red wine
350 ml (12 fl oz/1 ½ cups) vegetable stock (see Note)
2 tablespoons tomato purée (paste)

Sift the flour with 1 teaspoon salt and finely rub in one-quarter of the fat. Stir in half the herbs and work in enough iced water to form a soft dough. Knead lightly, wrap and chill for 30 minutes. Roll out pastry to a rectangle about 1 cm (½ in) thick, dot the top two-thirds with one-third of the remaining fat. Bring the bottom third of pastry up into the middle and the top third down over this. Press edges to seal, cover and chill for 30 minutes. Repeat the process twice and chill for a final 30 minutes.

Preheat oven to 200C (400F/Gas 6). Fry onions, garlic and the vegetables in the oil for 10 minutes. Add the wine and boil for 5 minutes. Add the stock and tomato purée (paste) and simmer for 20 minutes. Transfer to a 1.2 litre (2 pint/5 cup) pie dish.

Roll pastry out to a 0.5 cm (¼ in) rectangle, cut out a pie top a little larger than the dish. Cut remaining pastry into strips, dampen and press around edge of dish. Dampen edge of pastry, place pastry lid over pie and press edges to seal. Bake in the oven for 30 minutes.

Serves 6.

Note: To make your own stock, fry 1 roughly chopped onion and 1 trimmed and sliced leek in 2 teaspoons olive oil until softened. Add 2 chopped carrots, 1 diced large potato and 2 sliced sticks celery and fry for a further 5 minutes.

Add 4 roughly chopped ripe tomatoes, 115 g (4 oz) quartered mushrooms, 55 g (2 oz/⅓ cup) rice, 2 sprigs parsley, 2 sprigs thyme, 1 bay leaf, 1 teaspoon salt, 6 white peppercorns and 1.2 litres (2 pints/5 cups) water. Bring to the boil, cover and simmer gently for 30 minutes. Strain through a fine sieve.

FALAFEL

410 g (13 oz) can chick peas, drained
1 onion, quartered
2 cloves garlic
125 g (4 oz) fresh white bread
¼ teaspoon cumin seeds
4 small dried red chillies, crushed
1 tablespoon chopped fresh parsley
salt and pepper
1 egg, beaten
45 g (1½ oz/⅓ cup) golden breadcrumbs
vegetable oil for deep frying
4 warmed pitta bread, shredded lettuce, sliced onion and sliced tomato, to serve

Put chick peas, onion, garlic, bread, cumin seeds and chillies in a blender or food processor. Process ingredients until smooth, then turn mixture into a bowl. Add parsley, salt and pepper and beaten egg and mix well. Form into 8 balls and coat in breadcrumbs. Flatten each one slightly to form oval shapes.

Half-fill a deep fat pan or fryer with oil. Heat to 190C (375F) or until a cube of day-old bread browns in 40 seconds. Fry the falafel, a few at a time, for 3 minutes until golden brown. Drain on absorbent kitchen paper. Cut each pitta bread in half and open out to form pockets. Put a falafel in each pocket with a little shredded lettuce and a few slices raw onion and tomato. Serve hot.

Makes 8.

BEAN CURD & PEPPERS

225 g (8 oz) fresh bean curd, drained and cut into 2 cm (¾ in) cubes
1 tablespoon dark soy sauce
1 tablespoon ginger wine
2.5 cm (1 in) piece fresh root ginger, peeled and finely chopped
salt and freshly ground black pepper
1 tablespoon sunflower oil
1 fresh red chilli, seeded and finely chopped
2 cloves garlic, thinly sliced
1 red pepper (capsicum), thinly sliced
1 green pepper (capsicum), thinly sliced
1 yellow pepper (capsicum), thinly sliced
3 tablespoons chopped fresh basil

Place bean curd on a plate or in a shallow dish. Mix together the soy sauce, ginger wine, ginger and salt and pepper. Spoon over bean curd, cover and chill for 30 minutes.

Heat oil in a non-stick or well seasoned wok and stir-fry bean curd mixture, chilli and garlic for 2 minutes. Add peppers (capsicum) and stir-fry for 4 minutes. Stir in basil and serve immediately with noodles.

Serves 4.

PIZZAS, PASTA & RICE

DOLCELATTE MINI PIZZAS

55 g (2 oz/½ cup) stoned black olives
1 clove garlic, chopped
1 teaspoon chopped fresh thyme
1 tablespoon olive oil
1 quantity pizza dough (see opposite)
45 g (1½ oz/9 teaspoons) butter
2 red onions, thinly sliced
½ teaspoon fennel seeds
1 teaspoon chopped fresh rosemary
85 g (3 oz/½ cup) vegetarian dolcelatte cheese
grated zest 1 lemon

Purée olives, garlic, thyme and oil in a blender or food processor to a smooth paste.

Make up the pizza dough (see opposite), cover and leave to rise in a warm place for 30 minutes. Melt the butter and fry the onions over a low heat for 20-25 minutes until golden. Leave to cool. Preheat oven to 230C (450F/Gas 8) and place a baking sheet or pizza stone on the top shelf.

Divide the pizza dough in 4 and roll each piece out on a lightly floured surface to a 12.5 cm (5 in) round. Spread over the olive paste and onion mixture. Sprinkle over the fennel seeds and rosemary and crumble over the cheese. Sprinkle over the lemon zest and transfer the pizzas to the hot baking sheet. Cook for 10-12 minutes until bubbling and golden. Serve the pizzas hot with a tomato and green salad.

Serves 4.

GRILLED VEGETABLE PIZZA

225 g (8 oz/1⅔ cups) strong plain flour
½ teaspoon fast action dried yeast
½ teaspoon salt
100 ml (3½ fl oz/½ cup) warmed water
1 tablespoon olive oil
TOPPING:
1 red pepper (capsicum), quartered and seeded
1 small courgette (zucchini), sliced
1 small aubergine (eggplant), sliced
1 small onion, thinly sliced
6 large ripe tomatoes, quartered and seeded
2 tablespoons shop-bought pesto sauce
salt and pepper
150 g (5 oz) vegetarian Mozzarella cheese, grated

Mix the flour, yeast and salt together, make a well in the centre and work in the water and oil to form a stiff dough. Knead for 5 minutes, place in an oiled bowl, cover and leave to rise in a warm place for 30 minutes until doubled in size. Preheat oven to 230C (450F/Gas 8) and place a pizza plate or baking sheet on the top shelf. Preheat grill. Brush the peppers (capsicum), courgette (zucchini), aubergine (eggplant) and onion slices with a little oil and grill until charred on all sides.

Grill the tomato quarters, skin side up, until blistered. Peel and discard the skin and mash the flesh with the pesto sauce and salt and pepper. Roll out dough to a 23-25 cm (9-10 in) round. Spread over the tomato mixture and arrange the grilled vegetables over the top. Sprinkle over the cheese and transfer to the hot pizza plate or baking sheet. Bake for 25-30 minutes until bubbling and golden.

Serves 4.

PEPPER PIZZETTES

PIZZA DOUGH:
450 g (1 lb/4 cups) strong plain flour
Pinch salt
15 g (½ oz) packet dried yeast
1 teaspoon granulated sugar
200 ml (7 fl oz/scant cup) warm water
2 tablespoons extra virgin olive oil
Fresh herb sprigs to garnish
TOPPING:
2 red or yellow peppers (capsicums)
3 tablespoons sun-dried tomato paste
4 tablespoons capers in wine vinegar, drained
2 tablespoons chopped fresh oregano
Salt and freshly ground black pepper

Sieve flour and salt into a large mixing bowl. In a small bowl, mix yeast, sugar and warm water. Leave for 10-15 minutes, until frothy. Stir oil into yeast then gradually beat into flour using a wooden spoon to give a soft, but not wet, dough. Turn onto a floured surface; knead for 5 minutes until smooth and elastic. Put into an oiled mixing bowl, cover and leave in a warm place for 35-40 minutes until doubled in size.

Preheat grill. Cook whole peppers (capsicums) under the hot grill for about 10 minutes, turning occasionally, until evenly blistered and charred. Transfer to a plastic bag for a few minutes, then peel away and discard skins. De-seed peppers (capsicums) and cut into strips. Set aside.

Preheat oven to 230C (450F/Gas 8). Oil two baking sheets. Turn dough onto a lightly floured surface. Knead gently then cut into 16 equal pieces. Roll each piece into a small oval about 5 mm (¼ inch) thick.

Transfer to the baking sheets and prick dough with a fork. Divide sun-dried tomato paste, reserved peppers (capsicums), capers and oregano between dough ovals. Season with salt and freshly ground black pepper. Bake in the preheated oven for 8-10 minutes, until golden. Serve hot or warm garnished with herb sprigs.

Makes 16 pizzettes.

Variations:

Red onion and Gorgonzola Replace above topping with 115 g (4 oz) crumbled Gorgonzola cheese; ½ red onion, chopped and 2 tablespoons chopped fresh thyme.

Prawn and fennel Instead of the peppers (capsicums), capers and herbs use 1 small fennel bulb, brushed with olive oil, roasted at 180C (350F/Gas 4) for 35-40 minutes, then cooled and chopped, 115 g (4 oz) peeled prawns and 2 teaspoons fennel seeds.

PENNE WITH LEEKS & RICOTTA

450 g (1 lb) young leeks, washed and trimmed
2-3 tablespoons hazelnut oil
1 clove garlic, sliced
350 g (12 oz/4 cups) dried penne or other pasta shells
olive oil
225 g (8 oz/1 cup) ricotta cheese
4 tablespoons milk
45 g (1½ oz/⅓ cup) freshly grated Pecorino or Parmesan cheese
2 tablespoons mixed chopped fresh herbs
½ teaspoon grated lemon zest
½ teaspoon lemon juice
salt and pepper

Preheat oven to 220C (425F/Gas 7). Pat the leeks dry. Cut into thick slices, place in a roasting tin with 2 tablespoons oil and the garlic and roast for 25 minutes until lightly browned. After 10 minutes, bring a large pan of water to the boil, add the pasta, a little olive oil and return to the boil. Lower heat and simmer gently for 10 minutes until pasta is *al dente* (just cooked but with a firm bite).

Meanwhile, place all the remaining ingredients in a small pan and stir over a low heat until melted. Heat through for 5 minutes without boiling. Strain the pasta, stir in a little more hazelnut oil and toss with the cooked leeks. Carefully stir in the melted cheese mixture, season to taste and serve at once.

Serves 4.

RATATOUILLE PASTA SAUCE

1 onion
2 cloves garlic
3 teaspoons olive oil
1 aubergine (eggplant)
3 courgettes (zucchini)
1 green pepper (capsicum)
1 red pepper (capsicum)
400 g (14 oz) can chopped tomatoes
225 g (8 oz) can chopped tomatoes
1 tablespoon tomato purée (paste)
1 teaspoon dried basil
1 teaspoon dried oregano
salt and pepper

Slice onion and crush both cloves of garlic.

In a large saucepan, heat oil and cook onion and garlic for 3 minutes, stirring. Dice aubergine (eggplant), slice courgettes (zucchini), seed and slice peppers (capsicums) and add to saucepan.

Stir in tomatoes, tomato purée (paste), herbs and salt and pepper and mix well. Bring slowly to the boil, cover and simmer gently for 30 minutes, stirring occasionally. Adjust the seasoning before serving. Serve with freshly cooked pasta.

Serves 4.

TUNA, TOMATO & PENNE

2 tablespoons olive oil
1 onion, chopped
2 cloves garlic, finely chopped
800 g (28 oz) can peeled tomatoes
1 tablespoon tomato purée (paste)
1 tablespoon chopped fresh oregano or 1 teaspoon dried
55 g (2½ oz/⅓ cup) sun-dried tomatoes in oil, drained and chopped
salt and fresh ground black pepper
350 g (12 oz) penne or rigatoni
55 g (2½ oz/⅓ cup) black olives, coarsely chopped
2 tablespoons capers, drained
200 g (7 oz) can light tuna, drained
2 tablespoons chopped fresh parsley
Parmesan cheese, to garnish

Heat the wok until hot. Add the oil and swirl to coat wok. Add onion and garlic and stir-fry for 1-2 minutes until beginning to soften. Add the tomatoes, stirring to break up the large pieces. Stir in the tomato purée (paste), oregano and sun-dried tomatoes. Bring to the boil and simmer for 10-12 minutes until sauce is slightly thickened. Season with salt and pepper. Meanwhile, in a large saucepan of boiling water, cook penne according to packet directions.

Stir black olives, capers and tuna into the sauce. Drain pasta and add to sauce, stirring gently to mix well. Stir in chopped parsley and serve immediately from the wok, or spoon into 4 soup plates. Using a swivel-bladed vegetable peeler, shave flakes of Parmesan over each serving. Alternatively, grate Parmesan over each serving.

Serves 4.

BOLOGNESE PASTA SAUCE

1 onion
1 clove garlic
3 teaspoons sunflower oil
2 carrots
2 sticks celery
225 g (8 oz) mushrooms
55 g (2 oz) lean back bacon
450 g (1 lb) extra lean minced beef
400 g (14 oz) can chopped tomatoes
1 tablespoon tomato purée (paste)
150 ml (5 fl oz/⅔ cup) beef stock
150 ml (5 fl oz/⅔ cup) dry white wine
1 teaspoon dried mixed herbs
¼ teaspoon ground bay leaves or fresh bay leaves
salt and pepper

Chop onion and crush garlic. In a large saucepan, heat oil for 1 minute. Add onion and garlic and cook for 3 minutes, stirring. Chop carrots and celery finely and slice mushrooms. Add to saucepan and cook for 5 minutes, stirring. Trim rind and fat from the bacon and chop bacon finely. Add bacon to saucepan with minced beef, mixing well. Cook until the meat is browned all over, stirring.

Stir in tomatoes, tomato purée (paste), stock, wine, herbs and salt and pepper and mix well. Bring slowly to the boil, cover and simmer for 1½-2 hours. Remove the cover for the last 30 minutes of the cooking time and increase the heat slightly, to thicken the sauce. Adjust the seasoning before serving. Serve with freshly cooked spaghetti or pasta shapes.

Serves 6.

MACARONI WITH AUBERGINES

450 g (1 lb) aubergines (eggplants), cut into 0.5 cm (¼ in) matchstick strips
salt
450 g (1 lb) macaroni
3 tablespoons olive oil
3 cloves garlic, finely chopped
450 g (1 lb) plum or beefsteak tomatoes, peeled, seeded and chopped
1 fresh chilli, seeded and chopped
115 g (4 oz) Italian salami, cut into julienne strips
85 g (3 oz) black olives
2 tablespoons capers, rinsed and drained
4 tablespoons chopped fresh basil or oregano
115 g (4 oz) feta cheese, crumbled
25 g (1 oz/¼ cup) Parmesan cheese, grated
herb sprigs, to garnish

Place aubergine (eggplant) strips in a colander and sprinkle with salt. Toss to mix, then leave to stand, on a plate, for 1 hour. Rinse under cold running water and pat dry with absorbent kitchen paper. In a large saucepan of boiling water, cook macaroni according to packet directions. Drain and set aside.

Heat wok until very hot. Add olive oil and swirl to coat. Add aubergine (eggplant) and stir-fry for 3-5 minutes until browned. Drain on absorbent kitchen paper. Add garlic, tomatoes and chilli and stir-fry for 2 minutes until juices are absorbed. Add salami, olives, capers, basil or oregano, aubergine (eggplant) and macaroni and toss to coat well. Stir fry for 1-2 minutes to heat through. Add feta cheese and toss. Sprinkle with Parmesan cheese, garnish and serve hot.

Serves 6.

PORK & PRAWN NOODLES

200 g (7 oz) bean thread noodles
6 dried Chinese black mushrooms
2 tablespoons vegetable oil
350 g (12 oz) lean pork, very finely chopped
115 g (4 oz) cooked peeled large prawns
3 red shallots, finely chopped
4 spring onions (scallions), including some green, sliced
3 slim inner celery stalks, thinly sliced
55 g (2 oz) dried shrimps
2 tablespoons fish sauce
5 tablespoons lime juice
1½ teaspoons crushed palm sugar
2 fresh red chillies, seeded and chopped
15 g (½ oz) coriander leaves, chopped
whole cooked prawns and coriander, to garnish

Soak noodles in cold water for 15 minutes. Soak mushrooms in water for 30 minutes. Drain and chop. In a wok, heat oil, add pork and stir-fry for 2-3 minutes until cooked through. Using a slotted spoon, transfer to absorbent kitchen paper. Add noodles to a saucepan of boiling water and boil for 5 minutes. Drain well and set aside.

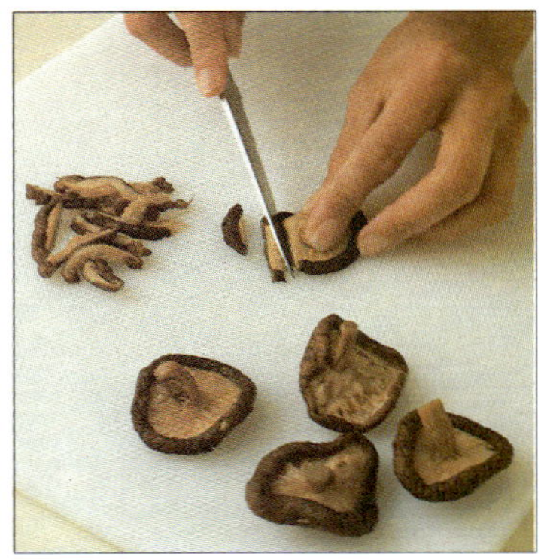

Cut each prawn into 3 and place in a bowl. Add shallots, spring onions (scallions), celery, mushrooms, noodles, pork and dried shrimps; toss together. In a small bowl, mix together fish sauce, lime juice and sugar. Pour into bowl, add coriander leaves and toss ingredients together. Serve garnished with whole prawns and coriander sprigs.

Serves 4.

PASTA WITH PEANUT SAUCE

450 g (1lb) thin spaghetti or egg noodles
2 tablespoons sesame oil
225 g (8 oz) lean minced pork
1 red pepper (capsicum), thinly sliced
115 g (4 oz) mange tout (snow peas), cut in half diagonally
1 tablespoon sugar
2.5 cm (1 in) piece fresh root ginger, grated
½ teaspoon crushed dried chillies
55 ml (2 fl oz/¼ cup) soy sauce
9 teaspoons cider vinegar
150 ml (5 fl oz/⅔ cup) peanut butter
8 spring onions, thinly sliced
2 tablespoons chopped fresh coriander
coriander sprigs, to garnish

In a large saucepan of boiling water, cook spaghetti or egg noodles according to packet directions. Drain and toss with 1 tablespoon sesame oil. Set aside. Place minced pork in a cold wok and cook over moderate heat, stirring and breaking up large pieces until pork is no longer pink. Add red pepper (capsicum), mange tout (snow peas) and sugar and stir-fry for 1 minute. Add ginger, chillies, soy sauce, vinegar, peanut butter and 150 ml (5 fl oz/⅔ cup) hot water, stirring until sauce bubbles and peanut butter thins out. Add a little more water if necessary.

Stir in spring onions and reserved spaghetti. Toss and stir-fry for 2-3 minutes until spaghetti is coated evenly with sauce and heated through. Sprinkle with chopped coriander and remaining sesame oil and toss. Serve hot, garnished with sprigs of coriander.

Serves 4-6.

SINGAPORE NOODLES

225 g (8 oz) thin round egg noodles
55 ml (2 fl oz/¼ cup) vegetable oil
2 cloves garlic, chopped
2.5 cm (1 in) piece fresh root ginger, peeled and finely chopped
1 fresh chilli, seeded and chopped
1 red pepper (capsicum), thinly sliced
115 g (4 oz) mange tout (snow peas), sliced if large
4-6 spring onions, finely sliced
175 g (6 oz) peeled cooked prawns, defrosted if frozen
115 g (4 oz) beansprouts, trimmed, rinsed and dried
70 ml (2½ fl oz/⅓ cup) tomato ketchup (sauce)
1 teaspoon chilli powder
1-2 teaspoons chilli sauce

In a large saucepan of boiling water, cook the noodles according to packet directions. Drain and toss with 1 tablespoon of the oil. Set aside. Heat the wok until hot. Add remaining oil and swirl to coat the wok. Add garlic, ginger and chilli and stir-fry for 1 minute. Add red pepper (capsicum) and mange tout (snow peas) and stir-fry for 1 minute.

Add spring onions, prawns and beansprouts and stir in the tomato ketchup (sauce), chilli powder, chilli sauce and 115 ml (4 fl oz/½ cup) water. Bring to the boil. Add noodles and toss. Stir-fry for 1-2 minutes until coated with sauce and heated through. Turn into large shallow serving bowl and serve at once.

Serves 4.

CARAMELISED CABBAGE & PASTA

1 red pepper (capsicum)
55 g (2 oz/¼ cup) butter
1 large onion, thinly sliced
1 clove garlic, chopped
1 small green cabbage (about 575 g/1¼ lb)
1 tablespoon brown sugar
85 g (3 oz/1 cup) dried shell pasta
salt
chopped fresh parsley, to garnish

Preheat oven to 200C (400F/Gas 6) and roast the pepper (capsicum) whole for 20 minutes. Place in a plastic bag and leave until cool enough to handle. Peel, deseed and cut the flesh into thin strips.

In a large non-stick frying pan, melt the butter and gently fry the onion and garlic for 10 minutes until lightly browned. Trim the outer leaves off the cabbage, cut the cabbage into quarters and discard the centre core. Roughly shred the rest and stir into the pan with the sugar. Stir well, cover and cook over a very gentle heat for 15 minutes, stirring from time to time, until cabbage is golden and just tender.

Cook the pasta in lightly salted, boiling water for 10 minutes until *al dente* (just cooked but with a firm bite). Drain, and stir into the cabbage with the pepper (capsicum) and salt and pepper and serve at once, garnished with chopped parsley.

Serves 6.

PASTA PRIMAVERA

450 g (1 lb) tagliatelle, linguine or thin spaghetti
2-4 tablespoons olive oil
225 g (8 oz) asparagus, cut into 5 cm (2 in) pieces
225 g (8 oz) broccoli florets, cut into small florets
2 yellow or green courgettes (zucchini), sliced
115 g (4 oz) mange tout (snow peas), cut in half if large
2-4 cloves garlic, finely chopped
400 g (14 oz) can chopped tomatoes
25 g (1 oz/2 tablespoons) butter
115 g (4 oz) frozen peas
4-6 tablespoons shredded fresh basil or chopped fresh dill
grated Parmesan, to serve

In the wok or a large saucepan, cook pasta according to packet directions.

Drain, turn into a large bowl, toss with 1 tablespoon olive oil and set aside. Heat the wok until hot. Add remaining oil and swirl to coat wok. Add asparagus and broccoli and stir-fry for 4-5 minutes until tender but still crisp. Remove to a bowl. Add courgettes (zucchini) and mange tout (snow peas) and stir-fry for 1-2 minutes until tender but still crisp. Remove to the bowl. Add garlic to oil remaining in wok and stir-fry for 1 minute. Stir in chopped tomatoes and their juice and simmer for 4-6 minutes until slightly thickened.

Stir butter into tomato sauce and add reserved vegetables, frozen peas, basil or dill and reserved pasta. Toss to coat well. Stir and toss for 2-3 minutes to heat through. Serve with grated Parmesan cheese.

Serves 4-6.

SPINACH GNOCCHI

350 g (12 oz) trimmed spinach leaves
175 g (6 oz/¾ cup) ricotta cheese
pinch of freshly grated nutmeg
45 g (1½ oz/⅓ cup) plain flour
1 large egg, lightly beaten
25 g (1 oz/¼ cup) grated Parmesan or vegetarian Cheddar cheese
2 tablespoons olive oil
salt and pepper
400 g (14 oz) can chopped tomatoes
1 clove garlic, crushed
1 tablespoon chopped fresh basil
pinch of sugar
115 g (4 oz) vegetarian dolcelatte cheese
2 tablespoons milk

Wash the spinach and wilt in a large pan over medium heat. Drain, squeeze out excess liquid and chop finely. Cool and beat in the ricotta, nutmeg, flour, egg, cheese, half the oil and salt and pepper. Chill for 2 hours.

Put tomatoes, remaining oil, garlic, basil and sugar in a small saucepan and cook gently for 30 minutes. Purée in a blender or food processor and keep warm.

Shape the ricotta mixture into walnut-sized balls, flatten out and place on a floured tray, to make 32 small gnocchi in total.

Bring a large pan of water to a steady simmer, drop in the gnocchi, in batches, and cook for 6 minutes. Drain on absorbent kitchen paper and keep warm while cooking the remainder in the same way. Preheat grill.

Gently heat the milk and dolcelatte, stirring until smooth. Pour the tomato sauce over the base of 4 gratin dishes or flameproof plates, arrange the gnocchi on top and drizzle over the cheese sauce. Place dishes under a hot grill for 3-4 minutes until bubbling and golden.

Serves 4.

GREEN RICE

300 g (10 oz/1¼ cups) long grain white rice, rinsed
800 ml (28 fl oz/3½ cups) vegetable stock
225 g (8 oz) small broccoli flowerets
225 g (8 oz) fresh spinach, tough stalks removed
1 tablespoon groundnut (peanut) oil
2 cloves garlic, finely chopped
1 fresh green chilli, seeded and chopped
1 bunch spring onions, finely chopped
225 g (8 oz) frozen peas
2 tablespoons light soy sauce
salt and freshly ground black pepper
4 tablespoons chopped fresh chives
fresh chives, to garnish

Place rice and stock in a large saucepan, bring to the boil, reduce heat and simmer gently for 25 minutes until the rice is cooked and the liquid has been absorbed. Blanch the broccoli in a saucepan of boiling water for 2 minutes. Drain and set aside. Blanch the spinach in a saucepan of boiling water for a few seconds until just wilted. Drain well, shred and set aside.

Heat oil in a non-stick or well seasoned wok and stir-fry garlic, chilli, spring onions and broccoli for 1 minute. Add cooked rice, spinach, frozen peas and soy sauce. Season well and cook gently for 5 minutes. Stir in chopped chives. Garnish with chives and serve with a mixed salad.

Serves 4.

ORIENTAL FRIED RICE

175 g (6 oz/1¼ cups) long-grain rice
300 ml (10 fl oz/1¼ cups) chicken stock
2 tablespoons sesame oil
1 cm (½ in) cube fresh root ginger, grated
1 clove garlic, crushed
175 g (6 oz) raw chicken, thinly sliced
6 spring onions, sliced
1 small red pepper (capsicum), deseeded and sliced
115 g (4 oz) cooked peeled prawns
2 large eggs
2 tablespoons light soy sauce
1 tablespoon chopped fresh coriander
55 g (2 oz/⅓ cup) toasted cashew nuts

Put the rice and stock into a pan, bring to the boil, cover and simmer gently for 10 minutes. Remove from the heat and leave for a further 10 minutes. Drain off any excess liquid and allow to cool slightly. Heat the sesame oil in a large frying pan or wok and add the ginger, garlic and chicken and stir-fry for 4-5 minutes until the chicken is cooked.

Add the onions, pepper (capsicum) and prawns and stir-fry for a further 1 minute. In a bowl, beat together the eggs and the soy sauce and stir in the rice. Tip onto the chicken mixture and continue to cook over a high heat for 1 minute, stirring. Remove from the heat and stir in the coriander. Serve garnished with toasted cashew nuts.

Serves 4.

SWEET SAFFRON RICE

250 g (8 oz/1½ cups) basmati rice
1 teaspoon saffron threads
3 tablespoons boiling water
3 tablespoons vegetable oil
6 cloves
6 green cardamom pods, bruised
7.5 cm (3 in) cinnamon stick
90 g (3 oz/½ cup) raisins
3 tablespoons sugar
salt
parsley sprigs, to garnish

Place rice in a sieve and wash under cold running water until water runs clear.

Put rice in a bowl with 625 ml (20 fl oz/2½ cups) water and soak for 30 minutes. Put saffron in a small bowl, add boiling water and leave to soak for 5 minutes. Heat oil in a heavy-based saucepan, add cloves, cardamom pods and cinnamon and fry for 1 minute. Drain rice and reserve the soaking water. Add rice to the pan and fry for 2-3 minutes, until opaque and light golden.

Stir in reserved water, saffron and its soaking water, raisins and sugar and season with salt. Bring to the boil, then lower the heat and simmer, covered, for 12-15 minutes, stirring once or twice, until liquid is absorbed and rice is very tender. Serve hot, garnished with parsley.

Serves 4.

Note: The whole spices in the rice are not meant to be eaten.

FRAGRANT FRIED RICE

185 g (6 oz/1¼ cups) basmati rice
3 tablespoons vegetable oil
8 cloves
4 black cardamom pods, bruised
1 bay leaf
7.5 cm (3 in) cinnamon stick
1 teaspoon black peppercorns
1 teaspoon cumin seeds
1 teaspoon coriander seeds
1 onion, sliced into rings
1 small cauliflower, cut into tiny flowerets
salt
onion rings and bay leaves, to garnish

Place rice in a sieve and wash under cold running water until water runs clear. Put in a bowl with 625 ml (20 fl oz/2½ cups) water and soak for 30 minutes. Heat oil in a heavy-based saucepan, add cloves, cardamom pods, bay leaf, cinnamon, peppercorns and cumin and coriander seeds and fry for 1 minute. Add onion and cook for 5 minutes, until softened. Drain rice and reserve the soaking water.

Add rice to the pan and fry for 2-3 minutes, until opaque and light golden. Stir in reserved water and cauliflower and season with salt. Bring to the boil, lower heat and simmer, covered, for 12-15 minutes, stirring once or twice, until liquid is absorbed and rice and cauliflower are tender. Serve hot, garnished with onion rings and bay leaves.

Serves 4.

Note: Do not eat the whole spices.

RADICCHIO RISOTTO

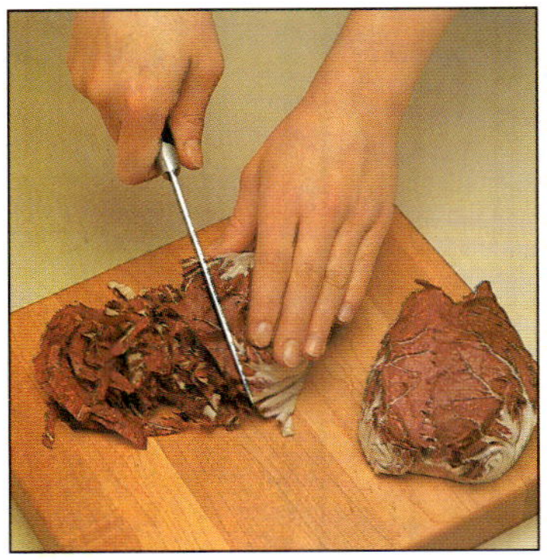

2 tablespoons olive oil
1 large onion, chopped
1 large clove garlic, chopped
1 teaspoon chopped fresh thyme
350 g (12 oz/2 cups) risotto rice
1 large head radicchio, shredded
150 ml (5 fl oz/⅔ cup) red wine
550 ml (20 fl oz/2½ cups) vegetable stock
2 tablespoons sun-dried tomato paste
salt and pepper
chopped fresh parsley, to garnish
freshly grated Parmesan cheese, to serve

In a large, heavy-based, non-stick frying pan, heat the oil and fry the onion, garlic and thyme for 5 minutes until softened. Add the rice and stir over a medium heat for 1 minute, until rice is transparent. Stir in the radicchio and immediately add the wine. Boil rapidly until all the liquid has evaporated.

Gradually add the stock in 3-4 batches, simmering over a low heat for 25 minutes or until all the stock is absorbed and the rice is tender. Stir in the tomato paste and seasoning. Garnish with chopped parsley. Serve hot with plenty of grated Parmesan cheese.

Serves 6-8.

LEEK & MUSHROOM PILAF

15 g (½ oz/¼ cup) dried ceps (mushrooms)
pinch of saffron strands
150 ml (5 fl oz/⅔ cup) boiling water
225 g (8 oz/1¼ cups) basmati rice
450 ml (16 fl oz/2 cups) vegetable stock
2 tablespoons olive oil
3 large leeks, trimmed
115 g (4 oz) fresh mushrooms, wiped
salt and pepper
whole or chopped chives, to garnish

Place the ceps and saffron in a small bowl and pour over the boiling water. Leave to soak for 10 minutes.

Wash the rice under cold running water for several minutes until the water runs clear and drain well. Place in a saucepan and add the stock and cep mixture. Bring to the boil, stir once, cover and simmer gently for 12 minutes.

Meanwhile, heat the oil and fry the leeks for 3 minutes, then add the fresh mushrooms and stir-fry for a further 3 minutes; keep warm. As soon as the rice is cooked, stir it into the pan and heat through for 1-2 minutes. Season, garnish with chives and serve at once.

Serves 6.

LEMON VEGETABLE RICE

juice 2 lemons
2 tablespoons caster sugar
vegetable stock (see method)
300 g (10 oz/1½ cups) long-grain rice
½ teaspoon salt
1 cinnamon stick
5 whole cloves
25 g (1 oz/6 teaspoons) butter
1 teaspoon cumin seeds
1 small onion, thinly sliced
2 small courgettes (zucchini)
55 g (2 oz/⅓ cup) cashew nuts, toasted
2 tablespoons chopped fresh mint

Mix the lemon juice and sugar together in a measuring jug. Make up to 550 ml (20 fl oz/ 2½ cups) with vegetable stock. Pour into a saucepan, add the rice, salt, cinnamon and cloves, bring to the boil, stir once and cook gently for 10 minutes until all the liquid is absorbed. Remove from the heat, cover with a tight-fitting lid and leave to sit undisturbed for a further 10 minutes.

In a small frying pan, melt the butter and stir-fry the cumin seeds for 1-3 minutes until they start to pop. Add the onion and fry for 5 minutes. Cut the courgettes (zucchini) into thin slices and add to the pan with the cashew nuts and mint. Stir-fry for 2-3 minutes until courgettes (zucchini) are tender, then stir in the rice. Heat through for 1 minute and serve.

Serves 4-6.

SPICED RICE & PEPPERS

4 tablespoons olive oil
225 g (8 oz) long-grain rice
2 cloves garlic
salt
1 teaspoon each cumin and coriander seeds
3 tablespoons tomato purée (paste)
2 teaspoons paprika
1 teaspoon chilli powder
pinch saffron threads, crushed and dissolved in 2 tablespoons boiling water
550 ml (20 fl oz/2½ cups) boiling chicken or vegetable stock or water
3-4 red peppers (capsicums), peeled, halved lengthways and seeded
extra virgin olive oil, to serve (optional)
chopped fresh herbs, to garnish

Heat oil in a paella pan or wide, heavy-based shallow saucepan. Stir in rice, then stir-fry for 2-3 minutes. Meanwhile, using a pestle and mortar, grind together garlic, salt, cumin and coriander seeds, then stir in tomato purée (paste), paprika, chilli and saffron liquid. Stir into rice. Stir in stock or water. Bring to boil, then cover and simmer for about 7 minutes.

Arrange peppers (capsicums) around sides of pan. Simmer for 7-10 minutes until rice is tender and plump, and liquid absorbed. Remove from heat and leave for 5 minutes. Trickle extra virgin oil over peppers (capsicums), if desired, and garnish with chopped herbs.

Serves 4.

RICE & CHICKEN

3 tablespoons olive oil
1.4 kg (3 lb) chicken, cut into 8 pieces, or 4 large chicken pieces, halved
1 Spanish onion, finely chopped
2 cloves garlic, chopped
1 large red pepper (capsicum), cut into strips
1 tablespoon paprika
225 g (8 oz) beefsteak tomatoes, peeled, seeded and chopped
350 g (12 oz) risotto rice
¼ teaspoon saffron threads, finely crushed
850 ml (1½ pints/3¾ cups) boiling chicken stock, or water
150 g (5 oz) small shelled fresh or frozen peas
2 tablespoons chopped fresh parsley
lime wedges, to garnish

Heat oil in a paella pan or large frying pan. Add chicken and cook for about 10 minutes until a light golden colour all over. Remove and set aside. Add onion, garlic and red pepper (capsicum) to pan and cook gently for 8-10 minutes until vegetables are soft. Stir in paprika, heat for about 30-60 seconds, then add tomatoes and cook for about 10 minutes until mixture is thick.

Add rice, stir for 2 minutes, then add saffron and stock or water and quickly bring to the boil. Return chicken to pan and simmer for 15 minutes. Add peas if using fresh ones and continue to simmer for about 10 minutes until chicken and rice are tender and most of liquid has been absorbed. Add frozen peas, if using. Remove from heat, cover pan and leave for 5-10 minutes. Sprinkle with parsley. Serve from pan if a paella pan has been used.

Serves 4.

CHICKEN & MUSHROOM RICE

175 g (6 oz/¾ cup) long-grain white rice
2 tablespoons vegetable oil
1 small onion, finely chopped
2 cloves garlic, finely chopped
2 fresh red chillies, seeded and cut into slivers
225 g (8 oz) chicken breast meat, finely chopped
85 g (3 oz) bamboo shoots, chopped or cut into matchstick strips
8 pieces dried Chinese black mushrooms, soaked for 30 minutes, drained and chopped
2 tablespoons dried shrimps
1 tablespoon fish sauce
about 25 Thai holy basil leaves
Thai holy basil sprig, to garnish

Cook rice, see page 144. In a wok, heat oil, add onion and garlic and cook, stirring occasionally, until golden. Add chillies and chicken and stir-fry for 2 minutes.

Stir in bamboo shoots, mushrooms, dried shrimps and fish sauce. Continue to stir for 2 minutes, then stir in rice and basil. Serve garnished with basil sprig.

Serves 4.

SIDE DISHES

POLANAISE CRUMBLE

250 g (8 oz) cauliflower flowerets
250 g (8 oz) broccoli flowerets

TOPPING: 30 g (1 oz/6 teaspoons) butter
60 g (2 oz/1 cup) soft white breadcrumbs
3 teaspoons chopped fresh parsley
1 hard-boiled egg, sieved

SAUCE: 30 g (1 oz/6 teaspoons) butter
30 g (1 oz/¼ cup) plain flour
315 ml (10 fl oz/1¼ cups) milk
salt and ground black pepper

To make topping, heat butter in a pan, add breadcrumbs and fry until golden. Put in a bowl; add parsley and egg.

To make sauce, put butter, flour, milk and salt and pepper to taste in a saucepan. Whisk together over a moderate heat until thick. Cook for 1-2 minutes, then keep warm.

Cook cauliflower and broccoli in boiling, salted water for 3-4 minutes until just tender. Drain and place in a warmed serving dish. Pour over sauce and sprinkle over topping. Serve hot.

Serves 4-6.

ALMOND BRUSSELS SPROUTS

500 g (1 lb) small Brussels sprouts
30 g (1 oz/6 teaspoons) butter
30 g (1 oz/¼ cup) flaked almonds
1 clove garlic, crushed
1 teaspoon finely grated lemon peel
1 teaspoon lemon juice
½ teaspoon salt
½ teaspoon ground black pepper
lemon twists and herb sprigs, to garnish

Trim stalks off sprouts and make a cut across each one. Cook in boiling, salted water for 4-5 minutes until just tender. Drain well and place in a warmed serving dish.

Meanwhile, melt butter in a small frying pan, add flaked almonds and garlic and fry until almonds are golden brown. Stir in lemon peel and juice and salt and pepper. Mix well.

Sprinkle almond mixture over sprouts and stir gently to mix. Serve immediately, garnished with lemon twists and herb sprigs.

Serves 4.

SPICY OKRA

375 g (12 oz) okra
2 tablespoons vegetable oil
2.5 cm (1 in) piece fresh root ginger, grated
1 teaspoon turmeric
½ teaspoon chilli powder
1 teaspoon chick-pea flour
salt
315 ml (10 fl oz/1¼ cups) natural yogurt
2 tablespoons chopped fresh coriander, to garnish

Wash okra and pat dry with absorbent kitchen paper, then cut into thick slices.

Heat oil in a saucepan, add okra and fry, stirring occasionally, for 4 minutes. Stir in ginger, turmeric, chilli powder and flour. Season with salt and fry for 1 minute more.

Stir in 3 tablespoons water, then cover and cook gently for 10 minutes or until okra is tender. Stir in yogurt and reheat gently. Serve hot, sprinkled with coriander.

Serves 4.

Note: Choose okra pods that are about 10 cm (4 in) long – larger pods are tough and stringy to eat.

PEPPERS WITH CAULIFLOWER

60 ml (2 fl oz/¼ cup) vegetable oil
1 large onion, sliced
2 cloves garlic, crushed
2 green chillies, seeded and chopped
1 cauliflower, cut into small flowerets
½ teaspoon turmeric
1 teaspoon Garam Masala
1 green pepper (capsicum)
1 red pepper (capsicum)
1 orange or yellow pepper (capsicum)
salt and pepper
1 tablespoon chopped fresh coriander, to garnish

Heat oil in a large saucepan, add onion and fry over a medium heat for 8 minutes or until soft and golden brown. Stir in garlic, chillies and cauliflower and fry for 5 minutes, stirring occasionally. Stir in turmeric and garam masala and fry for 1 minute.

Reduce heat, add 60 ml (2 fl oz/¼ cup) water and cook, covered, for 10-15 minutes, until cauliflower is almost tender. Cut peppers (capsicums) in half lengthwise, remove stalks and seeds, then slice peppers (capsicums) finely. Add to pan and cook for a further 3-5 minutes, until softened. Season with salt and pepper. Serve hot, garnished with chopped coriander.

Serves 4.

CHICORY-ASPARAGUS GRATIN

20 asparagus spears
4 small heads chicory
115 ml (4 fl oz/½ cup) virgin olive oil
1 clove garlic, crushed
grated zest and juice ½ lemon
1 tablespoon chopped fresh basil
45 g (1½ oz/⅓ cup) freshly grated Parmesan or Cheddar cheese
salt and pepper

Trim the asparagus spears, removing the woody ends, and peel almost to the tips. Steam the spears for 2 minutes until bright green.

Lightly oil 4 small gratin dishes. Preheat grill. Halve and trim the chicory and place 2 halves into each dish. Arrange the asparagus between the chicory.

Mix together the oil, garlic, lemon zest and juice and basil and pour over the vegetables. Place under a hot grill and cook for 3-4 minutes. Sprinkle over the cheese and return to the grill for 2-3 minutes until golden. Season and serve at once.

Serves 4.

COURGETTES WITH CHEESE

700 g (1½ lb) courgettes (zucchini)
6 teaspoons olive oil
1 large onion, chopped
1 teaspoon chopped fresh mint
2 eggs
175 g (6 oz/1½ cups) grated kefalotiri cheese
¼ teaspoon freshly grated nutmeg
salt and pepper

Preheat oven to 180C (350F/Gas 4). Trim courgettes (zucchini) ends, then cut into 1 cm (½ in) slices. Put courgette (zucchini) slices into a steamer above boiling water. Cook in batches, if necessary. Steam for a few minutes until just tender.

In a frying pan, heat oil, add onion and cook until soft. Mix courgettes (zucchini) and mint with the softened onion, then put in an ovenproof dish.

In a bowl, beat eggs with cheese, nutmeg, salt and pepper, then pour over the courgettes (zucchini). Bake in the oven for 20 minutes or until top is lightly browned.

Serves 4.

Variation: This dish may also be made with marrow instead of courgettes.

SWEET & SOUR VEGETABLES

5 teaspoons cornflour
427 g (15½ oz) can pineapple chunks in natural juice, drained, juice reserved
3-4 tablespoons light brown sugar, or to taste
70 ml (2½ fl oz/⅓ cup) cider vinegar
2 tablespoons soy sauce
2 tablespoons dry sherry or rice wine
55 ml (2 fl oz/¼ cup) tomato ketchup (sauce)
2 tablespoons vegetable oil
2 carrots, thinly sliced
1 red pepper (capsicum), cut lengthwise in half and thinly sliced
1 fennel bulb, trimmed, thinly sliced
175 g (6 oz) baby corn, trimmed
175 g (6 oz) mange tout (snow peas) or sugar snap peas
175 g (6 oz) courgettes (zucchini), thinly sliced

In a small bowl, dissolve the cornflour in the reserved pineapple juice. Stir in brown sugar, vinegar, soy sauce, dry sherry or rice wine and tomato ketchup (sauce) until well blended. Set aside.

Heat the wok until very hot. Add vegetable oil and swirl to coat wok. Add carrots, pepper (capsicum) slices and fennel and stir-fry for 3-4 minutes until carrots just begin to soften. Stir the cornflour mixture and stir into wok. Bring to the boil and stir until sauce bubbles and thickens. Add baby corn, mange tout (snow peas) or sugar snap peas and courgettes (zucchini) and simmer for 1-2 minutes. Stir in reserved pineapple chunks and toss for 30 seconds. Spoon into serving dish.

Serves 4.

SPINACH WITH RAISINS

50 g (2 oz) raisins
1 kg (2 lb) spinach
3 tablespoons olive oil
1 clove garlic, finely chopped
3 tablespoons pine nuts
salt and freshly ground black pepper
croûtons, to serve

Put raisins into a small bowl, cover with boiling water and leave to soak.

Wash spinach, shake off surplus water but do not dry the leaves. Put into a large saucepan, cover and cook until spinach wilts. Uncover and cook until excess moisture has evaporated. Chop coarsely. Drain raisins.

Heat oil in a frying pan, add garlic and pine nuts and fry, stirring occasionally, until beginning to colour. Stir in spinach and raisins, add salt and pepper and cook over low heat for 5 minutes. Serve with croûtons sprinkled over the top.

Serves 4.

SESAME GARLIC VEGETABLES

225 g (8 oz) broccoli
1 large green pepper (capsicum)
225 g (8 oz) courgettes (zucchini)
225 g (8 oz) asparagus
2 cloves garlic, thinly sliced
2 teaspoons sesame oil
1 tablespoon sesame seeds

Slice the broccoli into small flowerets. Slice courgettes (zucchini) into 2.5 cm (1 in) pieces and halve. Cut pepper (capsicum) into 8. Trim away tough ends from asparagus and slice into 5 cm (2 in) pieces. Place vegetables in a colander and rinse well.

Bring a wok or large saucepan of water to the boil. Arrange vegetables on a layer of baking parchment in a steamer and place over the water. Sprinkle with sliced garlic and sesame oil. Cover and steam for 10 minutes.

Remove vegetables from steamer and place on warmed serving plates. Sprinkle with sesame seeds and serve with soy sauce, for dipping.

Serves 4.

BROCCOLI WITH CHILLIES

450 g (1 lb) broccoli
olive oil
2 cloves garlic, sliced
2 dried red chillies, seeded and crushed
salt

Cut thick broccoli stems in half or thirds lengthways. Add all of broccoli to a saucepan of boiling salted water, boil for 2 minutes, then drain and rinse under cold running water.

Heat olive oil in a heavy-based frying pan sufficiently large to hold broccoli in a single layer. Add garlic and chillies to pan. Cook over a moderate heat until sizzling, 3-4 minutes.

Add broccoli, turn to coat in oil then reduce heat to very low. Pour in 115 ml (4 fl oz/ ½ cup) water, add salt and cover tightly. Cook very gently for about 20 minutes, turning broccoli carefully 2 or 3 times, until broccoli is very tender. If necessary, uncover and boil off excess liquid. Serve hot or warm.

Serves 4.

SZECHUAN AUBERGINE

450 g (1 lb) small aubergines (eggplants), cut into 2.5 cm (1 in) cubes or thin slices
salt
2 tablespoons groundnut oil
2 cloves garlic, finely chopped
2.5 cm (1 in) piece fresh root ginger, peeled and finely chopped
3-4 spring onions, finely sliced
2 tablespoons dark soy sauce
3-6 teaspoons chilli bean paste or sauce or 1 teaspoon crushed dried chillies
1 tablespoon yellow bean paste (optional)
2 tablespoons dry sherry or rice wine
3 teaspoons cider vinegar
1 tablespoon sugar
chopped fresh parsley, to garnish

Place aubergine (eggplant) cubes in a plastic or stainless steel colander or sieve, placed on a plate or baking sheet. Sprinkle with salt and leave to stand 30 minutes. Rinse aubergine (eggplant) under cold running water and turn out onto layers of absorbent kitchen paper; pat dry thoroughly. Heat wok until very hot. Add oil and swirl to coat wok. Add garlic, ginger and spring onions and stir-fry for 1-2 minutes until spring onions begin to soften. Add aubergine (eggplant) and stir-fry for 2-3 minutes until softened and beginning to brown.

Stir in remaining ingredients and 150 ml (5 fl oz/⅔ cup) water and bring to the boil. Reduce the heat and simmer for 5-7 minutes until aubergine (eggplant) is very tender, stirring frequently. Increase heat to high and stir-fry mixture until the liquid is almost completely reduced. Spoon into serving dish and garnish with parsley.

Serves 4-6.

SPICY STIR-FRIED CABBAGE

450 g (1 lb) bok choy
½ head Chinese leaves
1 tablespoon groundnut (peanut) oil
2 cloves garlic, finely chopped
1 tablespooon light soy sauce
1 teaspoon five-spice powder
1 teaspoon chilli sauce
salt and freshly ground black pepper
sliced fresh red chilli, to garnish

Discard damaged outer leaves from cabbages, Break bok choy leaves from stem, rinse well and dry on kitchen paper. Discard coarse stem at base of leaves then shred finely.

Bring a large saucepan of water to the boil and blanch the bok choy for a few seconds until just wilted. Drain well and rinse in cold water. Drain thoroughly and pat dry with kitchen paper. Remove core from Chinese cabbage leaves, and shred finely.

Heat oil in a non-stick or well seasoned wok and stir-fry bok choy and garlic for 2 minutes. Add the Chinese leaves and all the remaining ingredients except the garnish and stir-fry for 2 minutes. Garnish with sliced red chilli and serve immediately. Ideal accompaniment for Beef in Oyster Sauce, page 116.

Makes 4 servings.

CHILLI ROAST PEPPERS

1 large red pepper (capsicum)
1 large orange pepper (capsicum)
1 large green pepper (capsicum)
1 large yellow pepper (capsicum)
1 tablespoon dark soy sauce
1 teaspoon chilli sauce
1 tablespoon sunflower oil
freshly ground black pepper
2 tablespoons chopped fresh chives

Halve peppers (capsicum) lengthwise, remove the core and seeds then halve again. Place in a non-stick roasting tin.

Preheat oven to 190C (375F/Gas 5). In a small bowl, mix together the remaining ingredients except the chives and spoon over the peppers (capsicum), turning to make sure they are well coated. Roast for 30 minutes, basting occasionally, until softened.

Transfer roast peppers (capsicum) to warmed serving plates, sprinkle with chives and serve.

Serves 4.

BEANS IN TOMATO SAUCE

6 tablespoons olive oil
2 cloves garlic, chopped
1 small onion, finely chopped
2 sprigs fresh sage
1 kg (2 lb) broad beans, shelled
400 g (14 oz) can chopped plum tomatoes
1 tablespoon sun-dried tomato paste
Salt and freshly ground black pepper
Fresh sage leaves to garnish

Heat oil in a large, heavy-based saucepan. Add garlic, onion and sage and cook gently for 4-5 minutes to soften.

Stir in beans, tomatoes and sun-dried tomato paste and bring to the boil. Lower the heat, cover and cook for 20 minutes, stirring frequently, until beans are tender. Discard sage sprigs and season with salt and ground black pepper. Serve hot garnished with sage leaves.

Serves 4-6.

BUTTERY COUSCOUS

350 g (12 oz/2 cups) couscous
175 g (6 oz/1 1/3 cups) podded broad beans
200 g (7 oz) can sweetcorn kernels, drained
115 g (4 oz/1 cup) podded peas
115 g (4 oz/1/2 cup) butter
1 teaspoon ground cumin
1 teaspoon ground paprika
1 tablespoon chopped fresh coriander
25 g (1 oz/1/4 cup) chopped mixed nuts, toasted
juice 1/2 lime
salt and pepper

Wash the couscous until all the grains are moistened and set aside to soak for 5 minutes. Stir grains with a fork to separate and steam for 12-15 minutes until fluffed up and tender. Peel and discard the tough outer skins of the beans and blanch in boiling water for 2 minutes; drain and dry well. Blanch the sweetcorn for 2 minutes and the peas for 1 minute; drain and dry well.

In a large pan, heat the butter, stir in the spices and cook gently for 2 minutes. Add the blanched vegetables and fry for a further 2 minutes. Fork the cooked couscous to break up any lumps and stir into the pan until well coated with butter. Stir in the coriander, nuts, lime juice and season well. Serve hot.

Serves 4-6.

SPICED BROWN LENTILS

250 g (8 oz/1 1/4 cups) whole brown lentils
315 ml (10 fl oz/1 1/4 cups) Coconut Milk
1/4 teaspoon chilli powder
1/2 teaspoon turmeric
2 tablespoons vegetable oil
1 onion, finely chopped
4 curry leaves
1/2 stick lemon grass
7.5 cm (3 in) cinnamon stick
sprigs of lemon thyme, to garnish

Wash lentils, put in a bowl, cover with cold water and leave to soak for 6 hours or overnight.

Drain lentils and put them in a large saucepan with coconut milk, chilli powder and turmeric. Bring to the boil, then simmer, covered, for 30 minutes or until just tender. Heat oil in a separate pan, add onion, curry leaves, lemon grass and cinnamon and fry over a medium heat, stirring, for 8 minutes or until onion is soft and golden brown.

Stir into lentil mixture and simmer for a further 10 minutes or until liquid has evaporated and lentils are soft but not broken up. Remove whole spices and serve hot, garnished with thyme sprigs.

Serves 4.

Note: Substitute a few sprigs of lemon thyme if lemon grass is unavailable. Look for lemon grass at Asian and Oriental shops and the larger supermarkets.

SWEET POTATO 'CHIPS'

1-2 tablespoons olive oil
4 small sweet potatoes (about 700 g/1½ lb)
2 teaspoons paprika
½ teaspoon chilli powder
salt and pepper

Preheat oven to 230C (450F/Gas 8) and pour enough olive oil into a large roasting pan to just cover the base. Place in the oven for 2-3 minutes until hot.

Wash and dry the potatoes and cut each one into 8 wedges and carefully spoon into the hot oil, avoiding splashing. Bake at the top of the oven for 10 minutes, then turn potatoes over and return to the oven for a further 10 minutes until golden on the outside and cooked through.

Mix the spices together. Using a slotted spoon, transfer the potatoes to a serving dish. Add the spices and salt and pepper and stir well to coat evenly. Serve hot.

Serves 6.

Note: Reduce the quantity of oil, if wished.

GARLIC-ROASTED POTATOES

900 g (2 lb) new potatoes
12 unpeeled shallots
12 unpeeled cloves garlic
1 tablespoon chopped fresh sage
1 tablespoon chopped fresh thyme or rosemary
4 tablespoons hazelnut or olive oil
salt and pepper

Preheat oven to 200C (400F/Gas 6). Wash and dry the potatoes and halve any large ones. Trim the shallots, removing any dirt that may be trapped in the root ends and combine with the potatoes, garlic and herbs.

Put the oil into a roasting tin and place in the oven for 5 minutes until hot and starting to smoke. Add the potato and shallot mixture (taking care not to splash the hot oil) and stir until the potatoes, shallots, garlic and herbs are well coated.

Return to the oven and cook for 50-60 minutes until roasted and golden, turning from time to time to brown evenly. Transfer to a hot serving dish and serve at once.

Serves 6.

POTATOES WITH ALLIOLI

450 g (1 lb) small potatoes, preferably new, unpeeled
sea salt
1 tablespoon finely chopped fresh parsley
ALLIOLI SAUCE:
6-9 cloves garlic
salt and freshly ground black pepper
about 150 ml (5 fl oz/⅔ cup) olive oil

Add potatoes to a saucepan of boiling salted water and boil until tender.

Meanwhile, make sauce. Using a pestle and mortar, crush garlic with a little salt. Work in oil a drop at a time; as the sauce thickens the oil can be added more quickly. Season with salt and pepper.

Drain potatoes well. Immediately potatoes are cool enough to handle, cut into bite-size chunks and toss with sea salt and the allioli Sprinkle with parsley and serve warm.

Serves 4-6.

Variation: Pound 1 egg yolk with the garlic, then add juice of ½ lemon to finished sauce.

DRY POTATO CURRY

500 g (1 lb) waxy potatoes
salt
2 tablespoons vegetable oil
1 teaspoon mustard seeds
1 onion, finely sliced
2 cloves garlic, crushed
2.5 cm (1 in) piece fresh root ginger, grated
1 fresh green chilli, seeded and chopped
1 teaspoon turmeric
½ teaspoon cayenne pepper
1 teaspoon ground cumin
green pepper (capsicum) strips, to garnish, if desired

Cut potatoes into 2 cm (¾ in) chunks.

Cook potatoes in boiling salted water for 6-8 minutes, until just tender, then drain and set aside. Heat oil in a large saucepan, add mustard seeds and fry for 30 seconds or until they begin to pop. Add onion and fry for 5 minutes, until soft but not brown. Stir in garlic and ginger and fry for 1 minute more.

Add potatoes, chilli, turmeric, cayenne and cumin and stir well. Cook, covered, for 3-5 minutes, stirring occasionally, until potatoes are very tender and coated with spices. Serve hot, garnished with green pepper (capsicum) strips, if desired.

Serves 4.

SOUFFLÉ POTATOES

4 large potatoes
30 g (1 oz/6 teaspoons) butter
6 teaspoons single (light) cream
1 teaspoon salt
½ teaspoon ground black pepper
½ teaspoon grated nutmeg
2 eggs, separated

Preheat oven to 220C (425F/Gas 7). Scrub potato skins and remove any 'eyes'. Pierce each potato several times using a small, sharp knife, and arrange on a baking sheet. Cook in the oven for 1 hour, or until potatoes are tender.

Cut each potato in half, carefully scoop out the potato flesh and place in a bowl or an electric mixer fitted with a beater. Replace potato skins on a baking sheet and cook in the oven for 10-15 minutes until crisp and golden. Meanwhile mash or beat potato until smooth, add butter, cream, salt, pepper, nutmeg and egg yolks. Mash or beat until thoroughly blended.

Stiffly whisk egg whites, add to potato and fold in gently, using a spatula, until evenly mixed. Fill each potato skin with mixture and return to oven for 10-15 minutes or until risen and lightly browned. Serve immediately.

Serves 8.

Variations: Add 125 g (4 oz) chopped crispy bacon or grated cheese to filling for a change, or add chopped mixed herbs to taste.

BAKED POTATO LAYER

1 kg (2 lb) medium potatoes
30 g (1 oz/6 teaspoons) butter
1 clove garlic, crushed
1 teaspoon salt
1 teaspoon ground black pepper
125 g (4 oz/1 cup) grated Cheddar cheese
315 ml (10 fl oz/1¼ cups) milk
155 ml (5 fl oz/⅔ cup) single (light) cream
1 large egg, beaten
parsley sprigs, to garnish

Preheat oven to 190C (375F/Gas 5). Peel and very thinly slice potatoes. Using ½ the butter, lightly grease a 22.5 cm (9 in) shallow ovenproof dish.

Arrange a layer of potato slices over base and up sides of the dish. Sprinkle with some of the garlic, salt, pepper and cheese. Continue to layer until all these ingredients have been used, finishing with a layer of potatoes and a sprinkling of cheese.

Place milk, cream and egg in a bowl and whisk until smooth. Pour over potato layer and dot with remaining butter. Cook in the oven for 1 hour until golden brown and potatoes are tender. Garnish with parsley sprigs and serve hot.

Serves 4-6.

DESSERTS

TANGERINE SYLLABUB

grated peel and juice of 3 tangerines
grated peel and juice of 1 lemon
90 g (3 oz/⅓ cup) caster sugar
90 ml (3 fl oz/⅓ cup) cream sherry
315 ml (10 fl oz/1¼ cups) double (thick) cream
extra grated peel, to decorate, if desired

Put tangerine and lemon peel and both juices into a bowl with sugar and sherry and leave to infuse in a cool place for at least 1 hour.

In a large bowl, whip the cream while gradually pouring in the infused mixture. Keep whipping until mixture is thick enough to form soft peaks.

Pour mixture into a glass serving bowl or individual glasses and chill for at least 2 hours before serving. Decorate with extra peel, if desired.

Serves 4-6.

Note: Use a sharp grater to grate the peel of tangerines, otherwise the peel tends to tear. Warm citrus fruits slightly before squeezing and they will yield more juice.

CITRUS FLUMMERY

75 ml (2½ fl oz/⅓ cup) frozen concentrated orange and passion fruit juice
315 ml (10 fl oz/1¼ cups) double (thick) cream
1 egg white
30 g (1 oz/5 teaspoons) caster sugar (see Note)
orange wedges and passion fruit, to decorate
langues de chat biscuits, to serve

Thaw concentrated fruit juice and measure out required quantity. (Use remainder as a drink, making up with water.) In a bowl, whip cream to soft peaks.

Add juice gradually, continuing to whip cream, until fairly thick.

In a separate bowl, whisk egg white until stiff. Whisk in sugar, then fold into creamy mixture. Spoon into individual glasses and chill for 1 hour. Decorate with orange wedges and passion fruit. Serve with the biscuits.

Serves 4-6.

Note: Flavour the sugar for this and other desserts and cakes by keeping it in a jar with a vanilla pod. This will give the sugar a strong vanilla flavour.

COEURS À LA CRÈME

250 g (8 oz) ricotta or cottage cheese
30 g (1 oz/5 teaspoons) caster sugar
1 teaspoon lemon juice
315 ml (10 fl oz/1¼ cups) double (thick) cream
2 egg whites
TO SERVE
fresh fruit or Blackcurrant Sauce (see page 231)
double (thick) cream

Line 8 heart-shaped moulds with muslin. Press cheese through a sieve into a bowl. Stir in sugar and lemon juice.

In a separate bowl, whip cream until stiff. Stir into cheese mixture. Whisk egg whites until stiff, then fold into the cheese mixture.

Spoon into moulds, place on 2 plates and leave to drain overnight in the refrigerator. To serve, unmould onto individual plates and gently remove the muslin. Serve the hearts with fresh fruit with cream handed separately, or with whipped cream and Blackcurrant Sauce.

Serves 8.

Note: To add extra colour, decorate with sprigs of redcurrants and blackcurrants.

CHARLOTTE RUSSE

16 sponge fingers
3 teaspoons powdered gelatine
4 egg yolks
90 g (3 oz/⅓ cup) caster sugar
625 ml (20 fl oz/2½ cups) whipping cream
1 vanilla pod, split open
315 ml (10 fl oz/1¼ cups) thick sour cream
185 g (6 oz) fresh raspberries
whipped cream, to decorate

Line the base of 1.1 litre (35 fl oz/4¼ cup) charlotte mould with greaseproof paper. Stand sponge fingers, pressing against each other, round sides of mould and trim to fit.

Sprinkle gelatine over 3 tablespoons of water in a small bowl and leave to soften for 2-3 minutes. In a bowl, whisk egg yolks and sugar together until thick and mousse-like. Put 375 ml (12 fl oz/1½ cups) whipping cream in a saucepan with vanilla pod and bring almost to boiling point. Strain over egg mixture, stirring well. Pour back into saucepan and stir over low heat until mixture has thickened slightly. Do not boil.

Strain into clean bowl and add soaked gelatine. Stir until dissolved. Cool, then stand bowl in larger bowl of iced water and stir until mixture thickens. Whip remaining cream with sour cream and fold into mixture. Pour into prepared mould, cover with plastic wrap and refrigerate overnight. When ready to serve, turn out onto serving plate, remove greaseproof paper and decorate with the raspberries and whipped cream. Tie a ribbon round pudding.

Serves 6-8.

ATHOLL BROSE

45 g (1½ oz/3 tablespoons) medium oatmeal
60 g (2 oz/⅓ cup) whole blanched almonds
315 ml (10 fl oz/1¼ cups) double (thick) cream
60 ml (2 fl oz/¼ cup) whisky
90 g (3 oz/¼ cup) orange flower honey
1 tablespoon lemon juice

Toast oatmeal under a medium-hot grill until evenly browned. Toast the almonds in the same way, then chop them finely.

In a large bowl, whip cream to soft peaks, then gradually whisk in whisky, honey and lemon juice.

Fold oatmeal and half the chopped almonds into creamy mixture and spoon into 4 glasses. Chill in the refrigerator. When ready to serve, sprinkle remaining almonds on top of each pudding.

Serves 4.

Note: This traditional Scottish dessert is very rich and is perfect for a dinner party.

LYCHEE & PORT ICE CREAM

125 g (4 oz/½ cup) caster sugar
155 ml (5 fl oz/⅔ cup) ruby port
20 fresh lychees or 470 g (15 oz) can lychees
4 teaspoons fresh lime juice
315 ml (10 fl oz/1¼ cups) double (thick) cream
fresh or canned lychees and lime peel twists, to decorate

Place sugar and port in a saucepan and heat gently, stirring until sugar has dissolved. Peel lychees and remove stones, or drain canned lychees. Add lychees to port, bring to the boil, then cover and cook very gently for 2 minutes. Leave until cold.

Put port and lychees into a food processor fitted with a metal blade and process until smooth. Pour mixture into a sieve over a bowl and rub mixture through sieve using a wooden spoon. Stir in lime juice. Whip cream in a bowl until thick, add port mixture and fold in until evenly blended. Pour mixture into a plastic container, cover and freeze for 1-2 hours until mixture is almost frozen but still mushy.

Return mixture to processor and process until smooth and creamy. Return mixture to plastic container and freeze until firm. Scoop ice cream into serving dishes and decorate with lychees and lime peel.

Serves 6.

MAPLE BAVARIAN CREAM

1½ teaspoons powdered gelatine
3 tablespoons lemon juice and water, mixed
315 ml (10 fl oz/1¼ cups) double (thick) cream
5 tablespoons maple syrup
90 g (3 oz) crème fraîche
extra maple syrup for serving
langues de chat biscuits, to serve

Sprinkle gelatine over lemon juice and water in a small bowl and leave to soften for 2-3 minutes. In a bowl, whip cream lightly, adding half the maple syrup.

Stand gelatine bowl in a saucepan of hot water and stir until the gelatine has dissolved. Stir in remaining maple syrup, then pour into the cream, and whisk again until cream stands in soft peaks.

Fold crème fraîche into maple cream mixture. Spoon into individual glasses and chill until set. Top with extra maple syrup and serve with langues de chat biscuits.

Serves 4.

Note: Real maple syrup, as opposed to maple-flavoured syrup, is very expensive and not always easy to obtain. It is worth seeking out for this pudding, as it greatly improves the flavour of the cream.

NUTTY BROWN BREAD CREAM

60 g (2 oz/½ cup) hazelnuts
75 g (2½ oz/1¼ cups) fresh brown breadcrumbs
30 g (1 oz/2 tablespoons) demerara sugar
2 egg whites
90 g (3 oz/⅓ cup) caster sugar
315 ml (10 fl oz/1¼ cups) whipping cream
1-2 drops vanilla essence

Toast hazelnuts evenly, cool, then grind coarsely in a coffee grinder. Mix with breadcrumbs and demerara sugar in a bowl.

Tip crumb mixture onto a baking sheet and spread out evenly. Grill under medium-hot grill, turning and shaking, until brown. Leave to cool. Whisk egg whites in a large bowl, until stiff. Sprinkle in sugar and whisk for a further 2 minutes. In a separate bowl, whip cream with vanilla essence to soft peaks, then fold into egg whites with all but 1 tablespoon of breadcrumb mixture.

Spoon mixture into 6 glasses and chill until ready to serve. Sprinkle with reserved crumb mixture just before serving.

Serves 6.

Note: This mixture makes a delicious ice cream; simply turn the finished cream into a plastic container and freeze.

YOGURT FUDGE CREAM

315 ml (10 fl oz/1¼ cups) whipping cream
250 g (8 oz/1 cup) natural yogurt
250 g (8 oz/1½ cups) brown sugar
fresh strawberries or raspberries, to serve, if desired

In a large bowl, whip cream to stiff peaks. Fold in the yogurt.

Half fill 4 glasses with the creamy mixture. Sprinkle with about one-third of the sugar. Spoon remaining creamy mixture on top of the sugar, then pile on remaining sugar.

Chill in the refrigerator overnight. Serve puddings on their own, or with fresh strawberries or raspberries, if desired.

Serves 4.

Note: The brown sugar dissolves and forms a fudgy layer in these puddings. They must be prepared a day in advance to allow for this.

GRAPEFRUIT CHEESECAKE

250 g (8 oz) semi-sweet wheatmeal biscuits
125 g (4 oz/½ cup) butter, melted
2 pink grapefruit
3 teaspoons powdered gelatine
250 g (8 oz) cream cheese
155 ml (5 fl oz/⅔ cup) single (light) cream
2 tablespoons caster sugar
juice and grated peel of 1 lemon
4 egg whites

Crush biscuits to crumbs and mix with the melted butter.

Press two-thirds of the crumb mixture over base of a 22.5 cm (9 in) loose-bottomed or springform tin and chill. Cut off peel and pith from grapefruit, holding over a bowl to catch juice. Cut out segments from between membranes and set aside. Squeeze membranes into bowl to extract juice. Sprinkle gelatine over grapefruit juice and leave for 2-3 minutes to soften. Stand in a saucepan of hot water and stir until gelatine has dissolved. In a bowl, beat cream cheese, cream and sugar. Stir in gelatine, lemon juice and peel.

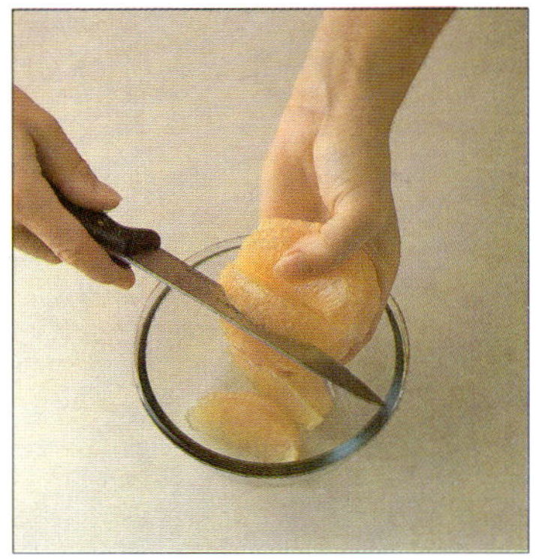

Whisk egg whites in a large bowl until stiff. Fold into creamy mixture. Pour over crumb mixture and return tin to refrigerator to set. To serve, remove cheesecake from tin and decorate with grapefruit segments. Press remaining crumbs evenly into sides of cake.

Serves 6-8.

Note: If liked, salt can be sprinkled onto the grapefruit to act as an alkali, making the grapefruit less acidic, so less sugar is needed to sweeten the fruit.

AMARETTI MOUSSE

100 g (3½ oz/½ cup) whole blanched almonds
60 g (2 oz) amaretti biscuits
3 eggs, plus 2 extra yolks
90 g (3 oz/⅓ cup) caster sugar
3 teaspoons powdered gelatine
2 tablespoons lemon juice
1-2 tablespoons Amaretto or kirsch
315 ml (10 fl oz/1¼ cups) whipping cream

Toast nuts under a medium grill to brown. Put with biscuits in food processor fitted with metal blade and process to crumbs.

In a bowl, whisk eggs, extra yolks and sugar together until thick and mousse-like. Sprinkle gelatine over lemon juice in a small bowl and leave to soften for 2-3 minutes. Stand bowl in saucepan of hot water and stir until gelatine has dissolved. Add to egg mixture with liqueur and three-quarters of nut and biscuit mixture. Whip cream stiffly and fold two-thirds into mixture.

Pour mixture into a 1 litre (32 fl oz/ 4 cup) soufflé dish and put in refrigerator to set. Just before serving, decorate with piped rosettes of reserved whipping cream and sprinkle remaining nuts and biscuits on top.

Serves 6-8.

Note: Amaretto is a very sweet liqueur made from almonds. Kirsch gives a more subtle flavour and makes the dessert less sweet.

BANANA BRÛLÉE

625 ml (20 fl oz/2½ cups) whipping cream
3 large bananas
juice of 1 small lemon
60 g (2 oz/¼ cup) caster sugar
few crumbled meringues (see page 169), if desired
125 g (4 oz/½ cup) granulated sugar

In a large bowl, whip cream until thick. Slice bananas thinly into a separate bowl and toss in lemon juice.

Fold bananas and caster sugar into whipped cream with crumbled meringues, if using. Spoon the mixture into a serving dish and place in the refrigerator.

Put granulated sugar and 1 tablespoon water into a small saucepan and place over a low heat to dissolve sugar. Do not stir. When sugar has dissolved, increase heat and boil syrup to a rich brown caramel. Immediately dribble this over banana cream mixture, then replace in refrigerator for caramel to harden. Serve within 1-2 hours.

Serves 6.

BREAD & BUTTER PUDDING

125 g (4 oz/¾ cup) sultanas and currants, mixed
8 slices thin white bread, buttered
30 g (1 oz/2 tablespoons) candied fruit, chopped
caster sugar for sprinkling

CUSTARD: 1 egg yolk
315 ml (10 fl oz/1¼ cups) milk
155 ml (5 fl oz/⅔ cup) single (light) cream
1 vanilla pod
1 teaspoon caster sugar

Put sultanas and currants into a bowl and cover with water. Leave to swell. Preheat oven to 180C (350F/Gas 4). Grease a 1 litre (32 fl oz/4 cup) pie dish.

Cut crusts from bread and sandwich 4 slices together. Cut into 6 pieces and place in prepared pie dish. Drain fruit and scatter over bread with chopped candied fruit. Top with remaining bread, butter side up.

Put egg yolk in a medium bowl. Put milk, cream, vanilla pod and sugar into a saucepan and bring almost to boiling point. Pour over egg, stir, then strain into pie dish, pouring down sides so top slices of bread are not soaked. Stand for 30 minutes, then sprinkle with caster sugar and place in a roasting tin. Pour in boiling water to come halfway up sides of dish and bake in the oven for 45-50 minutes, until top is golden brown.

Serves 4.

QUEEN OF PUDDINGS

500 ml (16 fl oz/2 cups) milk
155 ml (5 fl oz/⅔ cup) single cream
grated peel of 1 small lemon
90 g (3 oz/1½ cups) fresh white breadcrumbs
45 g (1½ oz/9 teaspoons) butter
250 g (8 oz/1¼ cups) caster sugar
3 small eggs, separated
3 tablespoons raspberry jam

Preheat oven to 180C (350F/Gas 4). Butter a 1.25 litre (40 fl oz/5 cup) pie dish. Put milk, cream and lemon peel in a saucepan.

Heat milk mixture gently for 5 minutes, then remove from heat and leave to infuse for 5 minutes. Put breadcrumbs, butter and one-quarter of the sugar into a bowl and pour the warm milk on top. Stir until butter and sugar have dissolved. In a small bowl, beat egg yolks, then stir them into breadcrumb mixture. Turn into prepared pie dish and bake for 45-50 minutes, until set. Remove from oven and cool slightly. Warm raspberry jam in a pan and spread over pudding.

Lower oven temperature to 160C (325F/Gas 3). In a large bowl, whisk egg whites until stiff, then fold in remaining sugar. Pile this meringue mixture onto pudding and return to oven for about 20 minutes, until meringue is crisp and golden. Serve warm or cold.

Serves 4.

Note: Sieve the warmed raspberry jam to remove pips, if desired.

MERINGUES WITH HONEY

2 egg whites
125 g (4 oz/½ cup) caster sugar

TO SERVE: 2 tablespoons clear honey
2 tablespoons toasted flaked almonds
315 ml (10 fl oz/1¼ cups) whipping cream

Preheat oven to 150C (300F/Gas 2). Line baking sheets with silicone paper. Put egg whites into a large bowl and whisk until stiff, but not dry.

Sprinkle 1 tablespoon sugar over egg whites and whisk for 1 minute more. Sprinkle half the remaining sugar over the mixture and fold in carefully, using a metal spoon. Then fold in remaining sugar. Spoon meringue into a piping bag fitted with a plain or star nozzle and pipe 12-16 small circles or ovals onto prepared sheets. Alternatively, simply place spoonfuls of meringue onto prepared sheets.

Bake meringues in the oven for 1-1½ hours, until crisp on the outside. Cool on a wire rack. When cold, pile onto a serving plate, dribble honey over the top and sprinkle with toasted flaked almonds. Whip cream until stiff and serve separately.

Makes 12-16 shells.

Note: An electric or hand whisk can be used to make meringues. Separate eggs carefully so there is no yolk with the white.

GINGER MARRONS GLACÉS

PAVLOVA: 3 egg whites
220 g (7 oz/1 cup) caster sugar
1 teaspoon white wine vinegar
1 teaspoon orange flower water
1 teaspoon cornflour

FILLING: 315 ml (10 fl oz/1¼ cups) whipping cream
3 pieces preserved stem ginger in syrup
vanilla ice cream
10 whole marrons glacés, each cut into 8 pieces

Preheat oven to 140C (275F/Gas 1). Line 3 baking sheets with non-stick baking paper, mark ten 8 cm (3 in) circles and invert paper.

Whisk egg whites in a bowl until stiff. Gradually add sugar, whisking well after each addition until thick. In a bowl, blend together the vinegar, orange flower water and cornflour. Add to meringue and whisk until very thick and glossy. Place meringue in a large piping bag fitted with a small star nozzle. Pipe a shell edging around the marked lines on the paper, then fill in centres with a thin layer of meringue. Pipe a second shell edging on top of the first edge.

Bake in the oven for 45 minutes. Turn off oven and leave in oven to cool. Remove when cold; store in an airtight container until required. Whip cream in a bowl until thick, place ½ in a piping bag fitted with a nozzle. Chop the ginger and fold into remaining cream and spread over each pavlova. Just before serving, top each with scoops of ice cream, whipped cream and a marron glacé.

Serves 10.

PANCAKES

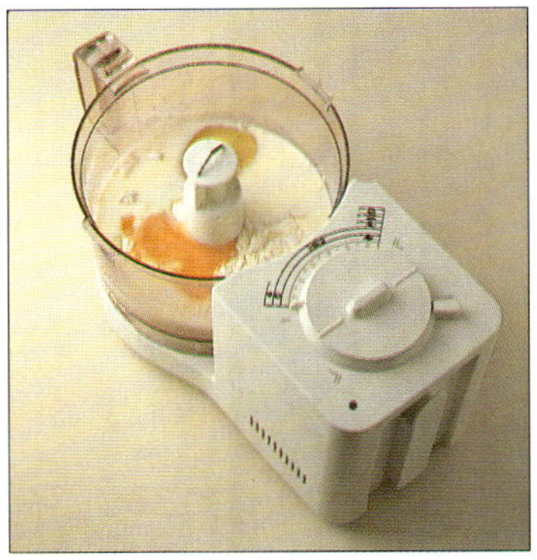

125 g (4 oz/1 cup) plain flour
pinch of salt
1 egg, plus 1 extra egg yolk
315 ml (10 fl oz/1¼ cups) milk
2 tablespoons oil or melted butter

TO SERVE: lemon wedges
caster sugar

Sift flour and salt onto a plate. Put into a food processor with egg, egg yolk and half the milk. Blend well, then add remaining milk and oil or melted butter and blend again. Stand for 30 minutes.

To make batter by hand, sift flour and salt into large bowl, make a well in the centre. Beat egg, egg yolk and half the milk together and tip into well. Using a wooden spoon, gradually stir flour into liquid, keeping batter smooth. Add remaining milk and beat well until bubbles appear round surface of batter. Leave to stand for 30 minutes – this allows flour to swell. Beat again before using.

Heat a 15-17.5 cm (6-7 in) heavy-based frying pan and grease lightly. Pour in just enough batter to cover bottom of pan. Cook over medium heat for 1-2 minutes, until underside is lightly browned. Turn or toss pancake and cook other side for same amount of time. Turn out and keep warm while cooking remaining pancakes. Serve sprinkled with lemon juice and sugar.

Serves 4.

ORANGE ROULADE

5 eggs, separated
185 g (6 oz/¾ cup) caster sugar, plus extra to sweeten cream
grated peel and juice of 2 oranges
icing sugar
315 ml (10 fl oz/1¼ cups) whipping cream
fresh orange segments, to decorate
Raspberry Sauce (see page 230), to serve if desired

Preheat oven to 180C (350F/Gas 4). Line a swiss roll tin with double thickness foil and grease very well. In a bowl, whisk egg yolks, sugar and orange peel until thick.

In a large bowl, whisk egg whites until stiff but not dry. Fold 1 tablespoon into egg yolk mixture, then tip egg yolk mixture onto whites and fold together carefully. Pour into prepared tin and spread evenly. Bake in the oven for 30 minutes, remove from oven and immediately cover with a damp tea towel. When quite cold, turn onto a piece of foil thickly dusted with icing sugar. Peel off bottom layer of foil, in long, thin strips.

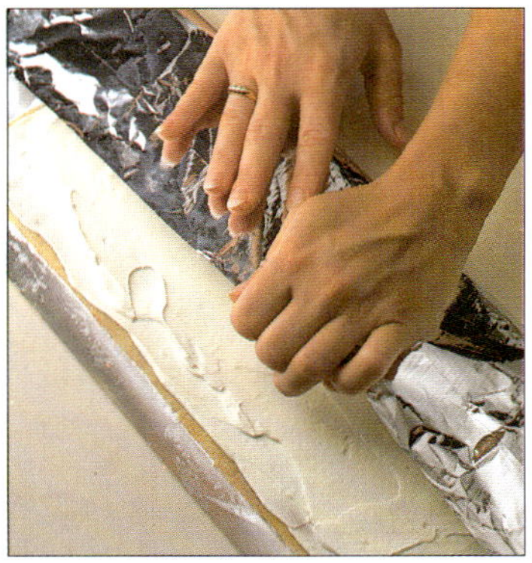

In a bowl, whip cream lightly and sweeten to taste. Gradually add orange juice, whisking all the time, until stiff. Reserve a little cream for decoration and spread remainder evenly over sponge. Roll up, using foil to help and transfer to a serving plate. Pipe rosettes along sides using reserved cream and decorate with fresh orange segments. Serve with Raspberry Sauce, if using.

Serves 6.

FRAMBOISE ZABAGLIONE

4 egg yolks
220 ml (7 fl oz/⅞ cup) Framboise liqueur
30 g (1 oz/5 teaspoons) caster sugar
strawberries or raspberries, to decorate, if desired
langues de chat biscuits, to serve

Put egg yolks, liqueur and sugar into a double boiler or a bowl set over a saucepan of simmering water.

Set over a medium heat and, using a balloon whisk, whisk the mixture until it is very thick and mousse-like in appearance – this will take about 20 minutes.

Pour mixture into glasses, decorate with strawberries or raspberries if desired, and serve immediately, while still warm, with langues de chat biscuits.

Serves 4.

Note: Although it is laborious it is important to use a hand whisk for this recipe. An electric whisk increases the volume of the eggs too quickly, so that they do not have a chance to cook. The mixture will then collapse when it is poured into glasses.

SOUFFLÉ LIME & CHOC LAYER

4 eggs, separated
90 g (3 oz/⅓ cup) caster sugar
3 teaspoons powdered gelatine
finely grated peel and juice of 1 lime
60 g (2 oz) plain (dark) chocolate, melted
315 ml (10 fl oz/1¼ cups) whipping cream
chocolate curls and lime peel, to decorate

Place egg yolks and sugar in a bowl over a saucepan of simmering water. Whisk until pale and thick. Remove bowl from saucepan, continue to whisk until mixture leaves a trail when whisk is lifted.

Sprinkle gelatine over 9 teaspoons water in a small bowl and leave to soften for 2-3 minutes. Stand bowl in a saucepan of hot water and stir until dissolved and quite hot. Stir gelatine into mixture until well blended. Pour ½ quantity of mixture into another bowl. Stir lime peel and juice into one mixture and chocolate into remaining mixture. Stir each until well blended. Whisk egg whites in a bowl until stiff. Whip cream until thick.

Add ½ quantity egg whites and cream to each mixture and fold in carefully until evenly blended. Spoon alternate spoonfuls of each mixture into 8 small glasses. Leave until set, then decorate with chocolate curls and lime peel.

Serves 8.

DACQUOISE

155 g (5 oz/1 cup) whole blanched almonds
5 egg whites
315 g (10 oz/1½ cups) caster sugar
185 g (6 oz/2¾ cups) dried apricots
juice of 1 lemon
375 ml (12 fl oz/1½ cups) whipping cream
toasted flaked almonds, to decorate

Preheat oven to 150C (300F/Gas 2). Line a baking sheet with silicone paper. Toast almonds under a medium grill to brown evenly. Cool, then grind finely in a coffee grinder or food processor. Set aside.

In a large bowl, whisk egg whites until stiff, but not dry. Sprinkle over 2 tablespoons of the caster sugar and whisk for a further 1 minute. Fold in remaining sugar with ground almonds, using a metal spoon. Spoon meringue onto lined baking sheet and spread evenly to a 25 cm (10 in) circle. Bake in the oven for 1½-2 hours, until dry and biscuit coloured. Peel off paper and cool meringue on a wire rack.

Put apricots and lemon juice into a saucepan, cover with water and simmer over medium heat for about 30 minutes, until tender. Cool, then purée apricots with a little cooking liquid in a blender or food processor to make a thick purée. Whip cream stiffly and fold half the purée into it. Pile onto meringue and dribble remaining purée, thinned with a little more cooking liquid, over top. Sprinkle with flaked almonds to decorate.

Serves 6-8.

CHERRY CLAFOUTI

750 g (1½ lb) stoned black cherries, fresh or frozen, thawed if frozen
90 g (3 oz/¾ cup) plain flour
pinch of salt
3 eggs
90 g (3 oz/⅓ cup) caster sugar
500 ml (16 fl oz/2 cups) milk
1 tablespoon cherry brandy or kirsch
icing sugar, to serve

Preheat oven to 200C (400F/Gas 6). Drain the cherries, if thawed. Butter a 1.25 litre (40 fl oz/5 cup) pie dish and put cherries in it.

Sift flour and salt together onto a plate. In a large bowl, beat eggs with sugar until creamy, then fold in flour. Warm milk slightly in a saucepan over a low heat and stir into egg mixture with cherry brandy or kirsch. Beat well to make batter smooth, then pour the batter over the cherries.

Bake in the oven for 30 minutes, until batter is set and golden. Serve warm, dusted with icing sugar.

Serves 6.

Note: Fresh cherries can taste a little bland when cooked. Add 1-2 drops almond essence to improve the flavour, if desired.

MIXED CHOCOLATE TERRINE

WHITE CHOCOLATE MOUSSE: **280 g (9 oz) white chocolate**
1½ teaspoons powdered gelatine
1 good tablespoon liquid glucose
2 egg yolks
155 ml (5 fl oz/⅔ cup) double (thick) cream
155 ml (5 fl oz/⅔ cup) thick sour cream

DARK CHOCOLATE MOUSSE: **185 g (6 oz) plain (dark) chocolate**
4 tablespoons strong black coffee
2 teaspoons powdered gelatine
125 g (4 oz/½ cup) butter, cut into cubes
2 egg yolks
315 ml (10 fl oz/1¼ cups) whipping cream

Line a 1 kg (2 lb) loaf tin with plastic wrap to overlap edges. To make the white chocolate mousse, break the white chocolate into small pieces and set aside. Sprinkle gelatine over 2 tablespoons water in a small bowl and leave to soften for 2-3 minutes. Put 3 tablespoons water in a saucepan with glucose and bring to the boil. Remove from heat and stir in gelatine until dissolved. Add chocolate and beat mixture until chocolate has melted and is smooth.

Beat in egg yolks, one at a time. In a bowl, whip the creams together lightly and fold into the chocolate mixture. Pour the chocolate into the loaf tin and refrigerate until set.

To make dark chocolate mousse, melt chocolate with coffee in the top of a double boiler or a bowl set over a pan of simmering water. Sprinkle gelatine over 3 tablespoons water in a small bowl and leave to soften for 2-3 minutes. Stand bowl in a pan of hot water and stir until gelatine has dissolved. Stir into chocolate with butter and beat until butter has melted and everything is well mixed. Leave to cool, then beat in egg yolks. In a bowl, whip cream lightly and fold into chocolate mixture.

Pour dark chocolate mixture over set white chocolate mousse in terrine. Return to refrigerator until set, then cover with overlapping plastic wrap and place in the refrigerator overnight.

When ready to serve, unfold plastic wrap from top of mousse and turn out onto a serving dish. Carefully peel off plastic wrap and serve terrine cut in slices.

Serves 8-10.

Note: Decorate the terrine with whipped cream and grated chocolate, if desired. Either mousse can be served as a dessert on its own and will serve 4 people.

CHOCOLATE CHERRY SLICE

185 g (6 oz) plain (dark) chocolate
4 eggs
60 g (2 oz/¼ cup) caster sugar
45 g (1½ oz/¼ cup) plain flour

FILLING: 220 g (7 oz/1 cup) unsweetened marron purée
125 g (4 oz) plain (dark) chocolate, melted
315 ml (10 fl oz/1¼ cups) double (thick) cream
9 teaspoons Morello cherry jam
185 g (6 oz/1 cup) fresh or canned cherries, stoned and halved

Preheat oven to 190C (375F/Gas 5). Line a 32.5 x 22.5 cm (13 x 9 in) Swiss roll tin with non-stick paper.

Melt chocolate in a bowl over a pan of hand-hot water. Whisk eggs and sugar until pale and thick enough to leave a trail. Stir in chocolate; sift in flour and fold in gently. Transfer to tin, shake to level and bake in the oven for 20-25 minutes until firm to touch. Cover with a damp tea towel; leave until cold. To make filling, put marron purée and chocolate in a food processor fitted with a metal blade. Process until puréed. Fold in ⅔ cream. Stiffly whip remaining cream; place in a piping bag fitted with a small star nozzle.

Turn cake out of tin; remove paper. Trim edges and cut into 3 short strips across width. Spread 2 strips of cake with jam, then cover with ⅓ marron mixture. Arrange ⅓ cherry halves on each; stack layers together on a serving plate with remaining cake layer on top. Spread top and sides with remaining marron mixture and pipe cream around top edge. Decorate with remaining cherry halves. Chill.

Serves 10.

RICH CHOCOLATE LOG

440 g (14 oz) can condensed milk
90 g (3 oz) plain (dark) chocolate
45 g (1½ oz/9 teaspoons) butter
500 g (1 lb) plain sponge cake
125 g (4 oz/⅔ cup) glacé cherries, halved
45 g (1½ oz/½ cup) walnuts, chopped
45 g (1½ oz/3 tablespoons) stoned dates, chopped

CHOCOLATE FUDGE ICING: 45 g (1½ oz/9 teaspoons) butter
60 g (2 oz/¼ cup) caster sugar
90 g (3 oz/½ cup) icing sugar
30 g (1 oz/¼ cup) cocoa

Put milk, chocolate and butter in a saucepan and stir over low heat until chocolate and butter have melted and ingredients are well combined. Remove from heat. Reduce cake to crumbs in a blender or food processor and stir into chocolate mixture. Stir in the cherries, walnuts and dates. Spoon mixture onto a large piece of greaseproof paper and form into a log shape. Roll up in the paper and chill overnight.

Two hours before serving, unwrap roll and place on serving dish. To make the fudge icing, melt the butter in a saucepan with caster sugar and 2 tablespoons water. Bring to boiling point. Sift icing sugar and cocoa into pan and beat well. Cool until fudgy, then spread over roll. Mark lines along roll with a fork to give a log effect.

Serves 8-10.

CHOCOLATE PEARS

60 g (2 oz) amaretti biscuits
3-4 tablespoons Cointreau
125 g (4 oz) plain (dark) chocolate
3 tablespoons strong black coffee
1 tablespoon orange juice
30 g (1 oz/6 teaspoons) butter
2 eggs, separated
4 ripe pears

Put amaretti biscuits into a bowl, pour over liqueur, then crush biscuits to rough crumbs using end of a rolling pin.

Melt chocolate with coffee and orange juice in the top of a double boiler or a bowl set over a saucepan of simmering water. When smooth, remove from heat and beat in butter and egg yolks. In a separate bowl, whisk egg whites until stiff and fold chocolate mixture into them. Set aside. Peel pears, leaving them whole with stalks intact. Hollow out as much core as possible from the base and fill cavity with crumb mixture.

Stand the pears on a plate, cutting off a small slice if necessary to make them stand upright. Spoon chocolate mixture over pears to coat evenly. Chill for several hours or overnight. Transfer to individual plates using a fish slice when ready to serve.

Serves 4.

MINTY CHOCOLATE MOUSSE

185 g (6 oz) plain (dark) chocolate
315 ml (10 fl oz/1¼ cups) double (thick) cream
1 egg
pinch of salt
few drops peppermint essence

TO DECORATE: mint leaves
1 small egg white
caster sugar
grated chocolate

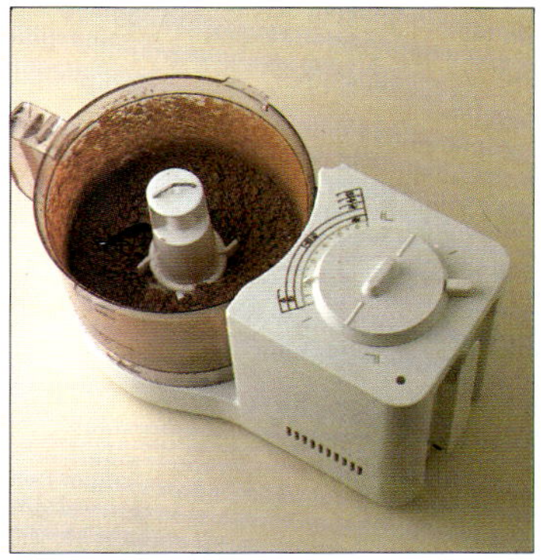

Break chocolate into small pieces and put into a blender or food processor fitted with a metal blade.

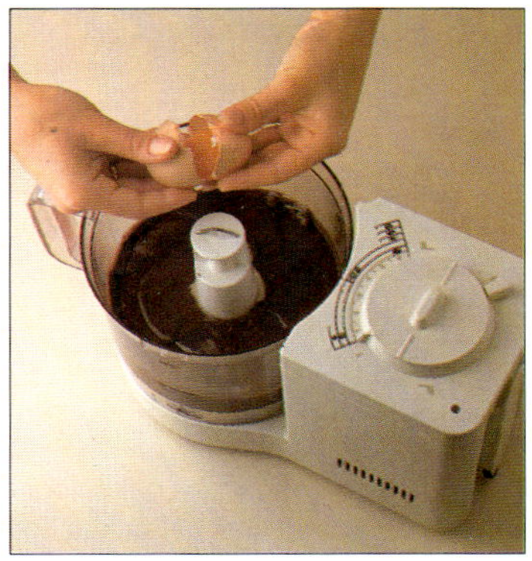

Heat cream in a small saucepan until almost boiling. Pour over chocolate and blend for 1 minute. Add egg, salt and peppermint essence and blend for 1 minute more. Pour into individual ramekin dishes or chocolate cups and refrigerate overnight.

To make the decoration, wash and dry mint leaves. Lightly whisk egg white in a shallow bowl and dip in mint leaves to cover. Dip them into caster sugar, shake off any excess and leave to harden on greaseproof paper. Place on each mousse just before serving and sprinkle with grated chocolate.

Serves 4-6.

Note: Peppermint essence has a very strong flavour; use it sparingly.

ROUND CHRISTMAS PUDDING

500 g (1 lb/3 cups) mixed dried fruit
60 g (2 oz/½ cup) chopped prunes
45 g (1½ oz/⅓ cup) chopped glacé cherries
60 g (2 oz/½ cup) chopped almonds
45 g (1½ oz/¼ cup) grated carrot
45 g (1½ oz/¼ cup) grated cooking apple
finely grated peel and juice of 1 orange
3 teaspoons black treacle (molasses)
90 ml (3 fl oz/⅓ cup) stout
3 teaspoons brandy plus extra for serving
1 egg
60 g (2 oz/¼ cup) butter, melted
60 g (2 oz/⅓ cup) dark soft brown sugar
¾ teaspoon ground allspice
60 g (2 oz/½ cup) plain flour
60 g (2 oz/1 cup) soft white breadcrumbs

In a large mixing bowl, put mixed fruit, prunes, cherries, almonds, carrot, apple, orange peel and juice, treacle, stout and the brandy. Mix well together. Stir in egg, butter, sugar, allspice, flour and breadcrumbs until well blended. Cover; leave in a cool place until ready to cook. Use a buttered round Christmas pudding mould, measuring 12.5 cm (5 in) in diameter, or a rice steaming mould, lined with double thickness foil. Fill each half of mould with mixture. Place two halves together, securing mould tightly.

Half-fill a saucepan with water, bring to the boil and place mould carefully into pan so that water comes just below join of mould. Cover and cook very gently for 6 hours. Cool in mould; turn out and wrap in foil until required. To re-heat pudding: unwrap and replace in mould. Cook as before for 2-3 hours. Turn onto a serving plate, decorate with holly, spoon over warmed brandy and set alight.

Serves 8.

PEARS IN WINE

2 eating pears
315 ml (10 fl oz/1¼ cups) sweet dessert wine, such as Beaume de Venise, or red wine
½ orange
½ lemon
60 g (2 oz/¼ cup) caster sugar
cream, to serve

Peal pears with a vegetable peeler, leaving stalks intact. Cut out as much core as possible from 'flower' end, then lay on their sides in a small saucepan: they should fit snugly. Cover with dessert wine.

Peel off as much peel as possible from the orange and lemon halves, using a canelle knife. Alternatively, use a vegetable peeler and peel thinly so as to get no pith, then cut peel into julienne strips. Squeeze juice from orange and lemon halves and add to pan with peel strips and sugar. Cover and poach pears on a low heat until just tender.

Remove with slotted spoon to a bowl. Pour over cooking liquid and leave to cool, then chill for 2 hours. Boil the cooking liquid vigorously until syrupy and reduced by half. Pour the syrup over the pears just before serving. Serve with the cream.

Serves 2.

Note: If you have wine left over from cooking or a meal, pour it over dried fruit and keep in a screw-top jar. The fruit will plump up and gives a lovely flavour to fruit cakes.

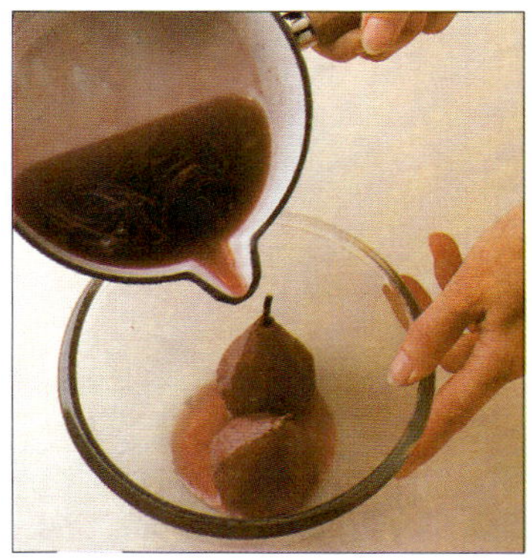

FRUIT FRITTERS

4 cooking or crisp tart eating apples
2-3 tablespoons calvados or cognac
3 tablespoons caster sugar
125 g (4 oz/1 cup) plain flour
pinch of salt
2 eggs, separated
155 ml (5 fl oz/⅔ cup) milk
1 tablespoon oil
oil for deep frying
icing sugar

Peel, core and cut apples into rings.

In a shallow dish, mix calvados or cognac with half the sugar. Add apples, turning them over to coat. Leave to macerate for 30 minutes. Sift flour and salt into a large bowl and mix in remaining sugar. Make a well in centre and drop in egg yolks. Using a wooden spoon, draw flour into yolks while gradually adding milk. Beat to a smooth batter, then leave to stand for 30 minutes. In a separate bowl, whisk egg whites until stiff and fold into batter with 1 tablespoon oil.

Heat oil for deep frying to 195C (385F). Drain fruit and dip each ring into batter to coat. Deep fry a few at a time, turning once, until puffed up and golden brown. Drain the fritters on absorbent kitchen paper and serve hot, sprinkled with a little icing sugar.

Serves 4.

Variations: Use pineapple, pears or bananas in place of apples, soaking them in an appropriate liqueur for 30 minutes.

TART LEMON MOULD

625 ml (20 fl oz/2½ cups) milk
90 g (3 oz/⅓ cup) granulated sugar
3 teaspoons powdered gelatine
3 small egg yolks
grated peel and juice of 1 large lemon
90 g (3 oz/⅓ cup) caster sugar
lemon twists and herb sprigs, to decorate

Put milk, granulated sugar and gelatine into a small saucepan and set over a low heat. Bring almost to boiling point (but do not boil), stirring constantly. Remove from heat.

In a bowl, beat egg yolks together lightly and gradually pour hot milk over them, stirring all the time. Pour into a 940 ml (30 fl oz/3¾ cup) mould. Leave at room temperature until cold, then refrigerate until set.

While mixture is cooling, put grated lemon peel and juice into a small saucepan with caster sugar and stir over a low heat until sugar has dissolved. Leave to cool. When ready to serve, turn out pudding onto a serving plate and pour lemon syrup around it. Decorate with lemon twists and herbs.

Serves 4.

APPLE CHARLOTTE

750 g (1½ lb) eating apples
grated peel of 1 lemon
90 g (3 oz/½ cup) brown sugar
125 g (4 oz/½ cup) butter
155 g (5 oz/2½ cups) coarse fresh breadcrumbs
apple slices and mint sprigs, to decorate

Peel, core and slice apples. Put into a saucepan with grated lemon peel, 60 g (2 oz/⅓ cup) of the sugar and 30 g (1 oz/6 teaspoons) of the butter. Simmer, covered, over a low heat until soft. Beat until pulpy.

Melt remaining butter in a frying pan and fry breadcrumbs until golden brown, stirring constantly to prevent burning. Stir in remaining sugar and leave to cool.

Spoon half the apple mixture into 4 glasses and cover with half the crumb mixture. Top with remaining apple and crumbs. Chill in the refrigerator for 2 hours before serving. Decorate with apple slices and sprigs of mint.

Serves 4.

SUMMER PUDDING

500 g (1 lb) redcurrants and blackcurrants, mixed
juice of ½ orange
125 g (4 oz/½ cup) caster sugar
250 g (8 oz) raspberries
12-16 slices thin white bread
extra raspberries, if desired, and whipping cream, to serve

Put currants into a saucepan with orange juice and sugar and cook over a low heat, stirring occasionally, until juicy and just tender. Gently stir in raspberries, then set aside to cool.

Cut crusts from bread. From 6 slices, cut circles the same size as the top of small ramekin dishes or dariole moulds. Use remaining bread to line 6 ramekin dishes or dariole moulds, overlapping bread to line dishes completely. Strain fruit, reserving juices, and spoon fruit into bread-lined dishes, pressing down quite firmly. Cover with bread circles. Pour some of the reserved juice into dishes to soak bread. Put a small weight on top of each pudding.

Chill puddings and remaining juice, for several hours or overnight. When ready to serve, turn puddings out onto individual plates and spoon a little of the reserved juices around them. Top with the extra raspberries, if desired. Whip cream lightly and dot a small amount in the juice and serve the remaining cream separately.

Serves 6.

FLAMING FRUIT SALAD

500 g (1 lb/7½ cups) mixed dried fruit, such as prunes, apricots, figs, apples, pears and peaches
2 tablespoons sherry
juice of ½ lemon
2 tablespoons clear honey
½ cinnamon stick
4 tablespoons brandy
90 g (3 oz/¾ cup) toasted almond flakes
60 g (2 oz/½ cup) walnuts, coarsely chopped
chilled single (light) cream or ice cream, to serve

Soak fruit overnight in 625 ml (20 fl oz/2½ cups) water and the sherry.

Put fruit and soaking liquid into a saucepan with lemon juice, honey and cinnamon stick. Cover and simmer on a low heat until fruit is just tender. Discard cinnamon stick, transfer fruit to serving dish and keep warm.

In a small pan, heat brandy and set alight. While still flaming, pour it over the fruit. Scatter with almonds and walnuts and serve immediately, with cream or ice cream.

Serves 5-6.

Note: The effect of flaming brandy is to burn off the alcohol and so concentrate the flavour. It is important to warm brandy first or it will not set alight.

PORT JELLY

625 ml (20 fl oz/2½ cups) ruby port
peel and juice of ½ orange
peel and juice of 1 lemon
90 g (3 oz/⅓ cup) caster sugar
1 cinnamon stick
5 teaspoons powdered gelatine

FROSTED FRUIT: 1 egg white
small bunches redcurrants and/or seedless grapes
caster sugar

Put port into a saucepan. Using a vegetable peeler, peel the orange half and the lemon thinly and add to port with lemon juice and squeezed lemon shell.

Add sugar and cinnamon stick and heat gently until sugar has dissolved. Leave to infuse for 20 minutes. Sprinkle gelatine on to squeezed orange juice in a small bowl and leave to soften for 2-3 minutes. Stand bowl in a saucepan of hot water and stir until gelatine has dissolved. Stir into port, then strain the mixture through a fine sieve into a wetted 815 ml (26 fl oz/3¼ cup) mould.

Place jelly in refrigerator to set. To make frosted fruit, lightly whisk egg white in shallow dish. Wash and dry fruit, dip into egg white and then into caster sugar to coat thoroughly. Put on a sheet of greaseproof paper to dry. When ready to serve, turn jelly out onto a serving dish and decorate with the frosted fruit.

Serves 4-6.

HOT ORANGE CAKE

125 g (4 oz/½ cup) butter, softened
125 g (4 oz/½ cup) caster sugar
2 large eggs, separated
125 g (4 oz/1 cup) self-raising flour
juice and grated peel of 3 small oranges
250 ml (8 fl oz/1 cup) double (thick) cream
icing sugar
fresh orange segments

Preheat oven to 180C (350F/Gas 4). Well grease a deep 20 cm (8 in) non-stick cake tin. In a large bowl, cream butter and sugar until light and fluffy. Beat egg yolks into mixture with 1 tablespoon flour and juice and grated peel of 1 orange.

In a separate bowl, whisk egg whites until stiff, but not dry. Fold into mixture with remaining flour and spoon into the prepared cake tin. Bake in the oven for 20-30 minutes, until golden brown and springy to touch.

While cake is cooking, whip cream stiffly in a bowl with remaining orange juice and peel. Leave cake in tin for 2-3 minutes, then turn out and cut in half horizontally. Working quickly, spread bottom with cream, cover with top half. Dust thickly with icing sugar and arrange orange segments on top. Serve the cake at once.

Serves 6.

Note: The cream will melt into the hot cake, so serve as quickly as possible.

CARAMEL FRUIT KEBABS

selection of fruit such as 2 bananas, 2 pears, 1 small pineapple, 2 peaches, grapes and strawberries
60 g (2 oz/¼ cup) butter, melted
2 tablespoons caster sugar
MARINADE
1 tablespoon lemon juice
3 tablespoons brandy
1-2 tablespoons clear honey
125 ml (4 fl oz/½ cup) orange juice
cinnamon stick, broken into pieces

In a large bowl, mix together all the ingredients for the marinade.

To prepare fruit, cut bananas into 2.5 cm (1 in) pieces, peel and core pears and cut in chunks, cut pineapple into thick slices then peel and discard core and cut flesh in chunks, skin peaches and cut flesh in chunks, leave grapes whole. Add these to the marinade and stir very gently to coat evenly, then leave for 2 hours. Add whole strawberries to marinade 15 minutes before end of marinating time.

Drain fruit, reserving marinade. Thread fruit onto 6 kebab sticks, brush with melted butter and sprinkle with sugar. Place under a medium grill for 7-8 minutes, turning frequently. Brush with any leftover butter and sprinkle with remaining sugar while turning. Strain marinade into a saucepan and heat gently.

Serves 6.

TREACLE CREAM FLAN

SHORTCRUST PASTRY: **250 g (8 oz/2 cups) plain flour**
pinch of salt
125 g (4 oz/½ cup) butter, cut into cubes
1 teaspoon sugar, if desired
2-3 tablespoons chilled water or milk

FILLING: **8 tablespoons golden syrup**
45 g (1½ oz/9 teaspoons) butter, cut into cubes
4 tablespoons thick sour cream
grated peel of 1 lemon
2 eggs, beaten

Sift flour and salt into a bowl. Using fingertips, rub butter into flour until mixture resembles breadcrumbs.

To bake blind, fold foil into 2.5 cm (1 in) strips using several thicknesses of foil and press round sides of pastry case. Prick base, then bake in the oven for 15-20 minutes, until dry and lightly coloured. Cool. Lower oven temperature to 180C (350F/Gas 4).

Stir in sugar, to make a sweet pastry if desired. Then, using a round-bladed knife, stir in sufficient water or milk to make a firm, but not sticky dough. Knead lightly on a floured surface. Wrap pastry in plastic wrap or foil and put in a cool place for 30 minutes. Resting pastry allows the flour to expand and helps to prevent pastry shrinking during cooking. Preheat oven to 190C (375F/Gas 5).

To make filling, warm syrup in a medium saucepan over a low heat. Remove from heat and add butter. Stir until butter has melted. Stir in sour cream and lemon peel. Whisk eggs into mixture, making sure they are thoroughly incorporated. Pour mixture into pastry case.

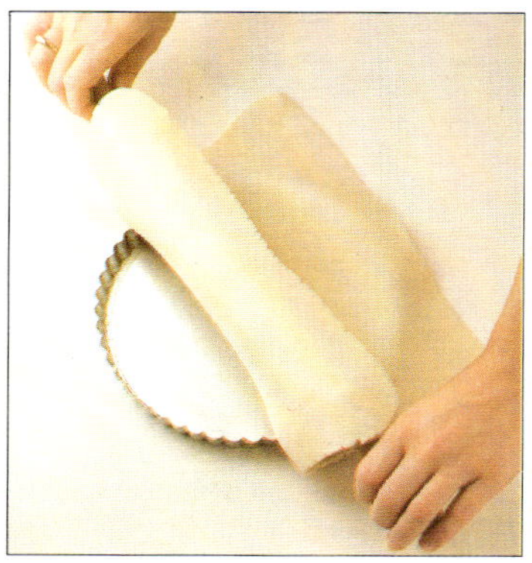

Unwrap the pastry and roll out on a lightly floured surface so that it is a good 2.5 cm (1 in) bigger all round than a 20 cm (8 in) flan ring or flan tin. Lift pastry on a rolling pin and lower into flan tin. Press gently into sides and trim off any excess with a sharp knife.

Bake the flan in the oven for 45-55 minutes, until filling is golden brown and puffed up. Serve warm or cold.

Serves 6.

Note: Serve the flan with whipped double (thick) cream and decorate with lemon slices or strips of peel and fresh herbs, if desired.

PECAN PIE

1 quantity Shortcrust Pastry, see page 181
3 eggs
315 g (10 oz/2 cups) soft brown sugar
1 tablespoon clear honey
30 g (1 oz/6 teaspoons) butter, melted
2 tablespoons whipping cream
pinch of salt
185 g (6 oz/1½ cups) pecan nuts, roughly chopped
icing sugar to serve, if desired

Preheat the oven to 190C (375F/Gas 5). Use the pastry to line a 25 cm (10 in) flan tin and bake blind as directed on page 181. Leave oven at 190C (375F/Gas 5).

In a large bowl, whisk eggs and brown sugar together until pale and thick. Stir in honey, butter, whipping cream and salt and mix together thoroughly. Fold in pecan nuts.

Pour mixture evenly into baked pastry case and bake in oven for 20 minutes. Lower oven temperature to 160C (325F/Gas 3) and cook for a further 45-50 minutes, until set. Serve warm, or allow to cool, and serve chilled. Dust with icing sugar, if desired.

Serves 6.

Note: Substitute walnuts for pecans in this pie if you prefer, or if you have difficulty in obtaining pecan nuts.

KUMQUAT CRANBERRY TARTS

WALNUT PASTRY: 185 g (6 oz/1½ cups) plain flour
125 g (4 oz/½ cup) butter
60 g (2 oz/½ cup) chopped walnuts
60 g (2 oz/¼ cup) caster sugar
1 egg, beaten

FILLING: 185 g (6 oz/¾ cup) caster sugar
250 g (8 oz) kumquats, sliced
250 g (8 oz/1½ cups) cranberries
185 g (6 oz/¾ cup) cream cheese
90 ml (3 fl oz/⅓ cup) Greek yogurt
1 teaspoon arrowroot

To make pastry, sift the flour into a bowl.

Add butter and rub in to form breadcrumbs. Stir in walnuts, sugar and enough egg to form a soft dough. Knead and roll out to line six 12 cm (4½ in) fluted flan tins. Trim edges and prick bases; chill 30 minutes. Preheat oven to 190C (375F/Gas 5). Heat sugar and 250 ml (8 fl oz/1 cup) water until dissolved. Bring to boil, add kumquats; cook for 3 minutes. Strain; return ⅓ syrup to pan; reserve remaining syrup. Add cranberries to syrup in pan, bring to boil, cover and cook for 3 minutes.

Strain, keeping individual syrups and fruit separate. Bake tart cases in oven for 10-15 minutes until lightly browned. Cool. Beat cream cheese with yogurt. Spread over base of tarts. Arrange alternate circles of fruit in tarts. Blend ½ teaspoon arrowroot into each syrup; bring each to boil. Glaze kumquats with clear syrup and cranberries with red syrup. Leave to set.

Serves 6.

TARTE FRANÇAISE

410 g (13 oz) puff pastry, thawed if frozen
1 egg yolk, beaten
6 tablespoons apricot jam, sieved
2 tablespoons lemon juice
about 750 g (1½ lb) mixed fresh fruit, such as grapes, strawberries and/or raspberries and bananas

Preheat oven to 220C (425F/Gas 7). Roll out pastry to a 30 x 20 cm (12 x 8 in) rectangle. Fold pastry in half, to a 15 x 20 cm (6 x 8 in) rectangle. Cut a rectangle from folded edge, 4 cm (1½ in) in from outside edges.

Unfold middle section and roll out to same size as 'frame' – 30 x 20 cm (12 x 8 in). Place on a baking sheet, dampen edges with water, then unfold 'frame' and place carefully on top of pastry rectangle. Press edges of pastry together, then 'knock up' using a blunt knife. Mark a pattern on frame and brush with beaten egg yolk. Prick centre of case all over.

Leave pastry in a cool place for 10 minutes, then bake for about 20 minutes, until golden brown. Leave to cool. Put jam and lemon juice into a saucepan and heat gently until jam has melted. To prepare fruit, halve and seed grapes, leave strawberries and/or raspberries whole and peel and slice bananas. Brush base of tart lightly with jam and arrange fruit in rows. Brush fruit with jam and serve as soon as possible.

Serves 6.

ORANGE MERINGUE PIE

1 quantity of Shortcrust Pastry (see page 181)
45 g (1½ oz/12 teaspoons) cornflour
315 ml (10 fl oz/1¼ cups) water
30 g (1 oz/6 teaspoons) butter
juice and grated peel of 2 small oranges
juice and grated peel of 1 small lime
2 eggs, separated
185 g (6 oz/¾ cup) caster sugar

Preheat oven to 190C (375F/Gas 5). Use the pastry to line a 25 cm (10 in) flan tin and bake blind as described on page 181. Lower oven to 160C (325F/Gas 3).

In a bowl, mix cornflour to a smooth paste with a little of the water. Stir in remaining water, then pour into a saucepan and add butter. Bring to the boil, stirring constantly. Simmer for 2-3 minutes, still stirring, then remove from heat. Beat in fruit juices and grated peel, egg yolks and one-third of the sugar. Spoon into flan case and cool slightly.

In a large bowl, whisk egg whites until stiff but not dry, add half remaining sugar and whisk again until mixture holds its shape. Fold in rest of sugar, then spoon or pipe meringue on top of flan, to cover filling and pastry. Bake in the oven for 20-30 minutes, until meringue is set and lightly golden. Serve warm or cold.

Serves 6-8.

MINCEMEAT JALOUSIE

410 g (13 oz) puff pastry, thawed if frozen
1 tablespoon milk
1 tablespoon caster sugar

MINCEMEAT: 2 eating apples
2 bananas
juice and grated peel of ½ lemon and 1 orange
60 g (2 oz) grapes
90 g (3 oz/⅔ cup) currants
90 g (3 oz/½ cup) raisins
90 g (3 oz/½ cup) sultanas
30 g (1 oz/¼ cup) almonds, roughly chopped
30 g (1 oz/⅓ cup) walnuts, roughly chopped
30 g (1 oz/⅓ cup) raw cane sugar
2 tablespoons brandy
45 g (1½ oz/9 teaspoons) butter, melted

To make the mincemeat, peel and chop apples and bananas. In a large bowl, quickly toss prepared fruit in lemon juice. Halve and seed grapes and add to fruit with orange juice and lemon and orange peel. Add currants, raisins and sultanas. Add nuts to mixture with sugar and brandy. Mix everything together well, then stir in melted butter. You only need one-third of this quantity for the jalousie, but it is not worth making a smaller amount. Use the remainder for mince pies.

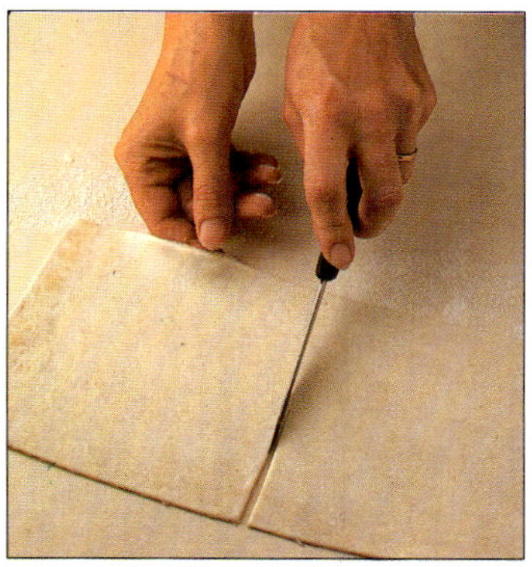

Preheat oven to 220C (425F/Gas 7). Roll out pastry to a 30 x 12.5 cm (12 x 5 in) rectangle. Cut pastry in half, to two 15 x 12.5 cm (6 x 5 in) rectangles.

Put one pastry half on a dampened baking sheet and spread mincemeat on top to within 2.5 cm (1 in) of edges. Moisten edges with water. Roll out remaining pastry to 2.5 cm (1 in) larger all round than other piece. Fold in half lengthwise and make cuts down from folded edge, 1 cm (½ in) apart to within 2.5 cm (1 in) of edge. Open and lifting carefully, place over mincemeat and pastry.

Press edges of pastry together and 'knock up' sides using a blunt knife. Chill jalousie for 30 minutes. Brush lightly with milk and sprinkle with caster sugar. Bake in the oven for 30-35 minutes, until pastry is puffed up and golden.

If the pastry starts to brown too quickly, cover it with foil.

Serves 6.

Note: Serve the jalousie with 250 ml (8 fl oz/ 1 cup) whipping cream, whipped with 1 tablespoon brandy and 1 tablespoon caster sugar.

The mincemeat can be made in advance and stored in a rigid plastic container in the refrigerator for up to 5 days.

NECTARINE BAKLAVA

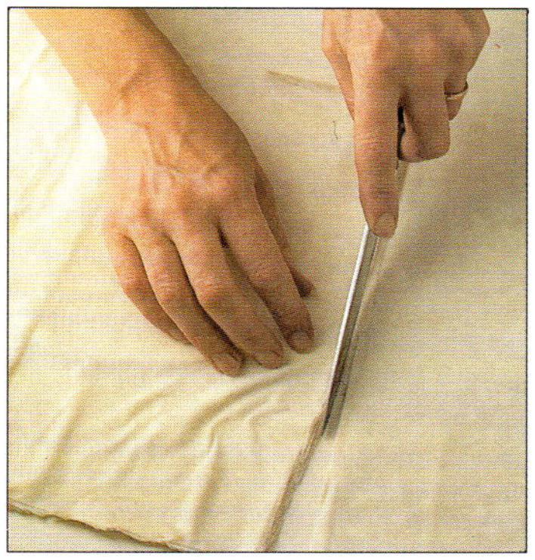

10 sheets filo pastry, thawed if frozen
155 g (5 oz/⅔ cup) butter, melted
220 g (7 oz/1¾ cups) chopped mixed nuts
1½ teaspoons ground cinnamon
8 tablespoons caster sugar
juice and grated peel of 2 lemons
1 tablespoon orange flower water
4 nectarines
icing sugar, to decorate

Preheat oven to 180C (350F/Gas 4). Cut pastry sheets in half, and each half into 4.

Working quickly, brush one cut sheet of pastry with melted butter. Line 8 individual 10 cm (4 in) Yorkshire pudding tins with one piece of pastry each. Brush 3 more cut sheets with butter and lay the pieces in the tins, so each tin has 4 pieces overlapping each other at different angles. Mix nuts, cinnamon and half the sugar, and spread half this mixture over pastry. Cover with 2 more layers of pastry, brushed with butter, then top with remaining nut mixture. Cover with rest of pastry, brushed with butter.

Press down pastry in tins and bake in the oven for 20-25 minutes, until golden brown. Meanwhile, dissolve remaining sugar in lemon juice over low heat. Stir in lemon peel and orange flower water. Bring to boil and simmer for 3 minutes. Cool slightly. Slice nectarines into syrup, turning them carefully to coat. Spoon into centre of pastries and dust edges with icing sugar. Serve lukewarm or cold, when pastries have absorbed some of the syrup.

Serves 8.

APRICOT HAZELNUT GALETTE

90 g (3 oz/½ cup) hazelnuts, skinned
90 g (3 oz/⅓ cup) butter, softened
90 g (3 oz/⅓ cup) caster sugar
125 g (4 oz/1 cup) plain flour
250 g (8 oz) fresh apricots, halved and stoned
315 ml (10 fl oz/1¼ cups) whipping cream
icing sugar for dusting

Preheat oven to 180C (350F/Gas 4). Lightly grease 2 baking sheets. Toast hazelnuts under a medium grill to brown evenly. Reserve 8 nuts, then grind remainder finely in a coffee grinder or food processor.

In a bowl, beat butter and two-thirds sugar together until light and fluffy. Fold in ground nuts and flour, then beat to a firm dough. Knead lightly on a lightly floured surface, then wrap in foil and chill for 30 minutes. Unwrap, cut in half and roll each piece out to a 17.5-20 cm (7-8 in) diameter circle. Carefully place on the greased baking sheets and bake in the oven for about 20 minutes, until golden. Cut one circle into 8 wedges and cool all pastry on a wire rack.

Poach apricots gently in 3 tablespoons water and remaining sugar, until just soft. Cool. In a bowl, whip cream stiffly. Transfer pastry circle to a serving plate and spread with half the cream. Remove apricots from pan with a slotted spoon and arrange over cream. Top with pastry sections and dust with icing sugar. Pipe a rosette onto each section with remaining cream and decorate with hazelnuts. Serve within 1 hour.

Serves 8.

INDIVIDUAL PEAR PUFFS

250 g (8 oz) puff pastry, thawed if frozen
2 large, ripe eating pears
1 egg yolk
1 tablespoon milk
caster sugar for sprinkling
Poire William liqueur, if desired

Preheat oven to 220C (425F/Gas 7). Roll out pastry to a rough rectangle, about 0.5 cm (¼ in) thick. Using a pear (halved, if easier) as a guide, cut out a pastry pear shape, 1 cm (½ in) larger than the pear.

Cut directly round pear, leaving a pear-shaped 'frame'. Roll out solid pear shape to same size as frame, dampen edges with water and fit frame on top. Press edges together lightly, then 'knock up' using a blunt knife. Make 3 more pastry pear shapes in same way. Peel and halve pears. Scoop out cores with a teaspoon, then cut across into thin slices. Fit neatly into pastry shapes.

Place pear puffs on baking sheet. Beat egg yolk with milk in a small bowl and brush edges of pastry with this. Bake in the oven for 15-20 minutes, until pears are tender and pastry edges are puffed up and golden. Remove from oven, sprinkle with caster sugar and place under a hot grill for 1 minute. Transfer to serving plates. Heat liqueur, if using, in a small saucepan, set alight and pour, flaming, over puffs. Serve at once.

Serves 4.

STRAWBERRY MILLE FEUILLE

410 g (13 oz) puff pastry, thawed if frozen
500 g (1 lb) fresh strawberries
315 ml (10 fl oz/1¼ cups) whipping cream
1-2 drops vanilla essence
caster sugar, to taste
5 tablespoons redcurrant jelly

Preheat oven to 220C (425F/Gas 7). Roll out the pastry to a thin rectangle and cut it into 3 even sections.

Place sections on baking sheets and prick all over with a fork. Bake in the oven for 15-20 minutes, until golden brown and crisp. Cool on a wire rack. When cold, trim edges with a very sharp knife to make even. Reserve trimmings. Cut half of the strawberries in half – choose even-sized ones for this. Slice remainder. In a bowl, whip cream fairly stiffly and flavour with vanilla essence and sugar. Fold sliced strawberries into cream.

Put a pastry slice onto a serving plate and spread with half the cream mixture. Lay another slice on top and spread with remaining cream mixture. Top with third slice. Put redcurrant jelly and 2 tablespoons water into a small saucepan and heat gently until jelly has dissolved. Brush top slice with a little jelly and arrange halved strawberries on top. Brush with remainder of jelly. Crush reserved pastry trimmings and press into sides of slice with the blade of a knife.

Serves 6-8.

BISCUITS & CAKES

ALMOND MACAROONS

2 egg whites
85 g (3 oz/3/4 cup) ground almonds
115 g (4 oz/1/2 cup) caster sugar
2 teaspoons ground rice or cornflour
few drops almond essence
12 split, blanched almonds

Preheat oven to 180C (350F/Gas 4). Line 2 baking sheets with rice paper or non-stick paper. Reserve 2 teaspoons egg white. Put remaining egg white in a large bowl and whisk until standing in soft peaks.

Fold in ground almonds, caster sugar, ground rice and almond essence until mixture is smooth. Put 6 spoonfuls of mixture onto each baking sheet and flatten slightly. Place a split almond in the centre of each round. Brush lightly with reserved egg white.

Bake in the oven for 20 minutes until very lightly browned. Allow to cool on baking sheets. When cold, remove macaroons from baking sheets and tear away excess rice paper or all the non-stick paper from each one.

Makes 12.

GINGERSNAPS

90 g (3 oz/1/3 cup) unsalted butter
90 g (3 oz/1/2 cup) light soft brown sugar
90 g (3 oz/1/4 cup) golden syrup
60 g (2 oz/2 tablespoons) black treacle
250 g (8 oz/2 cups) self-raising flour
1 teaspoon bicarbonate of soda
2 teaspoons ground ginger
1 teaspoon mixed spice

Preheat oven to 180C (350F/Gas 4). Butter 2 baking sheets. Put butter, sugar, syrup and treacle into a saucepan; stir over a gentle heat until melted.

Cool slightly. Sift flour, bicarbonate of soda, ginger and spice into a bowl. Make a well in centre, then pour in syrup mixture. Mix well to form a soft dough. Weigh dough into 15 g (1/2 oz) pieces, or divide into walnut-sized pieces. Roll pieces into smooth balls; place on baking sheets, spacing well apart. Flatten each ball to form a neat round.

Bake in the oven for 15 minutes until very lightly browned. Remove biscuits from oven, allow to cool for 2-3 minutes on baking sheets, then remove to a wire rack to cool completely. As biscuits cool they will become very crisp.

Makes 30.

DOUBLE CHOCOLATE COOKIES

115 g (4 oz/½ cup) butter
55 g (2 oz/¼ cup) granulated sugar
55 g (2 oz/⅓ cup) soft brown sugar
1 egg, beaten
few drops vanilla essence
130 g (4½ oz/1 cup plus 6 teaspoons) plain flour
15 g (½ oz/2 tablespoons) cocoa
½ teaspoon bicarbonate of soda
150 g (5 oz) white chocolate chips

Preheat oven to 180C (350F/Gas 4). Butter several baking sheets.

In a bowl, beat butter with granulated and soft brown sugar until creamy. Gradually add egg and vanilla essence. Sift flour, cocoa and bicarbonate of soda into bowl. Mix well, then stir in chocolate chips.

Drop teaspoonfuls of mixture, well spaced out, onto prepared baking sheets. Bake in the oven for 10-12 minutes until firm. Allow to cool on baking sheets for a few minutes, then remove to wire racks to cool completely.

Makes about 48.

– WHOLEWHEAT NUT BISCOTTI –

2 eggs
100 g (3½ oz/⅓ cup) caster sugar
225 g (8 oz/1¾ cups) wholewheat flour
1½ teaspoons baking powder
pinch of salt
1 tablespoon light olive oil
115 g (4 oz/¾ cup) Brazil nuts, toasted and ground
½ teaspoon caraway seeds
½ teaspoon freshly grated lemon zest

Preheat oven to 180C (350F/Gas 4) and lightly oil a baking sheet. Beat the eggs and sugar together until very thick and pale.

Beat in the flour, baking powder and salt to form a soft, sticky dough. Stir in the remaining ingredients and turn out onto a clean surface. Divide dough in half and roll into 2 logs about 5 x 20 cm (2 x 8 in) and transfer to the prepared baking sheet. Bake for 20 minutes. Remove from the oven and increase oven temperature to 200C (400F/Gas 6).

Using a serrated knife, cut the logs into 1 cm (½ in) biscuits, slicing diagonally. Place biscuits, cut-sides down, on the baking sheet and return to the oven for 8-10 minutes until browned around the edges. Cool on a wire tray.

Makes 32 biscuits.

Note: Sprinkle the biscuits with a little icing sugar, if wished.

TUILES

60 g (2 oz/¼ cup) unsalted butter
finely grated peel of 1 orange
2 teaspoons Grand Marnier
2 egg whites
125 g (4 oz/¾ cup) icing sugar, sifted
60 g (2 oz/½ cup) plain flour, sifted
60 g (2 oz/⅓ cup) blanched almonds, halved and cut into thin slivers

TO FINISH: icing sugar for sifting

Preheat oven to 230C (450F/Gas 8). Butter several baking sheets.

In a small saucepan, melt butter, then stir in orange peel and Grand Marnier. Cool. Whisk egg whites until softly peaking, then whisk in icing sugar. Fold in flour, then fold in butter mixture. Lightly mix almonds into batter. Drop small teaspoonfuls of mixture on baking sheets, spacing well apart. Using a fork dipped in cold water, flatten each mound to make a thin round. Bake, in batches, in the oven for 5 minutes, until lightly browned around edges.

Immediately biscuits are removed from oven, quickly remove them from baking sheet with a palette knife. Place on a rolling pin to cool into a curved shape (characteristic of Tuile biscuits which are meant to represent roof tiles). Sprinkle with sifted icing sugar before serving.

Makes 28-30.

BRANDY SNAPS

125 g (4 oz/½ cup) butter
125 g (4 oz/¾ cup) light soft brown sugar
125 g (4 oz/⅓ cup) golden syrup
4 teaspoons lemon juice
4 teaspoons brandy
125 g (4 oz/1 cup) plain flour
1 teaspoon ground ginger

Put butter, sugar, syrup, lemon juice and brandy into a saucepan and stir over a moderate heat until butter melts and sugar dissolves. Remove from heat, sift flour and ginger into pan and mix well. Allow mixture to cool completely.

Preheat oven to 190C (375F/Gas 5). Grease several baking sheets; line with non-stick paper. For ease of handling bake only 6 brandy snaps at a time, placing sheets in oven at 5 minute intervals. Non-stick paper may be re-used; wipe with absorbent kitchen paper before adding more mixture. Drop small teaspoonfuls of mixture onto baking sheets, spaced well apart. Bake in the oven for 8-10 minutes until very lightly browned. Have ready 6 chopsticks or pencils.

Allow brandy snaps to cool for a few seconds, then remove with a palette knife and wrap around chopsticks or pencils. When firm, remove chopsticks or pencils. Place on a tray. Should brandy snaps become too firm to roll up, simply reheat them for a few seconds to soften.

Makes 36.

CARAMEL SHORTBREAD

SHORTBREAD: 250 g (8 oz/2 cups) plain flour
pinch of salt
60 g (2 oz/¼ cup) caster sugar
185 g (6 oz/¾ cup) butter

CARAMEL: 125 g (4 oz/½ cup) unsalted butter
400 g (14.1 oz) can condensed milk
2 teaspoons instant coffee granules
60 g (2 oz/¼ cup) caster sugar
60 g (2 oz/2 tablespoons) golden syrup

TOPPING: 185 g (6 oz) plain (dark) chocolate, melted
30 g (1 oz) white chocolate, melted

Preheat oven to 180C (350F/Gas 4). To make shortbread, sift flour, salt and sugar into a bowl. Rub in butter until mixture forms coarse crumbs, then work together to form a soft dough. Roll out on a floured surface to an oblong a little smaller than a 32.5 x 22.5 cm (13 x 9 in) Swiss roll tin. Place shortbread in tin; press out to fit. Prick all over with a fork. Chill for 30 minutes. Bake in the oven for 25-30 minutes until lightly browned. Cool.

To make caramel, in a heavy saucepan, stir ingredients over moderate heat until melted. Stirring, bring to a gentle boil; boil until mixture thickens and holds a trail, about 6-8 minutes. Spread over shortbread. Cool. Spread plain chocolate over caramel. Put white chocolate into a paper piping bag, cut a small hole in bag; pipe lines across plain chocolate, 1 cm (½ in) apart. Pull a skewer through lines to decorate. Cut into squares when set.

Makes 48.

FRUIT FLAPJACKS

185 g (6 oz/¾ cup) butter
60 g (2 oz/¼ cup) demerara sugar
90 g (3 oz/¼ cup) golden syrup
250 g (8 oz/2¾ cups) rolled oats
90 g (3 oz/⅔ cup) dried apricots, chopped
90 g (3 oz/½ cup) stoned dates, chopped
90 g (3 oz/½ cup) stoned prunes, chopped

Preheat oven to 200C (400F/Gas 6). Butter a shallow tin measuring about 27.5 x 17.5 x 3 cm (11 x 7 x 1¼ in). Put butter, sugar and syrup into a large saucepan; stir continuously over a moderate heat until melted.

Stir oats into melted mixture, then spread half over base of tin to form a thin layer. Press with the back of a spoon to firm and smooth. In a bowl, mix apricots, dates and prunes together. Sprinkle evenly over oat mixture, then spread remaining oat mixture on top of fruits; press with spoon to firm and smooth.

Bake in the oven for 20-25 minutes until lightly browned. Allow to cool for 5 minutes, then mark into 24 squares: cutting into 4 lengthwise and 6 widthwise. Leave in tin until completely cold. Re-cut squares, then lift out with a small palette knife.

Makes 24.

JUMBLES

150 g (5 oz/⅔ cup) butter
150 g (5 oz/⅔ cup) caster sugar
1 egg, beaten
225 g (8 oz/2 cups) plain flour
55 g (2 oz/½ cup) ground almonds
grated rind 1 lemon
GLAZE:
6 teaspoons clear honey
6 teaspoons demerara sugar

In a bowl, beat butter with caster sugar until creamy. Gradually beat in egg.

Sift flour onto creamed mixture; add ground almonds and lemon rind. Mix well to make a firm dough. Knead lightly, wrap in plastic wrap and chill for 30 minutes. Preheat oven to 180C (350F/Gas 4). Grease several baking sheets. Divide dough into 32 pieces. Roll each piece into a pencil thin strip 10 cm (4 in) long. Twist into an S shape and place on a baking sheet. Bake in the oven for 15 minutes, until very lightly browned.

To glaze, brush the warm jumbles with honey and sprinkle with demerara sugar. Return to the oven for 2 minutes. Allow to cool on baking sheets for a few minutes, then remove to wire racks to cool completely.

Makes 32.

SHREWSBURY BISCUITS

155 g (5 oz/⅔ cup) butter
155 g (5 oz/⅔ cup) caster sugar
1 egg
few drops vanilla essence
375 g (12 oz/3 cups) plain flour
1 teaspoon baking powder
pinch of salt

In a bowl, beat butter with sugar until creamy. Beat in egg and vanilla to taste. Sift flour, baking powder and salt into bowl; blend in with spoon, then work by hand to form a dough. Knead lightly until smooth.

Wrap dough in plastic wrap or greaseproof paper. Chill for 45 minutes. Grease several baking sheets. Roll out dough on a floured surface to 0.3 cm (⅛ in) thick. Using a 6 cm (2 ½ in) fluted cutter, cut out as many rounds as possible from dough. Place, slightly apart, on baking sheets. Re-knead and re-roll trimmings: cut out more rounds to make 44 in total. Refrigerate for 30 minutes. Preheat oven to 180C (350F/Gas 4).

Bake biscuits in the oven for 15-20 minutes until very lightly coloured. Using a palette knife, carefully remove biscuits from baking sheets to wire racks to cool.

Makes 44.

Note: These biscuits can be sprinkled with icing sugar after baking, if desired.

CHERRY PRALINE RINGS

60 g (2 oz/½ cup) hazelnuts, skinned
155 g (5 oz/⅔ cup) caster sugar
125 g (4 oz/½ cup) butter
1 egg
375 g (12 oz/3 cups) plain flour
pinch of salt
1 teaspoon baking powder
185 g (6 oz/1 cup) glacé cherries, halved and thinly sliced

GLAZE: 1 small egg, beaten
3 teaspoons milk
2 teaspoons caster sugar

TO FINISH: caster sugar for sprinkling

Lightly oil a small baking sheet. Put nuts and 60 g (2 oz/¼ cup) sugar into a small saucepan; stir over low heat until sugar caramelizes. Pour onto baking sheet. When cold, break up and grind finely, then sieve. Preheat oven to 180C (350F/Gas 4). Grease several baking sheets. In a bowl, cream butter with remaining sugar. Beat in egg, then sieved praline. Sift flour, salt and baking powder into mixture; blend in with spoon, then work by hand to form a dough. Knead lightly until smooth.

Roll out dough on floured surface to 0.3 cm (⅛ in) thick. Using a 6 cm (2½ in) fluted cutter, cut out rounds from dough; remove centres with a 1 cm (½ in) cutter. Place rings, slightly apart, on baking sheets. Re-knead and re-roll trimmings to make 38-40 rings in total. Mix glaze ingredients together; brush over rings. Decorate with cherries. Bake for 15-20 minutes until lightly browned. Sprinkle with sugar. Cool on wire racks.

Makes 38-40.

PINWHEELS

185 g (6 oz/¾ cup) butter
185 g (6 oz/¾ cup) caster sugar
few drops vanilla essence
2 eggs
560 g (1 lb 2 oz/4½ cups) plain flour
2 teaspoons baking powder
salt
1 teaspoon brandy
2 tablespoons cocoa
1 egg white, very lightly beaten

Divide butter and sugar equally between 2 bowls.

To make vanilla dough, beat one portion of butter and sugar until creamy; beat in vanilla to taste and 1 egg. Sift half the flour, 1 teaspoon baking powder and a pinch of salt into bowl. Blend in with spoon, then work by hand to form dough. Wrap; chill 45 minutes. Make chocolate dough in same way with remaining butter, sugar and egg, adding brandy and sifting cocoa in with remaining flour and baking powder. Wrap and chill 45 minutes. Roll out doughs separately on a floured surface to oblongs about 32.5 x 27.5 cm (13 x 11 in).

Brush vanilla dough with egg white; place chocolate dough on top. Trim edges to neaten. Brush chocolate dough with egg white. Roll up, from one long side, to form a tight roll. Wrap and chill for 1 hour. Preheat oven to 180C (350F/Gas 4). Butter several baking sheets. Cut roll into 0.5 cm (¼ in) thick slices; place on baking sheets. Bake in the oven for 20 minutes until lightly browned. Remove to wire racks to cool.

Makes 48.

HAZELNUT SPECULAAS

250 g (8 oz/2 cups) hazelnuts
125 g (4 oz/1¼ cups) ground almonds
185 g (6 oz/¾ cup) caster sugar
185 g (6 oz/1 cup) icing sugar, sifted
2 teaspoons lemon juice
1 egg, beaten

SPICY DOUGH: 250 g (8 oz/2 cups) plain flour
¾ teaspoon baking powder
1 teaspoon mixed spice
90 g (3 oz/½ cup) light soft brown sugar
125 g (4 oz/½ cup) butter
2 small eggs
1 tablespoon milk
2 teaspoons caster sugar
20 blanched almonds, split into halves

Skin hazelnuts, then lightly toast nuts and grind finely. Put hazelnuts into a bowl with almonds and sugars; mix well. Mix with lemon juice and egg to make a firm paste. On a surface sifted with icing sugar, knead paste until smooth. Divide in half; shape each piece into a neat roll, about 30 cm (12 in) long. Wrap and chill for 30 minutes.

To make dough, sift flour, baking powder, spice and sugar into a bowl; rub in butter until mixture resembles fine breadcrumbs. Mix with 1 beaten egg to form a dough; knead lightly until smooth. Wrap and chill for 30 minutes. Preheat oven to 180C (350F/Gas 4). Butter a large baking sheet.

Roll out dough on lightly floured surface to a square a little larger than 30 cm (12 in) and trim edges to neaten. Cut in half to make two 15 cm (6 in) wide strips. Beat remaining egg, then brush over pastry strips. Place a roll of hazelnut paste on each strip; roll up neatly to enclose. Place rolls on baking sheet with joins underneath.

Mix remaining beaten egg with milk and caster sugar. Brush rolls with glaze. Decorate with almonds, placed slightly at an angle, in a long line on top. Brush almonds with glaze.

Bake in the oven for 30-35 minutes until golden. Using 2 large palette knives, very carefully remove rolls from baking sheet to a wire rack to cool. When cold, cut each roll, diagonally, into thin slices, cutting between almonds.

Makes 40.

LEMON SHORTBREAD

115 g (4 oz/½ cup) butter
55 g (2 oz/¼ cup) caster sugar
150 g (5 oz/1¼ cups) plain flour
¼ teaspoon ground nutmeg
25 g (1 oz/2 tablespoons) ground rice or cornflour
grated rind 1 lemon
TO FINISH:
caster sugar and nutmeg, for sprinkling

In a bowl, beat butter with sugar until creamy. Sift flour and nutmeg into bowl, then add ground rice and lemon rind. Blend in with a spoon, then work by hand to form a soft dough.

Knead dough lightly on a floured surface until smooth. Roll out to a smooth round, about 15 cm (6 in) in diameter. Very lightly flour a 17.5 cm (7 in) shortbread mould. Place shortbread, smooth side down, in mould. Press out to fit mould exactly. Very carefully unmould shortbread onto a baking sheet. Refrigerate for 1 hour. (If you do not have a shortbread mould, shape dough into a neat round. Place on baking sheet, prick well with a fork, then pinch edge to decorate.)

Preheat oven to 160C (325F/Gas 3). Bake shortbread in the oven for 35-40 minutes until cooked through, but still pale in colour. Immediately shortbread is removed from the oven, sprinkle lightly with caster sugar and nutmeg. Allow to cool on baking sheet for about 20 minutes, then very carefully transfer to a wire rack to cool completely.

Makes 1.

FLORENTINES

55 g (2 oz/¼ cup) unsalted butter
85 ml (3 fl oz/⅓ cup) double (thick) cream
85g (3 oz/⅓ cup) caster sugar
finely grated rind 1 lemon
1 teaspoon lemon juice
55 g (2 oz/½ cup) plain flour, sifted
85 g (3 oz/½ cup) slivered blanched almonds
115 g (4 oz/¾ cup) chopped mixed candied citrus peel
55 g (2 oz/⅓ cup) chopped glacé cherries
25 g (1 oz/2 tablespoons) sultanas
25 g (1 oz/2 tablespoons) chopped angelica
TO FINISH:
85g (3 oz) plain (dark) chocolate, chopped
85 g (3 oz) white chocolate, chopped

Preheat oven to 180C (350F/Gas 4). Grease several baking sheets. Line with non-stick paper. Put butter, cream, sugar, lemon rind and juice into a large saucepan and stir over a moderate heat until melted. Remove from heat and stir in flour, almonds, mixed peel, cherries, sultanas and angelica. Drop teaspoonfuls of mixture onto baking sheets; space well apart. Using a fork dipped in cold water, flatten each round to a circle about 6 cm (2½ in) in diameter.

Bake in the oven for 10-12 minutes until lightly browned around edges. Cool on baking sheets for a few minutes, then remove with a palette knife to wire racks to cool completely. Melt plain (dark) and white chocolate in bowls placed over pans of hot, not boiling, water. Spread flat sides of half the florentines with plain (dark) chocolate, and the remainder with white chocolate. Using a fork, mark chocolate into wavy lines. Leave to set, chocolate uppermost.

Makes 28.

VIENNESE FINGERS

250 g (8 oz/1 cup) butter
60 g (2 oz/1/3 cup) icing sugar, sifted
few drops vanilla essence
250 g (8 oz/2 cups) plain flour
pinch of salt
15 g (1/2 oz/1 tablespoon) pistachio nuts, skinned and chopped

TO FINISH: 60 g (2 oz) plain (dark) cake covering chocolate, chopped

Preheat oven to 180C (350F/Gas 4). Butter several baking sheets and dust lightly with flour.

In a bowl, beat butter with icing sugar until very light and creamy. Beat in vanilla to taste. Sift flour and salt into bowl; work into mixture with a wooden spoon to form a soft dough. Put into a piping bag fitted with a 1 cm (1/2 in) 10 point star nozzle. Pipe 6 cm (2 1/2 in) lengths of mixture on baking sheets, spaced apart, cutting mixture off at nozzle with a small knife when required length is reached. Sprinkle with pistachio nuts.

Bake in the oven for 20-25 minutes until very lightly browned. Cool on baking sheets for a few minutes, then remove to wire racks to cool completely. Melt chocolate in a double boiler or a small bowl placed over a saucepan of simmering water; stir until smooth. Dip both ends of biscuits in melted chocolate, scraping off excess on side of bowl. Place on foil. Leave in a cool place until set.

Makes 24.

LANGUES DE CHAT

60 g (2 oz/1/4 cup) butter
90 g (3 oz/1/3 cup) caster sugar
1 egg, beaten
60 g (2 oz/1/2 cup) plain flour

Preheat oven to 220C (425F/Gas 7). Grease several baking sheets; line with non-stick paper. In a bowl, beat butter with sugar until very light and fluffy. Gradually beat in egg. Sift flour into bowl and fold in to form a soft dough.

Put mixture into a piping bag fitted with a 10 mm (3/8 in) plain nozzle. Pipe 7.5 cm (3 in) lengths of mixture on baking sheets, cutting dough off at nozzle with a small knife when required length is reached. Space very well apart as biscuits will spread.

Bake in the oven for 6-8 minutes until golden brown around edges. Allow to cool on baking sheets for a few minutes. Using a palette knife, very carefully remove to a wire rack to cool.

Makes 36-40.

AMARETTI

1 egg white
2 teaspoons Amaretto di Saronno
155 g (5 oz/1⅓ cups) ground almonds
30 g (1 oz/¼ cup) bitter almonds, blanched and finely ground
250 g (8 oz/1½ cups) icing sugar, sifted

TO FINISH: icing sugar for sifting

Preheat oven to 180C (350F/Gas 4). Grease several baking sheets and line with non-stick paper. In a small bowl, very lightly whisk egg white and Amaretto together.

Put ground and bitter almonds and sugar into a large bowl, mix together and make a well in centre. Pour egg white into well, then mix to form a paste.

Divide mixture into 36 equal pieces; roll each one into a ball. Place on prepared baking sheets. Bake in the oven for 15-20 minutes until only just lightly browned. Remove from oven; immediately sift evenly with icing sugar. Cool on baking sheets.

Makes 36.

Note: If bitter almonds are unavailable, use 185 g (6 oz/1⅔ cups) ground almonds, adding a few drops of almond essence.

LINZER HEARTS

115 g (4 oz/½ cup) butter
55 g (2 oz/¼ cup) caster sugar
1 egg, beaten
few drops almond essence
200 g (7 oz/1¾ cups) plain flour
25 g (1 oz/3 tablespoons) cornflour
½ teaspoon baking powder
FILLING:
6 tablespoons raspberry jam
TO FINISH:
icing sugar, for sifting

In a bowl, beat butter and sugar together until creamy. Gradually beat in egg, then beat in almond essence, to taste.

Sift flour, cornflour and baking powder into bowl and blend together with a spoon, then work by hand to form a soft dough. Chill for 30 minutes. Preheat oven to 180C (350F/Gas 4). Butter several baking sheets. Roll dough out on a floured surface to 0.3 cm (⅛ in) thick. Using a 5 cm (2 in) heart cutter, cut out heart shapes from dough. Using a smaller heart cutter, cut out hearts from the centre of 20 of the hearts. Re-knead and re-roll trimmings and cut out more shapes to make 40 in total, half with the centre cut out.

Bake in the oven for 15 minutes until very lightly browned. Remove from baking sheets to wire racks to cool. Dust biscuits with cut-out centres with icing sugar. Spread whole hearts with raspberry jam and top with cut-out biscuits.

Makes 20.

ADVENT CRESCENTS

250 g (8 oz/2 cups) plain flour
pinch of salt
125 g (4 oz/½ cup) caster sugar
155 g (5 oz/1⅓ cups) ground almonds
250 g (8 oz/1 cup) butter, cut into small cubes
3 egg yolks
few drops almond essence

TO FINISH: icing sugar for sifting

Sift flour and salt into a bowl; mix in sugar and ground almonds. Make a well in centre.

Place butter, egg yolks and almond essence in centre of mixture. With fingertips, gently work butter with egg yolks, gradually incorporating flour, sugar and almonds until mixture forms a soft dough. Wrap in plastic wrap and refrigerate for 30 minutes. Preheat oven to 180C (350F/Gas 4).

Divide dough into 15 g (½ oz) pieces, about the size of a walnut. Shape each piece into a thin roll, about 10 cm (4 in) long. Curve round to form a crescent shape. Place on ungreased baking sheets. Bake in the oven for 15 minutes until lightly browned. Allow to cool on baking sheets. Sift liberally with icing sugar. Remove from baking sheets to a serving plate.

Makes 42.

EASTER BISCUITS

55 g (2 oz/⅔ cup) walnuts
115 ml (4 fl oz/½ cup) sunflower oil
55 g (2 oz/¼ cup) caster sugar
25 g (1 oz/2 tablespoons) currants
1 egg
175 g (6 oz/1½ cups) plain flour
1 teaspoon baking powder
¼ teaspoon vanilla essence
icing sugar

Preheat oven to 180C (350F/Gas 4). Grease 2 baking sheets. In a food processor, chop walnuts finely. In a bowl, mix walnuts, sunflower oil, sugar, currants and egg.

Sift in flour and baking powder. Add vanilla essence. Stir together to form a firm paste, adding more flour if necessary.

Roll mixture into small walnut sized balls, flatten slightly and place on prepared baking sheets. Bake in the oven for 10 minutes or until crisp and golden. Transfer to wire racks to cool. Dust with icing sugar as they cool.

Makes about 14.

FESTIVAL CRESCENTS

130 g (4½ oz) hazelnuts
250 g (9 oz/1¼ cups) unsalted butter, softened
55 g (2 oz/¼ cup) caster sugar
1 egg yolk
2 tablespoons brandy
55 g (2 oz/½ cup) cornflour
300 g (10 oz/2½ cups) plain flour
orange flower water
icing sugar

In a food processor, chop nuts finely, without reducing to ground hazelnuts. Preheat oven to 180C (350F/Gas 4). Butter 2 or 3 baking sheets.

In a bowl, cream butter and caster sugar until pale and fluffy. Beat in egg yolk and brandy. Stir in hazelnuts. Sift cornflour and flour over mixture. Stir in, adding more flour, if necessary, to make a firm dough. With floured hands, break off small pieces of dough and roll into 7.5 cm (3 in) lengths, tapering into pointed ends. Shape into crescents; place on baking sheets. Bake for 20-25 minutes until firm; reduce heat if browning. Cool on wire racks.

Pour orange flower water into a small bowl and icing sugar into a large one. Dip crescents very briefly into orange flower water, then into icing sugar, to coat completely. Pack loosely in a tin to avoid biscuits sticking together.

Makes about 40.

LEBKUCHEN

SPICED HONEY DOUGH: 375 g (12 oz/3 cups) self-raising flour
2 teaspoons mixed spice
pinch of salt
90 g (3 oz/¼ cup) clear honey
185 g (6 oz/1 cup) dark soft brown sugar
45 g (1½ oz/9 teaspoons) butter
1 egg, beaten
finely grated peel of 1 lemon
1 tablespoon lemon juice

TO DECORATE: 250 g (8 oz) plain (dark) cake covering chocolate, melted
1 egg white
250 g (8 oz/1½ cups) icing sugar, sifted
edible silver balls

Preheat oven to 180C (350F/Gas 4). Butter a large baking sheet. Sift flour, spice and salt into a bowl, then make a well in centre. Put honey, sugar and butter into a saucepan and stir over low heat until melted. Cool slightly. Pour into flour; add egg, lemon peel and juice. Mix to form a soft dough. Knead on a floured surface until smooth. Roll out to an oblong, about 27.5 x 22.5 cm (11 x 9 in). Place on baking sheet. Using a paper or cardboard template, cut out a large heart shape.

Remove trimmings from around heart and use to make gingerbread men. Bake heart in the oven for 20-25 minutes until lightly browned. If necessary trim to shape while still warm. Remove to wire rack to cool. When cold, place rack on a large baking sheet and coat heart with melted chocolate. Allow to set. In a bowl, beat egg white with icing sugar until mixture holds stiff peaks. Decorate heart, simply or elaborately, with icing and silver balls.

Makes 1.

PALMIERS

225 g (8 oz) puff pastry, thawed if frozen
55 g (2 oz/¼ cup) caster sugar
extra sugar, for rolling out
FILLING:
115 ml (4 fl oz/½ cup) double (thick) cream
4 teaspoons red jelly (such as redcurrant jelly)

Preheat oven to 220C (425F/Gas 7). On a surface dredged with caster sugar, roll out pastry to a 30 cm (12 in) square and sprinkle with half the sugar. Fold sides of pastry into the middle, sprinkle with half remaining sugar and fold sides into the middle again.

Sprinkle pastry with remaining sugar and fold in half down the middle. Press lightly. Cut pastry into 24 slices. Place slices, cut edge down, on dampened baking sheets. Press to flatten slightly. Bake in the oven for 10 minutes, or until crisp and a light golden brown. Turn over and bake for a further 2-3 minutes until second side is golden brown. Remove from baking sheets immediately and cool on wire racks.

In a bowl, whip cream until holding soft peaks. Spread a little jelly on 12 of the palmiers. Spread cream over jelly and top with remaining 12 palmiers.

Makes 12.

LITTLE GEMS

90 g (3 oz/⅓ cup) butter
60 g (2 oz/⅓ cup) icing sugar, sifted
1 egg yolk
125 g (4 oz/1 cup) plain flour
pinch of salt

ICING: 1 egg white
250 g (8 oz/1½ cups) icing sugar, sifted
few drops assorted food colourings

In a bowl, cream butter with icing sugar; beat in egg yolk. Sift flour and salt into bowl; blend in with a spoon, then work by hand to form a smooth dough. Wrap and chill for 30 minutes.

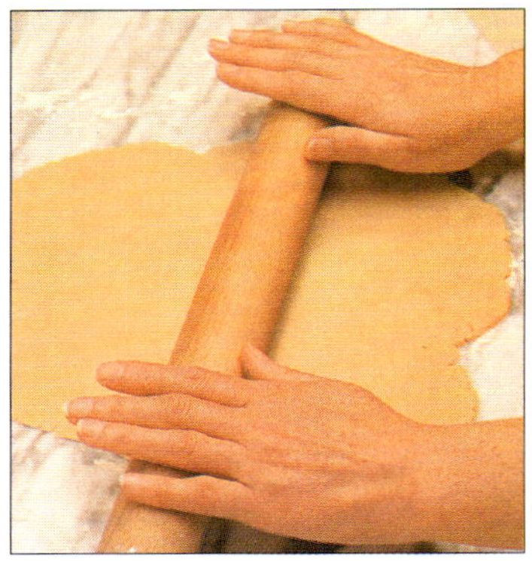

Preheat oven to 180C (350F/Gas 4). Butter 2 large baking sheets. Roll out dough on a floured surface to 0.3 cm (⅛ in) thick. Using a 2 cm (¾ in) fluted cutter, cut out as many rounds as possible; place on baking sheets. Re-roll and re-knead trimmings and cut out more rounds to make 110 in total. Bake in the oven for 8-10 minutes until very lightly browned. Remove from baking sheets to wire racks to cool.

To make icing, in a bowl, lightly whisk egg white. Beat in icing sugar, beating until very white and icing holds stiff peaks. Divide icing between 3 or 4 small bowls and add a few drops of a different food colouring to each one. Put icings in small paper piping bags, each one fitted with a small star nozzle. Pipe a rosette of icing on each biscuit. Allow to dry.

Makes 110.

EGG NOG BROWNIES

2 eggs
1 tablespoon brandy
few drops vanilla essence
125 g (4 oz/½ cup) butter
125 g (4 oz) bitter (unsweetened) chocolate
220 g (7 oz/1 cup) caster sugar
220 g (7 oz/1⅓ cups) light soft brown sugar
155 g (5 oz/1¼ cups) plain flour
125 g (4 oz/1 cup) chopped pecan nuts

Butter a shallow tin measuring about 27.5 x 17.5 x 3 cm (11 x 7 x 1¼ in). Line base with non-stick paper. Preheat oven to 180C (350F/Gas 4).

In a bowl, lightly whisk eggs with brandy and vanilla. Put butter and chocolate into a large saucepan and place over a moderate heat. Stir continuously until melted. Remove from heat; stir in caster and brown sugar, then egg mixture, flour and pecans. Pour into prepared tin and spread evenly. Bake in the oven for 30 minutes or until a cocktail stick inserted into centre comes out clean.

Allow brownie mixture to cool in tin. When cold, cut into 24 small squares: cutting evenly into 4 lengthwise and 6 widthwise. Remove from tin with a small palette knife. Brownies keep well for up to 1 week stored in an airtight tin, in a cool place.

Makes 24.

Note: Brownies are at their best if kept for 2-3 days before serving.

MADELEINES

4 eggs
185 g (6 oz/¾ cup) caster sugar
few drops vanilla essence
½ teaspoon orange flower water
185 g (6 oz/1½ cups) plain flour
125 g (4 oz/½ cup) unsalted butter, melted and cooled

TO FINISH: caster sugar for sprinkling

Preheat oven to 200C (400F/Gas 6). Butter and flour 1 or 2 Madeleine trays.

Put eggs, sugar, vanilla and orange flower water into a bowl, place over a saucepan of gently simmering water and whisk until very thick. Remove from heat and continue whisking until mixture is cool and will hold the trail of the whisk for 5 seconds. Carefully fold in flour, then gently fold in melted butter.

Three-quarters fill each Madeleine mould with mixture. Bake in the oven for 12-15 minutes until lightly browned and springy to the touch. Remove from moulds onto a wire rack, with shell pattern uppermost. Immediately sprinkle with caster sugar. Continue to bake Madeleines, in batches, until all the mixture is used.

Makes 42.

DATE & WALNUT LOAF

225 g (8 oz) stoned dates
grated rind and juice 1 lemon
175 g (6 oz/¾ cup) butter
175 g (6 oz/1 cup) light soft brown sugar
3 eggs, beaten
175 g (6 oz/1½ cups) self-raising flour
55 g (2 oz/½ cup) chopped walnuts
TO FINISH:
8 walnut halves

Preheat oven to 170C (325F/Gas 3). Grease and base line a 1 kg (2.2 lb) loaf tin. Chop dates into small pieces.

Put dates in a saucepan with lemon rind and juice and 70 ml (2½ fl oz/⅓ cup) water and cook for 5 minutes until a soft purée. In a bowl, beat butter and sugar together until light and fluffy. Gradually beat in eggs. Fold in flour and chopped walnuts. Spread one-third of mixture over base of prepared tin. Spread half the date purée over. Repeat layers, ending with cake mixture.

Arrange halved walnuts in a line down centre of loaf. Bake in the oven for 1-1½ hours until well risen and firm to the touch. Leave in tin for 10 minutes, then remove to a wire rack to cool. Serve sliced.

Makes 10-12 slices.

BRAMBLE MUFFINS

300 g (10 oz/2½ cups) plain flour
3 teaspoons baking powder
115 g (4 oz/½ cup) caster sugar
1 egg
300 ml (10 fl oz/1⅓ cups) milk
85 ml (3 fl oz/⅓ cup) sunflower oil
few drops vanilla essence
175 g (6 oz) blackberries
TO FINISH:
6 teaspoons demerara sugar

Preheat oven to 200C (400F/Gas 6). Grease a 12-hole muffin or deep bun tin. Sift flour and baking powder into a bowl, then stir in the caster sugar.

In a bowl, beat together egg, milk, sunflower oil and vanilla essence. Add to dry ingredients all at once. Mix until blended. Gently stir in blackberries.

Spoon batter into prepared muffin tin. Sprinkle with demerara sugar. Bake in the oven for 15-20 minutes until well risen and golden brown. Cool in the tin for 5 minutes, then transfer to wire racks to cool completely.

Makes 12.

LEMON CRUNCH CAKE

115 g (4 oz/½ cup) butter or margarine, softened
175 g (6 oz/¾ cup) caster sugar
2 eggs, beaten
finely grated rind 1 lemon
175 g (6 oz/1½ cups) self-raising flour
55 ml (2 fl oz/¼ cup) milk
TOPPING:
juice 1 lemon
115 g (4 oz/½ cup) granulated sugar

Preheat oven to 180C (350F/Gas 4). Grease and line a shallow oblong tin measuring 17.5 x 22.5 x 2.5 cm (7 x 9 x 1 in) and line with non-stick paper. In a bowl, beat together butter or margarine and sugar until light and fluffy.

Gradually beat in eggs. Stir in lemon rind. Fold in sifted flour, alternately with milk. Turn mixture into prepared tin and level surface. Bake in the oven for about 50 minutes until well risen and pale golden.

While cake is baking, make topping. In a bowl, mix together lemon juice and sugar. Spoon topping over hot cake. Leave in tin until completely cold, then turn out and cut into squares or diamonds.

Makes 12 squares or diamonds.

GINGER CAKE

225 g (8 oz/2 cups) self-raising flour
3 teaspoons ground ginger
1 teaspoon ground cinnamon
½ teaspoon bicarbonate of soda
115 g (4 oz/½ cup) butter or margarine
115 g (4 oz/¾ cup) light soft brown sugar
2 eggs
5 teaspoons golden syrup
5 teaspoons milk
TOPPING:
3 pieces stem ginger
115 g (4 oz/¾ cup) icing sugar
4 teaspoons stem ginger syrup

Preheat oven to 160C (325F/Gas 3). Grease a shallow oblong tin measuring 27.5 x 17.5 cm (11 x 7 in) and line with non-stick paper. Sift flour, ginger, cinnamon and bicarbonate of soda into a bowl. Rub in butter, then stir in sugar. In a bowl, whisk together eggs, syrup and milk. Pour into dry ingredients and beat until smooth and glossy. Pour into prepared tin. Bake in the oven for 45-50 minutes until well risen and firm to the touch. Leave in tin for 30 minutes, then remove to a wire rack to cool completely.

Cut each piece of stem ginger into quarters and arrange on top of cake. In a bowl, mix together sifted icing sugar, ginger syrup and sufficient water to make a smooth icing. Put icing into a greaseproof paper icing bag and drizzle over top of cake. Leave to set. Cut cake into squares.

Makes 12 squares.

DUNDEE CAKE

225 g (8 oz/1 cup) butter
225 g (8 oz/1½ cups) soft brown sugar
4 eggs, beaten
300 g (10 oz/2½ cups) plain flour, sifted
a little milk
55 g (2 oz/½ cup) ground almonds
115 g (4 oz/¾ cup) currants
115 g (4 oz/¾ cup) sultanas
115 g (4 oz/¾ cup) raisins
55 g (2 oz/⅓ cup) chopped mixed citrus peel
55 g (2 oz/⅓ cup) glacé cherries
grated rind 1 small orange and 1 small lemon
½ teaspoon bicarbonate of soda, dissolved in 1 teaspoon milk
55 g (2 oz/⅓ cup) blanched almonds

Preheat oven to 170C (325F/Gas 3). Grease and line a 20 cm (8 in) round cake tin. In a bowl, beat butter and sugar until light and fluffy. Gradually beat in eggs. Fold in flour to give a soft dropping consistency. If necessary, add a little milk. Carefully fold in ground almonds, currants, sultanas, raisins, peel, rinsed, dried and halved cherries and orange and lemon rind. Add bicarbonate of soda dissolved in milk. Stir to mix.

Turn mixture into prepared tin. Smooth the top. Arrange blanched almonds in circles over top of cake. Bake in the oven for 2½-3 hours until a skewer inserted into the centre of the cake comes out clean. Leave to cool in the tin for 30 minutes, then transfer to a wire rack to cool completely.

Makes about 12 slices.

COCONUT & CHERRY CAKE

225 g (8 oz/1 cup) butter, softened
225 g (8 oz/1¼ cups) caster sugar
4 eggs and 1 egg yolk
225 g (8 oz/2 cups) self-raising flour, sifted
55 g (2 oz/⅔ cup) desiccated coconut
175 g (6 oz/1 cup) glacé cherries, rinsed and quartered
TOPPING:
1 egg white
85 g (3 oz/½ cup) icing sugar, sifted
55 g (2 oz/1¼ cups) shredded coconut

Preheat oven to 180C (350F/Gas 4). Grease a 20 cm (8 in) loose-bottomed cake tin and line with non-stick paper.

In a bowl, beat butter and sugar until light and fluffy. In a bowl, whisk together eggs and egg yolk. Gradually beat into creamed mixture. Fold in flour, desiccated coconut and cherries. Spoon mixture into prepared tin and bake in the oven for 45-50 minutes until just firm.

To make the topping, whisk egg white in a bowl until stiff; gradually whisk in icing sugar. Spread over top of cake. Scatter over shredded coconut. Return to the oven and cook for a further 20 minutes until golden brown and a skewer inserted into the centre of cake comes out clean. Cover lightly with foil if topping is browning too quickly. Leave to cool in tin for 10 minutes; transfer to a wire rack to cool completely.

Makes 8-10 slices.

JEWEL-TOPPED MADEIRA CAKE

225 g (8 oz/1 cup) butter, softened
225 g (8 oz/1¼ cups) caster sugar
grated rind 1 lemon
4 eggs, beaten
300 g (10 oz/2½ cups) self-raising flour
2-3 tablespoons milk
TOPPING:
8 teaspoons clear honey
225 g (8 oz) crystallised fruits and angelica

Preheat oven to 160C (325F/Gas 3). Grease and line a 20 cm (8 in) deep, round cake tin. In a bowl, beat together butter, sugar and lemon rind until light and fluffy.

Gradually beat in eggs. Fold in sifted flour, alternating with sufficient milk to give a soft dropping consistency. Spoon mixture into prepared tin. Bake in the oven for 1½-1¾ hours, until a skewer inserted into the centre of cake comes out clean.

Leave to cool in tin for 5 minutes, then transfer to a wire rack to cool. Gently heat honey. Brush over cake and arrange fruits and angelica on top.

Makes 8-10 slices.

Variation: A traditional Madeira cake has a thin slice of candied peel on top. This should be placed on cake after it has been cooking for about 1 hour.

CHOCOLATE MARBLE CAKE

55 g (2 oz) plain (dark) chocolate
3 teaspoons strong coffee
225 g (8 oz/2 cups) self-raising flour
1 teaspoon baking powder
225 g (8 oz/1 cup) soft margarine
225 g (8 oz/1¼ cups) caster sugar
4 eggs, beaten
55 g (2 oz/½ cup) ground almonds
6 teaspoons milk
FROSTING:
130 g (4½ oz) plain (dark) chocolate
25 g (1 oz/6 teaspoons) butter

Preheat oven to 180C (350F/Gas 4). Grease a 1.7 litre (60 fl oz/7½ cup) ring mould. Put chocolate and coffee in a basin. Set over a pan of simmering water; heat until melted. Leave to cool. Sift flour and baking powder into a bowl. Add margarine, sugar, eggs, ground almonds and milk. Beat well until smooth. Spoon half the mixture evenly into prepared tin. Stir cooled, soft chocolate into the remaining mixture, and spoon into tin. Draw a knife through mixture in a spiral. Smooth the surface.

Bake in the oven for 50-60 minutes until well risen and a skewer inserted into the centre, comes out clean. Leave in tin for 5 minutes, then turn out onto a wire rack to cool, completely. To make frosting, put chocolate, butter and 6 teaspoons water in a bowl, then set over a pan of simmering water until melted. Stir and pour over cake, working quickly to coat top and sides. Leave to set before serving.

Makes 10-12 slices.

SUMMER SPONGE CAKE

175 g (6 oz/¾ cup) soft butter
175 g (6 oz/¾ cup) caster sugar
3 eggs, beaten
175 g (6 oz/1½ cups) self-raising flour
4 teaspoons boiling water
FILLING:
85 g (3 oz/⅓ cup) soft unsalted butter
115 g (4 oz/¾ cup) icing sugar, sifted
few drops vanilla essence
ICING:
175 g (6 oz/1 cup) icing sugar, sifted
2 teaspoons lemon juice
TO DECORATE:
crystallised flowers

Preheat oven to 180C (350F/Gas 4). Grease two 20 cm (8 in) sandwich tins and line bases with non-stick paper. In a bowl, beat together butter and sugar until light and fluffy. Gradually beat in eggs, then fold in flour. Stir in the boiling water to make a soft dropping consistency. Divide mixture between prepared tins. Bake in the oven for 25-30 minutes until cakes are lightly browned and spring back when pressed. Leave in tins for 5 minutes, then transfer to wire racks to cool.

To make filling, in a bowl, beat together the unsalted butter and icing sugar. Stir in vanilla essence. Sandwich cakes together with filling. To make icing, in a bowl, mix together icing sugar, lemon juice and sufficient water to make a spreading consistency. Spread icing over cake and decorate with crystallised flowers.

Makes 8 slices.

OLIVE OIL & APPLE CAKE

250 g (9 oz/2 cups plus 2 tablespoons) self-raising flour
¾ teaspoon ground cinnamon
85 g (3 oz/⅓ cup) caster sugar
finely grated rind and juice 1 lemon
2 eggs, beaten
3 tablespoons sweet sherry
160 ml (5½ fl oz/⅔ cup) olive oil
450 g (1 lb) crisp apples

Preheat oven to 180C (350F/Gas 4). Grease an 18 cm (7 in) cake tin. In a bowl, stir together flour, cinnamon, sugar and lemon rind. Make a well in centre and gradually add eggs, sherry, olive oil and lemon juice, stirring to make a smooth mixture.

Peel, core and chop apples. Fold into cake mixture and turn into prepared tin. Bake for 40-45 minutes until golden brown and firm to the touch in centre. Leave for a few minutes before turning onto a wire rack to cool.

Makes 8 slices.

DOUBLE CHOCOLATE GÂTEAU

225 g (8 oz/1 cup) soft butter
225 g (8 oz/1¼ cups) caster sugar
4 eggs, beaten
175 g (6 oz/1½ cups) self-raising flour
55 g (2 oz/½ cup) cocoa
FILLING:
250 ml (9 fl oz/1 cup) whipping cream
150 g (5 oz) white chocolate
FROSTING:
350 g (12 oz) plain (dark) chocolate
115 g (4 oz/½ cup) butter
85 ml (3 fl oz/⅓ cup) double (thick) cream
TO DECORATE:
115 g (4 oz) plain (dark) chocolate
2 teaspoons icing sugar and cocoa mixed

Preheat oven to 180C (350F/Gas 4). Grease a 20 cm (8 in) deep round tin and line the base with non-stick paper. In bowl, beat together butter and sugar until light and fluffy. Gradually beat in eggs. Sift together flour and cocoa. Fold into mixture, then spoon into tin. Bake in the oven for 45-50 minutes until springy to the touch and a skewer inserted into the centre comes out clean. Leave in tin for 5 minutes, then remove to a wire rack to cool completely.

To make the filling, heat the cream in a saucepan to just below boiling point. In a food processor, chop white chocolate. With motor running, pour hot cream through feed tube and process for 10-15 seconds until smooth. Transfer to a bowl, cover with plastic wrap and chill overnight. The next day whisk the filling until just beginning to hold soft peaks.

To make the frosting, melt chocolate in a bowl over pan of hot water. Stir in butter and cream. Leave to cool, stirring occasionally until mixture is a thick spreading consistency.

To make chocolate curls for decoration, melt chocolate in a bowl over a pan of hot water. Spread one-quarter of the chocolate over a baking sheet. Chill sheet for a few minutes until chocolate loses its gloss and is just set, but not hard. Using a palette knife, scrape off large shavings of chocolate, transferring them to a baking sheet lined with non-stick paper. Chill until set. Make 3 more batches of shavings in the same way.

Slice the cake horizontally into 3 layers. Sandwich layers together with white chocolate filling. Cover top and sides of cake with chocolate frosting. Arrange chocolate shavings over top of cake. Sift mixed icing sugar and cocoa over cake.

Makes 10 slices.

ARTEMIS CAKE

400 g (14 oz) plain (dark) chocolate
5 eggs, separated
225 g (8 oz/1 cup) butter, softened
115 g (4 oz/¾ cup) icing sugar, sifted
6 teaspoons plain flour, sifted
1 teaspoon ground cinnamon
icing sugar, to decorate

Preheat oven to 180C (350F/Gas 4). Butter and line a 20 cm (8 in) cake tin (preferably a loose-bottomed tin). Break chocolate into a bowl and stand bowl over a pan of hot water until melted. Leave until almost cold.

In a bowl, whisk egg whites until stiff. In a bowl, beat butter and icing sugar until light and creamy. Beat in egg yolks. Add chocolate; stir in lightly. It does not need to be thoroughly mixed.

Stir in flour and cinnamon and then fold in whisked egg whites. Pour mixture into prepared tin. Bake in the oven for 45 minutes until well risen and firm to the touch. Leave in tin until almost cool, then transfer to a wire rack. Sift icing sugar over the top and place on a serving plate.

Serves 8.

FROSTED WALNUT CAKE

175 g (6 oz/¾ cup) soft butter
175 g (6 oz/¾ cup) caster sugar
3 eggs, beaten
55 g (2 oz/½ cup) chopped walnuts
175 g (6 oz/1½ cups) self-raising flour
FROSTING:
225 g (8 oz/1¼ cups) caster sugar
2 egg whites
6 walnut halves

Preheat oven to 180C (350F/Gas 4). Grease two 20 cm (8 in) deep round cake tins and line bases with non-stick paper. In a bowl, beat together butter and sugar until light and fluffy.

Gradually beat in eggs. Fold in walnuts and sifted flour. Divide mixture between prepared tins. Bake in the oven for 25-35 minutes until risen and golden brown. Leave in the tins for 5 minutes, then transfer to wire racks to cool. To make frosting, put sugar in a saucepan with 70 ml (2½ fl oz/⅓ cup) water. Stir over low heat until sugar has dissolved.

Bring to boil and boil to 116C (240F) on a sugar thermometer. Remove from heat. In a bowl, whisk egg whites until stiff. Pour hot syrup onto egg white, beating constantly. Continue beating as mixture cools. Use some frosting to sandwich cakes together; cover cake with the remainder. Decorate with walnut halves. Leave to set overnight.

Serves 8.

COFFEE CARAMEL CAKE

225 g (8 oz/2 cups) self-raising flour
175 g (6 oz/¾ cup) soft butter
175 g (6 oz/¾ cup) caster sugar
3 eggs, beaten
100 ml (3½ fl oz/⅓ cup) strong black coffee
ICING:
115 ml (4 fl oz/½ cup) creamy milk
130 g (4½ oz/½ cup plus 3 teaspoons) butter
9 teaspoons caster sugar
575 g (1¼ lb/3¾ cups) icing sugar
TO DECORATE:
chocolate coffee beans

Preheat oven to 180C (350F/Gas 4). Grease two 20 cm (8 in) sandwich tins; line bases with non-stick paper.

Sift flour 3 times and set aside. In a bowl, beat together butter and sugar until light and fluffy. Gradually beat in eggs. Fold in flour and coffee. Divide mixture between prepared tins and bake in oven for 30 minutes until risen and slightly shrinking from sides of tin. Cool in tins for 5 minutes, then transfer to wire racks to cool. To make icing, warm milk and butter in a saucepan.

In another heavy-based saucepan, heat caster sugar over a gentle heat until it dissolves and turns a golden caramel. Off the heat, stir in warm milk, taking care as it may splutter. Return to the heat and stir until caramel has dissolved. Remove from heat. Gradually stir in icing sugar, beating until icing is a smooth spreading consistency. Sandwich cakes together with some icing; spread remainder over top and sides. Decorate with chocolate coffee beans.

Serves 8-10.

CHOC ORANGE RING CAKE

2 small oranges
85 g (3 oz) plain (dark) chocolate
200 g (7 oz/1¾ cups) self-raising flour
1½ teaspoons baking powder
175 g (6 oz/¾ cup) soft margarine
175 g (6 oz/¾ cup) caster sugar
3 eggs, beaten
TO GLAZE:
225 g (8 oz/1½ cups) icing sugar
6 teaspoons orange juice
55 g (2 oz) plain (dark) chocolate

Preheat the oven to 160C (325F/Gas 3). Thoroughly grease an 850 ml (30 fl oz/3¾ cup) fluted or plain ring mould.

Cut skin and pith from oranges. Cut oranges into segments by cutting down between membranes. Chop segments into small pieces. Reserve as much juice as possible. Grate chocolate coarsely. Sift flour and baking powder into a bowl. Add margarine, sugar, eggs and any reserved orange juice. Beat thoroughly until mixture is smooth. Fold in chopped oranges and grated chocolate. Spoon mixture into prepared tin.

Bake in the oven for 40 minutes until well risen and golden brown. Leave in tin for 5 minutes, then transfer to a wire rack to cool completely. To make icing, sift icing sugar into a bowl and stir in enough orange juice to make a coating consistency. Using a spoon, drizzle icing over cake. Break chocolate into a bowl and melt over a pan of simmering water. Drizzle chocolate over cake. Leave to set.

Makes 8-10 slices.

CHRISTMAS CAKE

1.15 kg (2¼ lb/6¾ cups) mixed dried fruit
185 g (6 oz/¾ cup) quartered glacé cherries
90 g (3oz/¾ cup) flaked almonds
finely grated peel and juice of 1 orange
125 ml (4 fl oz/½ cup) brandy or sherry
375 g (12 oz/3 cups) plain flour
3 teaspoons ground mixed spice
75 g (2½ oz/⅔ cup) ground almonds
280 g (9 oz/1½ cups) dark soft brown sugar
280 g (9 oz/1½ cups) butter, softened
6 teaspoons black treacle (molasses)
5 eggs
9 teaspoons apricot jam, boiled and sieved
875 g (1¾ lb) marzipan
1 kg (2 lb) ready-to-roll fondant icing
red and green food colourings

Preheat oven to 140C (275F/Gas 1). Line a 20 cm (8 in) square or 22.5 cm (9 in) round cake tin with double thickness greased greaseproof paper. Tie a double thickness band of brown paper around tin and stand tin on double thickness lined baking sheet. Place dried fruit, cherries and almonds in a large bowl; stir until well mixed. Add orange peel and juice and brandy or sherry; mix well together.

In another bowl, put flour, spice, ground almonds, sugar, butter, treacle (molasses) and eggs. Stir all ingredients together using a wooden spoon to mix, then beat until smooth and glossy. Add fruit mixture to cake mixture; stir until evenly mixed.

Spoon mixture into prepared tin, level top with back of metal spoon, making a slight depression in centre. Cook in the oven for 3¼-3½ hours or until a skewer inserted in the centre comes out clean. Leave cake in tin to cool; turn out, remove paper and place on a cake board.

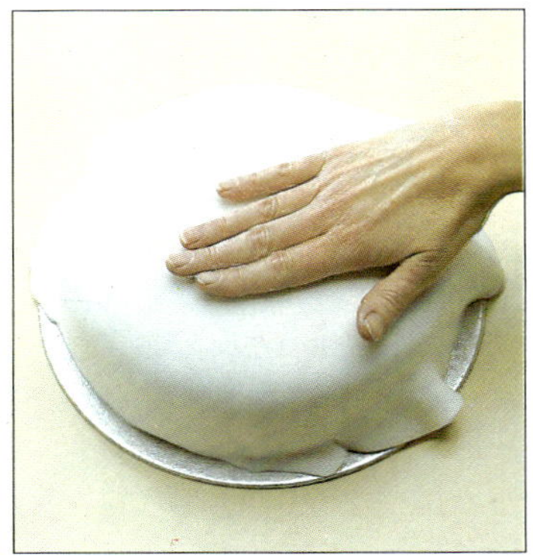

Brush top and side of cake with apricot jam. Knead marzipan, roll out to 0.5 cm (¼ in) thickness and use to cover top and sides of cake; trim to fit neatly at base. Roll out fondant icing on a lightly-sugared surface and use to cover cake; press icing over top and down side of cake. Trim off excess icing at base.

Knead icing trimmings together; colour ⅓ red and remainder green with food colourings. Make tiny berries with some of the red icing; roll and cut out holly leaves from green icing, mark leaf veins with a knife and leave decorations to set. Arrange on top of cake, securing with jam. Cut out 'NOEL' from red icing and place on cake. Tie ribbon around outside of cake. Leave cake to dry overnight.

Makes 30 slices.

RUM TRUFFLE CAKE

220 g (7 oz) plain (dark) chocolate
125 g (4 oz/½ cup) unsalted butter
75 ml (2½ fl oz/⅓ cup) dark rum
3 eggs, separated
125 g (4 oz/½ cup) caster sugar
90 g (3 oz/¾ cup) plain flour
60 g (2 oz/½ cup) ground almonds

ICING: 220 g (7 oz) plain (dark) chocolate
315 ml (10 fl oz/1¼ cups) double (thick) cream
3 teaspoons dark rum
60 g (2 oz) white chocolate, grated

Butter and flour a 20 cm (8 in) round cake tin and line base with greaseproof paper.

Preheat oven to 180C (350F/Gas 4). Place chocolate and butter in a bowl over a saucepan of hand-hot water. Stir occasionally until melted. Add rum and stir well.

Place egg yolks and sugar in a bowl over a saucepan of simmering water. Whisk until thick and pale, remove bowl from pan and continue to whisk until mixture leaves a trail when whisk is lifted. Stir in chocolate mixture until evenly blended. Mix together flour and ground almonds, add to mixture and fold in carefully using a spatula.

Whisk egg whites until stiff, fold in ⅓ at a time until all egg white has been incorporated. Pour mixture into tin and bake in the oven for 45-55 minutes until firm to touch in centre. Turn out of tin and cool on a wire rack.

To make the icing, melt 125 g (4 oz) of the chocolate with 60 ml (2 fl oz/¼ cup) cream in a bowl over a pan of hot water. Stir in rum until well blended. Leave to cool. Whip 125 ml (4 fl oz/½ cup) cream in a bowl until thick, add ½ chocolate rum mixture and fold in to make a smooth icing.

Cut cake in half, sandwich together with the chocolate icing and spread remainder over top and sides. Chill cake and remaining ½ of chocolate rum mixture until firm. Melt remaining chocolate and cream in a bowl, stir until smooth; cool and pour mixture over cake to cover evenly. Shape firmed chocolate rum mixture into 16 truffles, coat in grated white chocolate. Arrange on top of cake; chill to set.

Makes 10-12 slices.

CHOC ALMOND MERINGUE

MERINGUE:
4 egg whites
225 g (8 oz/1¼ cups) caster sugar
115 g (4 oz/1¼ cups) ground almonds
FILLING:
175 g (6 oz) plain (dark) chocolate
45 g (1½ oz/9 teaspoons) unsalted butter
9 teaspoons black coffee
9 teaspoons brandy
175 ml (6 fl oz/¾ cup) whipping cream
TO DECORATE:
chopped, toasted almonds

Preheat oven to 140C (275F/Gas 1). Line 2 baking sheets with non-stick paper.

To make meringue, whisk egg whites in a bowl until stiff; whisk in half the sugar. In another bowl, mix together remaining sugar and ground almonds. Carefully fold into meringue mixture. Pipe or spread meringue in two 20 cm (8 in) rounds on the prepared baking sheets. Bake in the oven for about 1½ hours until completely dry. Transfer to wire racks to cool.

To make filling, break chocolate into pieces and put into a bowl with butter, coffee and brandy. Set over a pan of simmering water. When melted, stir and set aside to cool. Whip cream lightly; stir in chocolate mixture. Sandwich meringue rounds together with most of the chocolate cream. Put remaining cream into a piping bag and pipe rosettes on top of cake. Decorate with toasted almonds.

Serves 8.

LIME & TANGERINE GÂTEAU

12 trifle sponges
155 ml (5 fl oz/⅔ cup) double (thick) cream
9 teaspoons fromage frais
25 g (1 oz/¼ cup) chopped pistachio nuts
lime and tangerine wedges, to decorate

FILLING: 3 eggs, separated
250 g (8 oz/1 cup) curd cheese
125 g (4 oz/½ cup) caster sugar
finely grated peel and juice of 2 tangerines
finely grated peel and juice of 2 limes
5 teaspoons powdered gelatine

To make filling, put egg yolks, curd cheese and sugar in a bowl. Beat until smooth.

Stir in fruit peels and ½ of juices. Sprinkle gelatine over 9 teaspoons water in a bowl; leave to soften. Stand bowl in a pan of hot water; stir until dissolved. Stir into cheese mixture; leave until thick. Line a 17.5 cm (7 in) square tin with plastic wrap. Cut sponges into 3 thin layers; line base and sides of tin. Sprinkle with ⅓ of remaining fruit juice. Stiffly whisk egg whites; fold into cheese mixture. Pour ½ into tin, cover with a layer of sponge; sprinkle with ⅓ juice.

Top with remaining sponge and juice. Cover with plastic wrap and chill until set. Turn gâteau onto a serving plate; remove plastic wrap. Whip cream and fromage frais until thick, place ¼ in a piping bag fitted with a small star nozzle. Spread remaining cream over gâteau; press pistachio nuts onto sides. Pipe a border around top and base of gâteau. Decorate with lime and tangerine wedges.

Serves 12.

BREADS

CRUMPETS

450 g (1 lb/4 cups) strong plain white flour
1 teaspoon salt
1 teaspoon caster sugar
2 teaspoons easy blend dried yeast
550 ml (20 fl oz/2½ cups) tepid milk
150 ml (5 fl oz/⅔ cup) tepid water
oil, for cooking
TO SERVE:
butter

Sift flour into a bowl. Stir in salt, sugar and yeast.

Make a well in the centre of flour and pour in the tepid milk and water. With a wooden spoon, gradually work flour into liquid, then beat vigorously to make a smooth batter. Cover bowl with a cloth and leave in a warm place for about 1 hour or until mixture has doubled in size.

Thoroughly grease a heavy frying pan or griddle and several crumpet rings. Arrange as many rings as possible in the pan. Heat the pan and pour in enough of the mixture to half fill each ring. Cook crumpets for 5-6 minutes until bubbles appear and burst on the surface. Remove rings and turn crumpets over. Cook on other side for a further 2-3 minutes. Serve crumpets hot, generously buttered.

Makes about 16.

SEEDED BREAD STICKS

1 tablespoon dried yeast
4 teaspoons honey
125 g (4 oz/½ cup) butter, chopped
1 teaspoon salt
1 egg, beaten
440 g (14 oz/3¼ cups) plain flour
1 egg
caraway, sesame and poppy seeds

In a small bowl mix together yeast, 125 ml (4 fl oz) warm water and 1 teaspoon honey. Set aside and allow yeast to become foamy. In a saucepan, combine butter, remaining honey, salt and 125 ml (4 fl oz) water.

Heat gently until butter and honey melt. Pour liquid into large warmed bowl. Add beaten egg and yeast to mixture. Beat in flour. Do not knead dough. Cover and place in refrigerator until cold. Divide dough into 12 pieces. On a floured board, roll each piece to a 30-cm (12-in) length. Cut in 2 to form 2 even lengths. Place lengths on greased baking sheets about 10-cm (4-in) apart.

In a small bowl beat remaining egg with 1 teaspoon water. Brush egg mixture over dough lengths. Sprinkle with seeds. Let rise in a warm place 30 minutes or until not quite doubled in size. Preheat oven to 220C (425F). Bake 15 minutes, or until golden brown. Cool on a wire rack.

Makes 24 sticks.

SPANISH COUNTRY BREAD

225 g (8 oz/2 cups) strong flour
2 teaspoons salt, preferably coarse
3 teaspoons easy-blend dried yeast
oil for brushing
cornmeal for sprinkling

Sift flour and salt into a large bowl, stir in yeast and form a well in centre. Slowly pour 175 ml (6 fl oz/¾ cup) tepid water into well, stirring with a wooden spoon, to make a dough. Beat well until dough comes away from sides of bowl.

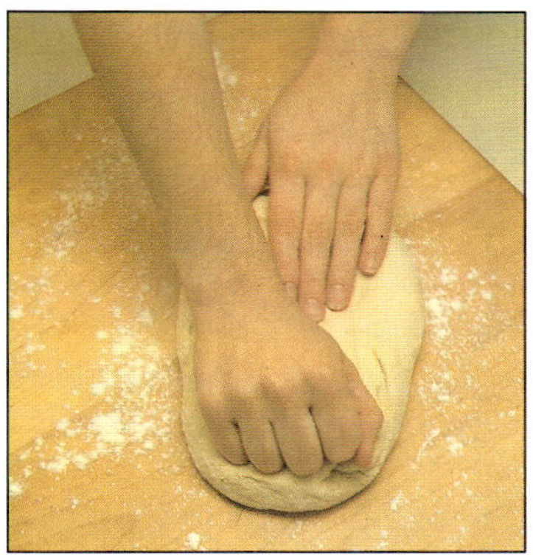

Turn dough onto a lightly floured surface and knead for 10-15 minutes until smooth and elastic; add a little more flour if dough is sticky. Put dough in an oiled bowl, cover and leave in a warm place until doubled in volume, about 2½ hours. Lightly sprinkle a baking sheet with cornmeal. Turn dough onto lightly floured surface, punch down then roll to a rectangle about 15 x 40 cm (6 x 16 in). Roll up like a Swiss roll and pinch seam to seal.

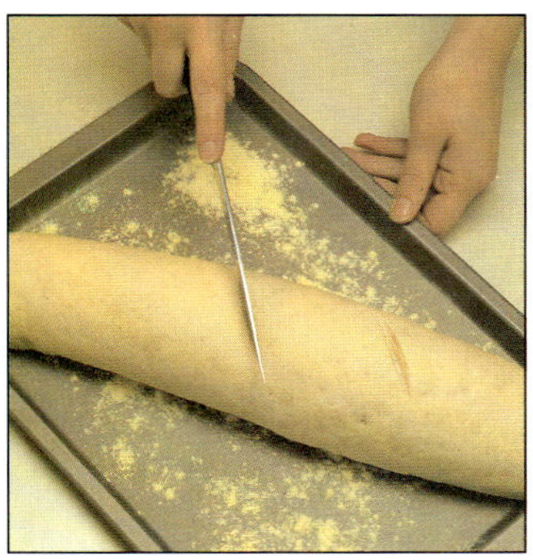

Place roll, seam-side down, on baking sheet. Using a very sharp knife, make 3 diagonal slashes on roll at equal distances. Brush top lightly with water. Leave in a warm place until doubled in volume, about 1 hour. Preheat oven to 230C (450F/Gas 8) and place a pan of water in the bottom. Brush loaf again with water and bake for 5 minutes. Remove pan of water. Brush loaf once more with water. Bake for about 20 minutes until loaf sounds hollow underneath.

Makes 1 loaf.

PITTA BREAD

800 g (1¾ lb/7 cups) strong white bread flour
1 sachet easy blend dried yeast
2 teaspoons salt
6 teaspoons olive oil

Sift flour into a large bowl. Stir in yeast and salt. Add oil and 425 ml (15 fl oz/scant 2 cups) tepid water. Mix together, then turn dough out onto a floured surface.

Knead dough thoroughly for 10 minutes until smooth and elastic. Cut into 12 equal pieces. Roll each piece into a ball, then roll out to an oval shape 18 cm (7 in) long. Place on floured trays; cover with a cloth; leave in a warm place for 1 hour or until puffed up to double the original size.

Preheat oven to 240C (475F/Gas 9). Oil 2 baking sheets and place in the oven to heat up. Place 3 pitta breads on each baking sheet and sprinkle with water. Bake in the oven for 5 minutes until puffed up and lightly browned. Remove from baking sheets and wrap in a cloth while baking remaining bread.

Makes 12.

CHAPATI

155 g (5 oz/1¼ cups) plain flour
155 g (5 oz/1¼ cups) wholewheat flour
salt
60 g (2 oz/¼ cup) butter or ghee, melted, for serving

Sift flours and salt together into a mixing bowl and tip in any bran caught in sieve. Mix in about 185 ml (6 fl oz/¾ cup) water to make a soft dough.

Knead dough on a lightly floured surface for about 5 minutes, until smooth and pliable, then, with wet hands, knead dough for 1 minute more to make it extra smooth. Wrap in plastic wrap and chill for 30 minutes. Divide dough into 12 pieces and roll each out on a lightly floured surface to a 12.5 cm (5 in) round.

Heat a griddle or heavy-based frying pan on a medium heat and cook dough rounds, 1 at a time, floury side down, for 1-2 minutes, until beginning to bubble on surface. Turn over and cook second side for ½-1 minute, pressing with a folded dry cloth during cooking to make them puff up. Wrap each chapati in a dry cloth as soon as it is ready. Serve them warm, brushed with melted butter or ghee.

Makes 12.

NAAN

500 g (1 lb/4 cups) plain flour
1 teaspoon baking powder
½ teaspoon bicarbonate of soda
salt
1 egg, beaten
6 tablespoons natural yogurt
45 g (1½ oz/9 teaspoons) butter or ghee, melted
about 250 ml (8 fl oz/1 cup) milk
3 teaspoons poppy seeds

Sift flour, baking powder and bicarbonate of soda together into a mixing bowl. Season with salt.

Stir in egg, yogurt and 30 g (1 oz/6 teaspoons) butter or ghee. Gradually mix in enough milk to make a soft dough. Cover bowl with a damp cloth and put in a warm place for 2 hours. Preheat oven to 200C (400F/Gas 6). Knead dough on a lightly floured surface for 2-3 minutes, until smooth, then divide dough into 8 pieces.

Roll each piece into a ball, then roll out to make ovals about 15 cm (6 in) long, pulling ends to stretch dough into shape. Brush ovals with water and place wet-side down on greased baking trays. Brush dry side with melted butter or ghee and sprinkle with poppy seeds. Bake for 8-10 minutes, until puffy and golden brown. Serve at once.

Makes 8.

WALNUT BREAD

15 g (½ oz) sachet dried yeast
150 ml (5 fl oz/⅔ cup) warm milk
1 tablespoon clear honey
350 g (12 oz/3 cups) strong plain flour
350 g (12 oz/3 cups) plain wholemeal flour
1½ teaspoons salt
25 g (1 oz) butter, diced
150 g (5 oz/1¼ cups) walnuts, chopped
2 teaspoons fennel seeds, lightly crushed
½ teaspoon grated nutmeg
Milk to glaze

In a small bowl or jug mix yeast with warm milk and honey. Leave for 10-15 minutes until frothy.

Sieve flours and salt into a large mixing bowl. Rub in butter until mixture resembles breadcrumbs. Stir in walnuts, 1 teaspoon of the fennel seeds and the grated nutmeg.

Using a wooden spoon, stir yeast liquid into flour mixture with sufficient warm water to form a soft, but not wet, dough.

Oil a mixing bowl. Turn dough out onto a lightly floured surface and knead for 5 minutes until elastic. Put into an oiled mixing bowl, cover and leave in a warm place for 35-40 minutes until doubled in size. Turn onto a lightly floured surface and knead again for 5 minutes.

Preheat oven to 220C (425F/Gas 7). Oil a deep 15 cm (6 inch) round cake tin. Divide dough into seven equal sized pieces and shape into balls. Arrange in the cake tin. Brush tops with milk and sprinkle with remaining 1 teaspoon fennel seeds. Leave in a warm place for 25 minutes then bake in the oven for about 45 minutes until the top is well browned and the bottom sounds hollow when tapped.

Turn bread onto a wire rack and leave to cool. Serve as part of the antipasti.

Makes 1 large loaf.

Note: This bread is delicious served with cheese and fish dishes, for soaking up olive oil dressings and is particularly good toasted.

FOCACCIA

450 g (1 lb/4 cups) strong plain flour
Pinch salt
15 g (½ oz) packet dried yeast
225 ml (8 fl oz/1 cup) warm milk
1 teaspoon granulated sugar
4 tablespoons extra virgin olive oil, plus extra for brushing
2 teaspoons fresh rosemary leaves
Coarse sea salt

Sieve flour and salt into a large mixing bowl. In a small bowl, mix together yeast, milk and sugar. Leave for 10-15 minutes, until frothy.

Stir in oil then gradually beat into flour mixture using wooden spoon to give a soft, but not wet, dough; add a little more warm milk if necessary. Turn dough onto a floured surface; knead for 5 minutes until smooth and elastic. Place in an oiled bowl, cover and leave in a warm place for about 40 minutes until doubled in size. Turn onto a floured surface and knead for 5 minutes.

Preheat oven to 230C (450F/Gas 8). Oil a baking sheet. Roll dough to a large circle about 1.5 cm (½ inch) thick and transfer to the baking sheet. Brush with olive oil and sprinkle over rosemary and sea salt, pressing in lightly. With a clean finger make deep indentations over surface of dough. Leave to rise for 25 minutes. Bake in the preheated oven for 20-25 minutes until golden. Brush again with olive oil. Serve warm.

Makes 1 loaf.

OLIVE BREAD

70 ml (2½ fl oz/⅓ cup) olive oil
1 onion, finely chopped
800 g (1¾ lb/7 cups) strong white bread flour
1 sachet easy blend dried yeast
2 teaspoons salt
225 g (8 oz/1⅓ cups) black olives, stoned and chopped

In a frying pan, heat oil. Add onion and cook until soft. Leave to cool. Sift flour into a large bowl. Stir in yeast and salt. Add 6 teaspoons oil and 425 ml (15 fl oz/scant 1 cup) tepid water. Mix together, then turn dough onto a floured surface.

Knead dough thoroughly for 10 minutes until smooth and elastic. Knead in 3 teaspoons oil, the fried onion and chopped olives. Cut dough in half and shape into 2 round loaves. Place on lightly oiled baking sheets.

Cover with oiled plastic wrap and leave in a warm place for 1 hour or until doubled in size. Preheat oven to 180C (350F/Gas 4). Brush with a little of the oil. Bake loaves for 30-40 minutes until base of each sounds hollow when tapped. Brush tops of loaves with remaining oil. Return to the oven for 2 minutes, then transfer to wire racks to cool.

Makes 2 loaves.

LEEK & BACON KNOTS

1 leek, finely chopped
55 g (2 oz/¼ cup) butter
175 g (6 oz) streaky bacon, chopped
225 g (8 oz/2 cups) strong plain white flour
225 g (8 oz/2 cups) plain wholemeal flour
1 teaspoon salt
1 teaspoon caster sugar
2 teaspoons easy blend dried yeast
150 ml (5 fl oz/⅔ cup) tepid milk
175 ml (6 fl oz/¾ cup) tepid water
TO FINISH:
beaten egg and sesame seeds

Put leek and half the butter in frying pan. Cook until leek is soft. Remove from pan.

Gently cook bacon in frying pan until fat begins to run. Continue cooking until just beginning to turn crisp. Leave to cool. Sift white flour into a bowl. Stir in wholemeal flour, salt, sugar and yeast. Rub in remaining butter. Stir in leek and bacon and make a well in centre. Pour in milk and tepid water. Stir until a soft dough is formed. Turn out onto a floured surface and knead for about 10 minutes until smooth. Put in an oiled bowl, cover and leave in a warm place until doubled in size.

Grease 2 baking sheets. Turn dough onto a floured surface; knead for 3-4 minutes until smooth. Divide into 12 pieces and roll each into a sausage about 30 cm (12 in) long. Tie each one in a knot and place on baking sheets. Cover with plastic wrap and leave in a warm place until doubled in size. Preheat oven to 220C (425F/Gas 7). Brush rolls with egg and sprinkle with sesame seeds. Bake in the oven for 15 minutes until golden.

Makes 12.

CHEESE & CHIVE PLAIT

450 g (1 lb/4 cups) strong plain white flour
1 teaspoon salt
1 teaspoon caster sugar
1½ teaspoons easy blend dried yeast
25 g (1 oz/6 teaspoons) butter
115 g (4 oz/1 cup) coarsely grated Cheddar cheese
3 tablespoons chopped fresh chives
4 spring onions, chopped
150 ml (5 fl oz/⅔ cup) tepid milk
175 ml (6 fl oz/¾ cup) tepid water
beaten egg, to glaze

Sift flour into a bowl. Stir in salt, sugar and yeast. Rub in butter.

Stir in cheese, chives and spring onions and make a well in the centre. Mix milk with the tepid water and pour into the well. Mix until a soft dough is formed. Turn dough onto a lightly floured surface. Knead for about 10 minutes until smooth and elastic. Place in an oiled bowl, cover and leave in a warm place for about 1 hour, until doubled in size. Preheat oven to 220C (425F/Gas 7). Turn dough out onto a floured surface and knead for about 3 minutes.

Divide dough into 3 pieces. Roll each one out to a rope shape and plait together, pinching ends to seal. Place on a baking sheet, cover with oiled plastic wrap and leave in a warm place for about 45 minutes until doubled in size. Brush with beaten egg and bake in the oven for 20 minutes. Reduce temperature to 180C (350F/Gas 4) and bake for a further 15 minutes until golden brown and the base sounds hollow when tapped. Serve loaf warm or cold.

Makes about 10 slices.

WHOLE SWEETCORN BREAD

225 g (8 oz/1⅔ cups) coarse cornmeal
225 g (8 oz/2 cups) plain flour
1 teaspoon fast action dried yeast
1 teaspoon sugar
½ teaspoon salt
200 g (7 oz) can sweetcorn kernels
150 ml (5 fl oz/⅔ cup) milk
25 g (1 oz/6 teaspoons) butter, melted

Combine the cornmeal, flour, yeast, sugar and salt in a large bowl and make a well in the centre.

Drain the sweetcorn, reserve the juices and pour into a small pan. Add the milk and heat gently until tepid. Stir into the cornmeal mixture with the melted butter and gradually work to form a soft dough. Knead on a lightly floured surface for 6-8 minutes until smooth, then carefully begin working in the sweetcorn kernels, adding a little more flour, if necessary. Place in an oiled bowl, cover and leave to rise in a warm place for 45 minutes until doubled in size.

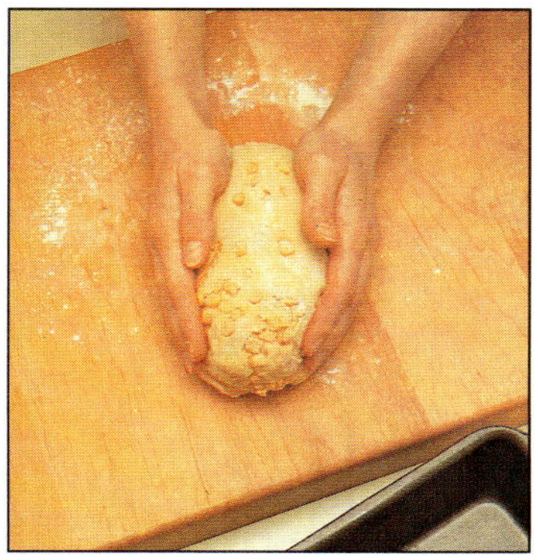

Preheat oven to 220C (425F/Gas 7). Knock back risen dough, form into a log shape and press into an oiled 23 x 12.5 cm (9 x 5 in) loaf tin. Cover and leave to rise for 30 minutes until dough reaches the top of the tin. Bake for 25 minutes until risen and golden and the base sounds hollow when tapped. Leave to cool on a wire rack before serving.

Makes 1 large loaf.

EASTER BREAD

800 g (1¾ lb/7 cups) strong white bread flour
1 sachet easy blend dried yeast
55 g (2 oz/¼ cup) caster sugar
2 teaspoons caraway seeds
115 g (4 oz/½ cup) butter, melted
2 eggs, beaten
225 ml (8 fl oz/1 cup) warm milk
1 egg, beaten, for glazing
6 teaspoons flaked almonds, to decorate

Sift flour into a large bowl. Stir in yeast, sugar and caraway seeds. Stir in butter, eggs and milk. Mix together, then turn dough out onto a floured surface.

Knead dough thoroughly for 10 minutes until smooth and elastic. Cut dough in half and divide each half into 3 pieces. Roll each piece into a rope 50 cm (20 in) long. Plait 3 ropes, then shape plait into a ring, pressing the ends together firmly. Repeat with remaining 3 ropes. Place the 2 rings on oiled baking sheets. Cover with a cloth and leave in a warm place for 1 hour or until doubled in size. Preheat oven to 190C (375F/Gas 5).

Brush loaves with beaten egg. Scatter flaked almonds over the top. Bake for 40 minutes or until loaves are lightly browned and sound hollow when tapped on the bases. Leave on wire racks to cool. Serve sliced and buttered.

Makes 2 loaves.

Note: Traditionally these loaves have red dyed eggs tucked into the braids before baking.

SAUCES & SALAD DRESSINGS

BASIC WHITE SAUCE

25 g (1 oz/6 teaspoons) low fat spread
25 g (1 oz/1/4 cup) plain flour
300 ml (10 fl oz/1 1/4 cups) semi-skimmed milk
salt and pepper

In a saucepan, melt low fat spread over a low heat. Stir in flour and cook for 1 minute, stirring.

Remove pan from heat and gradually stir or whisk in the milk. Bring slowly to the boil, stirring or whisking, and continue to cook until the mixture thickens.

Simmer gently for 3 minutes. Remove pan from heat and season with salt and pepper. Serve with meat, poultry, fish or vegetables.

Makes 300 ml (10 fl oz/1 1/4 cups/20 tbsp).

WHITE SAUCE VARIATIONS

CHEESE SAUCE

Follow the recipe for Basic White Sauce. Before seasoning with salt and pepper, stir in 55 g (2 oz/1/2 cup) grated reduced-fat Cheddar cheese and 1 teaspoon prepared mustard. Serve with fish, poultry, ham, vegetables or egg dishes.

PARSLEY SAUCE

Follow the recipe for Basic White Sauce. After seasoning with salt and pepper, stir in 2 tablespoons finely chopped fresh parsley. Serve with fish, ham or bacon.

CAPER SAUCE

Follow the recipe for Basic White Sauce. Before seasoning with salt and pepper, stir in 2 tablespoons capers and 2 teaspoons vinegar from the jar of capers. Reheat gently before serving. Serve with lamb.

ESPAGNOLE SAUCE

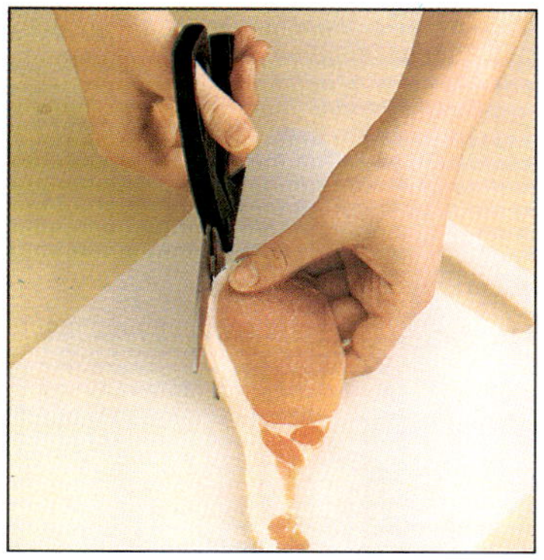

1 rasher lean back bacon
25 g (1 oz/6 teaspoons) low fat spread
1 small onion or shallot
1 small carrot
55 g (2 oz) mushrooms
9 teaspoons plain flour
550 ml (20 fl oz/2½ cups) beef stock
1 bouquet garni
4 black peppercorns
1 bay leaf
2 tablespoons tomato purée (paste)
salt and pepper

Trim the rind and fat from the bacon and chop the bacon finely.

In a saucepan, melt low fat spread over a low heat. Add bacon and cook for 2 minutes, stirring. Chop onion or shallot, carrot and mushrooms finely. Add vegetables to the bacon and cook for 5-10 minutes until lightly browned, stirring occasionally. Stir in flour and cook until lightly browned, stirring continuously. Remove pan from heat and gradually stir in stock. Add all the remaining ingredients and bring slowly to the boil, stirring, until the mixture thickens. Cover and simmer gently for 1 hour, stirring occasionally.

Strain the sauce, remove bouquet garni and rub the pulp through a sieve. Discard the remaining pulp and return sauce to a saucepan. Reheat gently and adjust the seasoning before ~~serving. Serve with~~ red meats or game.

Makes 425 ml (15 fl oz/1¾ cups/28 tbsp).

BÉCHAMEL SAUCE

1 small onion or shallot
1 small carrot
½ stick celery
1 bay leaf
6 black peppercorns
several stalks parsley
300 ml (10 fl oz/1¼ cups) semi-skimmed milk
25 g (1 oz/6 teaspoons) low fat spread
25 g (1 oz/¼ cup) plain flour
salt and pepper

Slice the onion or shallot and carrot. Chop the celery roughly. Put vegetables and flavourings in a saucepan with milk and bring slowly to the boil.

Remove pan from heat, cover and set aside to infuse for 30 minutes. Strain into a jug, reserving the milk. In a saucepan, melt low fat spread over a low heat. Stir in flour and cook for 1 minute, stirring.

Remove pan from heat and gradually stir or whisk in flavoured milk. Bring slowly to the boil, stirring or whisking, and continue to cook until the mixture thickens. Simmer gently for 3 minutes. Remove pan from heat and season with salt and pepper. Serve with poultry, fish, vegetables or egg dishes.

Makes 300 ml (10 fl oz/1¼ cups/20 tbsp).

TRADITIONAL GRAVY

1 small onion
25 g (1 oz/6 teaspoons) low fat spread
25 g (1 oz/¼ cup) plain flour
300 ml (10 fl oz/1¼ cups) beef stock
1 tablespoon tomato purée (paste)
1 teaspoon sugar
1 teaspoon yeast extract
1 teaspoon dried mixed herbs
salt and pepper

Chop onion finely. In a saucepan, melt low fat spread over a low heat. Add onion and cook for 5 minutes until soft, stirring.

Stir in flour and cook gently for 1 minute, stirring. Remove pan from heat and gradually stir in stock. Add the remaining ingredients and bring slowly to the boil, stirring. Continue to cook until the mixture thickens, then simmer gently for 3 minutes.

Adjust the seasoning and serve with grilled or roast red meats, such as beef, lamb or pork.

Makes 425 ml (15 fl oz/1¾ cups/28 tbsp).

Variation: Use chicken stock instead of beef stock, if serving the gravy with poultry.

ONION SAUCE

1 onion
25 g (1 oz/6 teaspoons) low fat spread
25 g (1 oz/¼ cup) plain flour
450 ml (16 fl oz/2 cups) semi-skimmed milk
salt and pepper

Chop onion finely. In a saucepan, melt low fat spread over a low heat. Add onion and cook for 8-10 minutes, until soft, stirring occasionally.

Stir in flour and cook for 1 minute, stirring. Remove pan from heat and gradually stir in milk. Bring slowly to the boil, stirring, and continue to cook until the mixture thickens.

Simmer gently for 3 minutes. Remove pan from heat and season with salt and pepper. Serve with lamb or egg dishes.

Makes 550 ml (20 fl oz/2½ cups/36 tbsp).

MUSHROOM SAUCE

1 small onion
1 small carrot
½ stick celery
1 bay leaf
6 black peppercorns
450 ml (16 fl oz/2 cups) semi-skimmed milk
175 g (6 oz) button mushrooms
55 g (2 oz/¼ cup) low fat spread
55 g (2 oz/½ cup) plain flour
salt and pepper

Slice the onion and carrot. Chop celery roughly. Put vegetables and flavourings in a saucepan with the milk and slowly bring to the boil.

Remove pan from heat, cover and set aside to infuse for 30 minutes. Strain into a jug, reserving the milk. Slice mushrooms thinly. In a saucepan, melt low fat spread over a low heat. Add mushrooms and cook for 5 minutes until soft, stirring occasionally. Stir in flour and cook for 1 minute, stirring. Remove pan from heat and gradually stir in the flavoured milk.

Bring slowly to the boil, stirring, and continue to cook until the mixture thickens. Simmer gently for 3 minutes. Remove pan from heat and season with salt and pepper. Serve with fish or vegetables such as broccoli or potatoes.

Makes 550 ml (20 fl oz/2½ cups/36 tbsp).

MUSTARD SAUCE

25 g (1 oz/6 teaspoons) low fat spread
25 g (1 oz/¼ cup) plain flour
300 ml (10 fl oz/1¼ cups) semi-skimmed milk
6 teaspoons wholegrain mustard
salt and pepper

In a saucepan, melt low fat spread over a low heat. Stir in flour and cook for 1 minute, stirring.

Remove pan from heat and gradually stir or whisk in the milk. Bring slowly to the boil, stirring or whisking, and continue to cook until mixture thickens. Simmer gently for 3 minutes.

Stir in mustard and season with salt and pepper. Reheat gently before serving. Serve with oily fish, ham, bacon, vegetables or cheese dishes.

Makes 350 ml (12 fl oz/1½ cups/23 tbsp).

ROMESCO SAUCE

3 cloves garlic, unpeeled
225 g (8 oz) beefsteak tomatoes
1 red pepper (capsicum)
25 g (1 oz) blanched almonds, lightly toasted
1 dried hot red chilli, soaked in cold water for 30 minutes, drained and seeded
3 tablespoons red wine vinegar
about 150 ml (5 fl oz/⅔ cup) olive oil
salt

Preheat oven to its hottest setting. Bake garlic, tomatoes and red pepper (capsicum) for 20-30 minutes, removing tomatoes and garlic when soft and pepper (capsicum) when soft and lightly browned.

Peel tomatoes and pepper (capsicum) and discard seeds. Peel garlic. Mix vegetables with almonds and chilli in a blender or food processor, then, with the motor running, slowly pour in vinegar and enough oil to make a thick sauce.

Add salt to taste. Leave to stand for 3-4 hours before serving with meat, fish and vegetable dishes.

Serves 6.

Variation: True Romesco Sauce is made from romesco peppers (capsicums). If available, substitute 2 dried romesco peppers for the red pepper (capsicum) and chilli.

TOMATO SAUCE

2 tablespoons olive oil
½ Spanish onion, finely chopped
½ clove garlic, chopped
1 red pepper (capsicum), chopped
900 g (2 lb) beefsteak tomatoes, peeled, seeded and chopped
sugar or tomato purée (paste), (optional)
salt and freshly ground black pepper

Heat oil in a frying pan, add onion and cook slowly for 5 minutes.

Stir in garlic and pepper (capsicum) and continue to cook slowly for a further 10 minutes, stirring occasionally.

Stir tomatoes into pan. Simmer gently for 20-30 minutes, stirring occasionally, until thickened. Add sugar or tomato purée (paste), if desired, and season with salt and pepper. Mix in a blender or food processor, or pass through a non-metallic sieve, if desired.

Serves 4-6.

BARBECUE SAUCE

3 tablespoons corn oil
1 small onion
1 clove garlic, crushed
½ teaspoon dry mustard
2 tablespoons malt vinegar
1 tablespoon Worcestershire sauce
2 tablespoons light soft brown sugar
3 tablespoons tomato ketchup (sauce)
½ teaspoon chilli seasoning
185 ml (6 fl oz/¾ cup) chicken stock
sprig of parsley, to garnish

Heat oil in a small saucepan. Add onion and garlic and cook gently for 2 minutes, stirring frequently.

Stir in mustard, vinegar, Worcestershire sauce, sugar, tomato ketchup (sauce), chilli seasoning and chicken stock. Bring to the boil.

Cover and simmer sauce gently for 7-8 minutes until slightly thickened. Serve hot as a sauce, garnished with sprigs of parsley, with beefburgers, hot dogs or fried chicken. Or, if preferred, allow to cool and use to brush over meats, poultry and fish while baking or grilling.

Makes 315 ml (10 fl oz/1¼ cups).

SPICY CHILLI SAUCE

1 clove garlic
1 Spanish onion, quartered
2 fresh green chillies, seeded
2 tablespoons corn oil
½ teaspoon ground ginger
250 g (8 oz) can tomatoes
60 g (2 oz/⅓ cup) seedless raisins
1 tablespoon lemon juice
1 tablespoon dark soy sauce
30 g (1 oz/2 tablespoons) light soft brown sugar
salt and pepper
sprig of parsley, to garnish

In a blender or food processor, finely chop garlic, onion and chillies.

Heat oil in a saucepan. Add onion mixture and ginger and cook gently for 3 minutes. Add tomatoes and break up with a spoon. Stir in raisins, lemon juice, soy sauce, sugar and 315 ml (10 fl oz/1¼ cups) water.

Bring to the boil, then reduce heat and simmer, uncovered, for 15 minutes. Blend to a smooth purée in a blender or food processor. Reheat and season with salt and pepper. Serve hot, garnished with a sprig of parsley, with grilled steak or fried chicken.

Makes 625 ml (20 fl oz/2½ cups).

Note: This sauce is also delicious served with grilled white fish.

HORSERADISH SAUCE

4 tablespoons grated fresh horseradish
1 teaspoon caster sugar
2 teaspoons smooth mustard
salt and pepper
2 tablespoons malt vinegar
9 teaspoons low fat plain yogurt

Place the grated horseradish in a bowl. Add sugar, mustard and salt and pepper and mix well.

Stir in vinegar, then gently stir in the yogurt, mixing well. Leave the horseradish sauce in a cool place for 30 minutes before serving, to allow the flavours to develop.

Serve with beef or oily fish.

Makes 150 ml (5 fl oz/⅔ cup/10 tbsp).

Variation: Use reduced fat single (light) cream in place of the plain yogurt, but remember this will increase the calorie and fat contents of the sauce.

MINTY APPLE SAUCE

1 small onion
450 g (1 lb) cooking apples
small bunch fresh mint
25 g (1 oz/5 teaspoons) caster sugar

Chop onion finely. Peel, core and slice apples. Put onion and apples in a saucepan with 2 tablespoons water.

Cover saucepan and heat mixture gently until the apples and onion are soft. Remove pan from heat and mash the apples and onion lightly.

Chop mint finely and add to saucepan with the sugar, mixing well. Reheat sauce gently until the sugar has dissolved. Serve hot or cold with lamb or pork.

Makes 400 ml (14 fl oz/1¾ cups/26 tbsp).

CRANBERRY SAUCE

225 g (8 oz) cranberries
115 g (4 oz/½ cup) caster sugar
12 teaspoons ruby port

Place cranberries in a saucepan with 150 ml (5 fl oz/⅔ cup) cold water.

Bring to the boil and boil rapidly until cranberries are soft. Reduce the heat and stir in the sugar.

Heat gently until sugar has dissolved, then stir in port. Reheat gently and serve with turkey or pork.

Makes 450 ml (16 fl oz/2 cups/30 tbsp).

Variation: In place of the ruby port, add medium sherry to the sauce.

BRANDY SAUCE

6 teaspoons cornflour
300 ml (10 fl oz/1¼ cups) semi-skimmed milk
6 teaspoons caster sugar
9 teaspoons brandy

In a bowl, blend cornflour with 2 tablespoons milk until smooth. Put remaining milk in a saucepan and bring slowly to the boil.

Pour hot milk onto cornflour mixture, whisking. Return the sauce to the saucepan and bring slowly to the boil, stirring continuously, until the sauce thickens. Simmer gently for 3 minutes.

Remove pan from heat and stir in sugar and brandy. Reheat the sauce gently. Serve with Christmas pudding or mince pies.

Makes 300 ml (10 fl oz/1¼ cups/20 tbsp).

Variation: Replace the brandy with rum, sherry or whisky.

RASPBERRY SAUCE

250 g (8 oz) fresh or frozen raspberries
2 tablespoons lemon juice
60-90 g (2-3 oz/¼-⅓ cup) caster sugar
75 ml (2½ fl oz/⅓ cup) Framboise liqueur or water

Put all ingredients into a saucepan and bring slowly to boiling point.

Simmer for a few minutes, then either serve immediately, or rub through a nylon sieve (if you do not have a nylon one, use a wooden – not metal – spoon to rub fruit through a metal sieve, otherwise fruit will have a metallic taste). Serve the sauce cold.

Serves 4-6.

Note: Serve Raspberry Sauce with Orange Roulade (see page 170).

DARK CHOCOLATE SAUCE

185 g (6 oz) plain (dark) chocolate
125 ml (4 fl oz/½ cup) strong black coffee or water
60 g (2 oz/¼ cup) caster sugar

Break chocolate into pieces and put in the top of a double boiler or a bowl set over a saucepan of simmering water. Add the coffee or water and sugar.

Stir over medium heat until the chocolate has melted and the sauce is smooth and creamy. Serve hot or cold.

Serves 4-6.

Note: Serve Dark Chocolate Sauce with Mixed Chocolate Terrine (see page 173), or serve it hot with vanilla ice cream.

BLACKCURRANT SAUCE

250 g (8 oz) fresh or frozen blackcurrants, thawed if frozen
60 g (2 oz/1/4 cup) caster sugar
2 tablespoons crème de cassis

Put blackcurrants into a saucepan with the sugar and 125 ml (4 fl oz/1/2 cup) water, and cook them over a medium heat until they are tender.

Drain fruit, reserving juice. Push fruit through a sieve with a little juice to make a purée. Stir in cassis and enough of reserved juice to give desired consistency. Serve cold.

Serves 4-6.

Note: Serve Blackcurrant Sauce with Coeurs à la Crème (see page 163).

HOT LEMON SAUCE

juice and grated peel of 3 lemons
90 g (3 oz/1/3 cup) butter
90 g (3 oz/1/3 cup) caster sugar
1 rounded teaspoon cornflour

Put lemon juice and peel in a saucepan with butter and sugar. Stir over gentle heat until butter has melted and sugar dissolved.

Mix cornflour to a smooth paste with a little water and stir into the pan. Bring the sauce to the boil, stirring constantly.

Simmer for 1-2 minutes, stirring all the time. Keep warm until ready to serve.

Serves 4-6.

CARAMEL SAUCE

115 g (4 oz/¾ cup) soft brown sugar
115 g (4 oz/½ cup) caster sugar
3 teaspoons arrowroot

Put sugars in a saucepan with 450 ml (16 fl oz/ 2 cups) water. Heat mixture gently until sugar has dissolved. Bring slowly to the boil and simmer gently for 10 minutes, stirring occasionally.

In a small bowl, blend arrowroot with 2 tablespoons water. Whisk arrowroot mixture into sugar, mixing well. Reheat the sauce gently, until sauce thickens, stirring continuously.

Serve with fruit such as oranges or bananas.

Makes 425 ml (15 fl oz/1¾ cups/28 tbsp).

Variation: Once the sauce has thickened, add 2-3 tablespoons brandy or a liqueur such as Cointreau to the sauce and reheat gently.

BLACKBERRY & APPLE SAUCE

225 g (8 oz) cooking apples
225 g (8 oz) blackberries
55 g (2 oz/¼ cup) caster sugar
115 g (4 oz) low fat soft cheese
150 ml (5 fl oz/⅔ cup) reduced fat single (light) cream

Peel, core and slice apples thinly. Put apples and blackberries in a saucepan with 3 tablespoons water. Cover and cook gently until fruit is soft, stirring occasionally.

Remove pan from heat and stir in sugar. Set aside to cool. Once cool, purée the fruit in a blender or food processor until smooth. Press the fruit through a nylon sieve, discarding pips.

Whisk soft cheese and cream together, then whisk fruit in, mixing thoroughly. Serve with steamed and baked puddings, meringues or poached fruit such as peaches or pears.

Makes 550 ml (20 fl oz/2½ cups/36 tbsp).

Variation: In place of blackberries, use raspberries, loganberries or blackcurrants.

MINT & YOGURT DRESSING

1 clove garlic
300 ml (10 fl oz/1¼ cups) low fat plain yogurt
6 teaspoons semi-skimmed milk
2 tablespoons chopped fresh mint
salt and pepper

Peel and crush garlic. Put garlic, yogurt, milk, mint and salt and pepper in a bowl.

Whisk the ingredients together until thoroughly mixed. Cover and leave the dressing in a cool place for 30 minutes before serving, to allow the flavours to develop. Adjust the seasoning before serving.

Serve with a mixed bean salad or chicken salad.

Makes 350 ml (12 fl oz/1½ cups/23 tbsp).

Variation: In place of the garlic and mint, add the finely grated rind and juice of 1 lemon or 1 lime.

FRENCH DRESSING

12 teaspoons olive oil
4 tablespoons white wine vinegar
4 tablespoons tarragon vinegar
150 ml (5 fl oz/⅔ cup) white grape juice
2 teaspoons chopped fresh mixed herbs, such as parsley, thyme, mint and rosemary
2 teaspoons wholegrain mustard
pinch caster sugar
salt and pepper

Put olive oil, vinegars, grape juice, herbs, mustard, sugar and salt and pepper in a bowl. Whisk ingredients together until thoroughly mixed.

Alternatively, put all the ingredients in a clean jam jar. Screw top on jar and shake until ingredients are thoroughly mixed.

Adjust seasoning before serving. Serve with a fresh mixed salad or a selection of raw or cooked vegetables.

Makes 325 ml (11 fl oz/1⅓ cups/21 tbsp).

COCONUT YOGURT DRESSING

300 ml (10 fl oz/1¼ cups) low fat plain yogurt
6 tablespoons desiccated coconut
6 teaspoons clear honey
juice of 1 lime

Put yogurt and desiccated coconut in a bowl and mix well.

Whisk in honey and lime juice, mixing well. Cover and leave the dressing in a cool place for 30 minutes before serving, to allow the flavours to develop.

Serve with a bean salad or a mixed salad.

Makes 400 ml (14 fl oz/1¾ cups/26 tbsp).

Variation: For a special dressing, add 6 teaspoons coconut liqueur, such as Malibu, to the dressing with the honey.

TARTARE SAUCE

55 g (2 oz) gherkins
1 tablespoon capers
300 ml (10 fl oz/1¼ cups) reduced calorie mayonnaise
1 tablespoon tarragon vinegar
1 tablespoon chopped fresh parsley
1 tablespoon chopped fresh chives
2 teaspoons chopped fresh tarragon
salt and pepper

Using a sharp knife, chop gherkins and capers finely.

Put gherkins and capers in a bowl and stir in the mayonnaise, mixing well.

Stir in vinegar, parsley, chives, tarragon and salt and pepper and mix thoroughly. Cover and leave in a cool place for at least 30 minutes before serving, to allow the flavours to develop. Serve with grilled or baked fish.

Makes 400 ml (14 fl oz/1¾ cups/26 tbsp).

THOUSAND ISLAND DRESSING

55 g (2 oz) gherkins
2 tablespoons chopped red pepper (capsicum)
2 tablespoons chopped green pepper (capsicum)
300 ml (10 fl oz/1¼ cups) reduced calorie mayonnaise
4 tablespoons low fat plain yogurt
6 teaspoons tomato ketchup (sauce)
1 tablespoon chopped fresh parsley
salt and pepper

Chop gherkins finely. In a bowl, mix together gherkins and red and green pepper (capsicum).

Stir in mayonnaise, yogurt, tomato ketchup (sauce), parsley and salt and pepper and mix thoroughly. Cover and leave in a cool place for 30 minutes before serving, to allow the flavours to develop.

Serve with a fresh mixed seafood salad.

Makes 600 ml (21 fl oz/2¾ cups/40 tbsp).

Variation: Add two cold hard-boiled eggs, mashed or finely chopped, to the dressing.

MILD CURRY MAYONNAISE

6 spring onions
15 g (½ oz/3 teaspoons) low fat spread
6 teaspoons mango chutney
3 teaspoons mild curry powder
3 teaspoons desiccated coconut
300 ml (10 fl oz/1¼ cups) reduced calorie mayonnaise
150 ml (5 fl oz/⅔ cup) low fat plain yogurt
salt and pepper

Trim and chop spring onions finely. In a saucepan, melt low fat spread over a low heat. Add spring onions and cook for 5 minutes, stirring.

Remove pan from heat and stir in chutney, curry powder and coconut, mixing well. Set aside to cool.

Once cool, mix with mayonnaise, yogurt and salt and pepper. Cover and leave the sauce in a cool place for 30 minutes before serving, to allow the flavours to develop. Serve with potato salad or coleslaw.

Makes 500 ml (18 fl oz/2¼ cups/33 tbsp).

RASPBERRY VINAIGRETTE

400 g (14 oz) can raspberries in fruit juice
8 tablespoons red wine vinegar
5 tablespoons sunflower oil
1 teaspoon caster sugar
1 teaspoon dried sage
salt and pepper

Put raspberries and juice in a blender or food processor and blend until smooth.

Strain raspberry purée through a nylon sieve and discard pips. Put raspberry juice, vinegar, oil, sugar, sage and salt and pepper in a bowl. Whisk the ingredients together until thoroughly mixed.

Alternatively, put all the ingredients in a clean jam jar. Screw top on jar and shake until ingredients are thoroughly mixed. Adjust the seasoning before serving. Serve with fresh salad leaves, rice salad, avocado or cold sliced meats such as chicken.

Makes 500 ml (18 fl oz/2¼ cups/33 tbsp).

GARLIC & GINGER DRESSING

2 cloves garlic
2.5 cm (1 in) piece fresh root ginger
7 tablespoons cider vinegar
6 teaspoons light soy sauce
3 teaspoons sunflower oil
3 teaspoons sesame oil
salt and pepper

Peel and crush garlic cloves. Peel and chop or grate ginger finely.

Put garlic, ginger, vinegar, soy sauce, sunflower oil, sesame oil and salt and pepper in a bowl. Whisk ingredients together until thoroughly mixed. Alternatively, put all the ingredients in a clean jam jar. Screw top on jar and shake until all the ingredients are thoroughly mixed.

Adjust the seasoning before serving. Serve with a fresh mixed salad, root vegetables, a mixed bean salad or grilled chicken or turkey.

Makes 175 ml (6 fl oz/¾ cup/11 tbsp).

PRESERVES

LEMON CURD

4 lemons
350 g (12 oz/1 3/4 cups) caster sugar
115 g (4 oz/1/2 cup) butter
4 eggs

Finely grate rind from all 4 lemons into a heatproof bowl. Squeeze lemons and pour juice into the bowl. Stir in sugar. Cut butter into small pieces and add to other ingredients in bowl.

Set bowl over a saucepan one-quarter filled with simmering water, until butter has melted and sugar dissolved. In a bowl, break up eggs with a fork and strain into lemon and butter mixture.

Cook gently, stirring frequently, for 10-15 minutes until mixture is thick and creamy. Pour into clean warm jars and seal while hot. Keep in the refrigerator.

Makes about 700 g (1 1/2 lb).

Variations: For Lime Curd, use limes instead of lemons.

For Lemon & Elderflower Curd, add 2 handfuls of elderflowers, well shaken and flowers removed from stems, after adding the butter to the bowl.

APPLE BUTTER

1.2 litres (40 fl oz/5 cups) dry cider
1 kg (2.2 lb) dessert apples
450 g (1 lb) cooking apples
granulated sugar
grated rind and juice 1/2 orange
grated rind and juice 1/2 lemon
1/2 teaspoon ground cinnamon
1/2 teaspoon ground cloves

Put cider in a large saucepan. Boil rapidly until reduced by one-third. Peel, core and slice apples and add to pan.

If necessary, add sufficient water to just cover apples. Half-cover the pan and simmer gently until apples are very soft and pulpy and well reduced. Stir occasionally and crush pulp down in the pan as it cooks. Measure pulp and process to a purée if it is lumpy. Return to saucepan. Add 300 g (10 oz/1 1/4 cups) sugar for every 550 ml (20 fl oz/2 1/2 cups) of apple pulp. Stir in the orange and lemon rind and juice and cinnamon and cloves.

Cook gently until sugar has dissolved. Simmer, stirring frequently, until most moisture has been driven off. The mixture is ready when a spoon drawn across the surface will leave an impression. Pot in clean, warm jars and store in the refrigerator. Once a jar is opened the apple butter should be consumed within 3-4 days.

Makes 4 or 5 small jars.

GRAPEFRUIT MARMALADE

2 kg (4 lb) grapefruit, well scrubbed
sugar, see recipe

Cut grapefruit into quarters, remove seeds and pithy centres. Put the seeds and centres in a 15-cm (6-in) square of muslin, tie into a bag. Peel grapefruit. Cut peel into julienne strips. Slice peeled fruit crosswise into thin slices. Separate slices into individual sections. Place fruit and bag in a large bowl; just cover with water. Soak 12 hours. Remove bag.

In large preserving pan or saucepan, simmer fruit and soaking water 1 hour. For every cup of fruit and water add 115 g (5 oz/¾ cup) sugar. Bring to a boil; boil about 20 minutes or to proper consistency. Test marmalade for doneness immediately after boiling. Proper consistency is reached when candy thermometer reaches 105C (220F). Or test by spoon test. Pour a small amount of marmalade onto a cold plate. Let stand until cold. If marmalade forms a skin and wrinkles when pushed with a finger or spoon, it is ready.

Remove pan from heat while test preserve is cooling. Cool 10 minutes; stir gently to mix skin through marmalade. Pour into sterilized jars to within 1-cm (½-in) of top. Seal with sterilized lids. Invert jars for a few seconds. Cool in upright position. Store in cool, dark place.

Makes about 2.3 kg (5 lb/10 cups).

ROSE PETAL JAM

225 g (8 oz) red, fragrant rose petals
450 g (1 lb/2 cups) granulated sugar
juice of 2 lemons

Cut off white area from base of each petal. Put petals in a bowl and sprinkle with enough of the sugar to cover them. Leave overnight.

In a saucepan, put remaining sugar, 1 litre (35 fl oz/4½ cups) water and the lemon juice. Heat gently until sugar has dissolved. Stir in rose petals and simmer for 20 minutes. Bring to the boil and boil for 5 minutes until mixture thickens.

Pour jam into clean, warm jars. Cover and label. Store in a cool place.

Makes about 450 g (1 lb).

APRICOT & ALMOND CONSERVE

450 g (1 lb) dried apricots, quartered
1.13 l (2 pts/5 cups) water
1.25 kg (2½ lb/6 cups) sugar
½ teaspoon almond liqueur or almond essence
60 g (2 oz/½ cup) blanched, slivered almonds

Soak apricots overnight in water. Strain apricots; reserve liquid.

In a heavy-bottomed saucepan combine reserved liquid and sugar, bring to boil over a low heat stirring until sugar is dissolved. Add apricots and simmer until oven temperature reaches 105C (220F). Or test using spoon method described in Grapefruit Marmalade, page 239.

Immediately stir in liqueur and almonds. Remove from heat. Allow jam to stand at room temperature 10 minutes, stirring occasionally, to keep fruit and nuts in suspension. Pour conserve to within ¼-cm (⅛-in) of top of sterilized jars; seal tightly with sterilized lids. Store in a cool, dark place.

Makes 1.8 kg (4 lb/8 cups).

SPICED CITRUS SLICES

3 thin-skinned oranges
4 thin-skinned lemons
5 limes
625 ml (20 fl oz/2½ cups) white wine vinegar
1.25 kg (2½ lb/4½ cups) granulated sugar
2 cinnamon sticks
7g (¼ oz/2 teaspoons) whole cloves
6 blades of mace

Scrub fruit thoroughly, then cut into 0.3 cm (⅛ in) thick slices. Lay slices in a stainless steel or enamel saucepan and just cover with water. Bring to boil, then cover and cook very gently for about 15 minutes until peel is tender. Drain slices and reserve liquor.

In another saucepan, gently heat vinegar, sugar and spices, stirring occasionally, until sugar has dissolved. Bring to boil, then add fruit slices. Add reserved liquor to cover fruit if necessary, then cook very gently for 15 minutes until peel looks transparent.

Arrange fruit slices in small, clean, hot jars, alternating slices, or packing each separately, as desired. Bring syrup to the boil, discard cinnamon and immediately fill each jar to top. Cover with airtight, vinegar-proof lids. When cold, label and store in a cool place for up to 6 months.

Makes 4 small jars.

MIXED CURRANT JELLY

1 kg (2 lb) redcurrants, washed
1 kg (2 lb) blackcurrants, washed
1.75 l (60 fl oz/7½ cups) water
sugar, see recipe

In a preserving pan combine fruit and water. Bring to a boil and simmer until very soft.

Mash fruit with a wooden spoon and spoon into a jelly bag to drip overnight. Measure fruit juice and allow 220 g (7 fl oz/1 cup) sugar for each 250 ml (8 fl oz/1 cup) of juice.

Place sugar and liquid back in pan and bring to a boil, stirring to dissolve sugar. Boil 7 minutes until temperature reaches 105C (220F). Or, test using spoon method, page 239. Pour into sterilized jars; cover; seal tightly with sterilized lids. Store in a cool, dark place.

Makes about 3.6 kg (8 lb)/16 cups).

BRANDIED MINCEMEAT

500 g (1 lb/3 cups) raisins
500 g (1 lb/3 cups) sultanas
500 g (1 lb/3⅓ cups) currants
125 g (4 oz/1 cup) dried apricots
125 g (4 oz/¾ cup) stoned dates
185 g (6 oz/1 cup) candied peel
125 g (4 oz/¾ cup) whole almonds
500 g (1 lb) cooking apples, peeled and cored
finely grated peel and juice of 2 lemons
375 g (12 oz/2¼ cups) light soft brown sugar
250 g (8 oz/1 cup) unsalted butter, melted
3 teaspoons ground mixed spice
155 ml (5 fl oz/⅔ cup) brandy

In a bowl, put raisins, sultanas and currants.

Chop or mince apricots, dates, candied peel, almonds and apples. Add to bowl with lemon peel and juice and mix well together. Stir in sugar, butter, mixed spice and brandy. Stir the mixture until evenly blended, cover bowl with plastic wrap and leave in a cool place for 2 days.

Preheat the oven to 200C (400F/Gas 6). Thoroughly wash and dry six 500 g (1 lb) jam jars, stand them on a paper-lined baking sheet and place in the oven until hot. Stir mincemeat thoroughly, then spoon into hot jars, filling each to the top. Place a wax disc on top of each and cellophane covers over the jars, securing each with an elastic band. Label clearly and store in a cool, dry place for up to 6 months.

Makes 3 kg (6 lb).

FIGS IN BRANDY

14 dried whole figs
105 g (3½ oz/½ cup) sugar
1 cinnamon stick
approximately 250 ml (8 fl oz/1 cup) brandy

In a large saucepan or frying pan, place figs in one layer with sugar and cinnamon stick. Just cover with water, poach over low heat 5 minutes. Discard cinnamon stick. Drain figs.

Pack figs in sterilized jar. Reduce syrup to half by simmering uncovered.

Half fill jar of figs with brandy. Pour reduced syrup in jar to within 1.5-cm (½-in) of top, cover. Store in a cool dark place – allow to mellow at least 1 month before using.

Makes 750 g (1½ lb/3 cups).

FRUITS IN CHARTREUSE

10 fresh lychees or 470 g (15 oz) can lychees
250 g (8 oz/2 cups) cherries or 470 g (15 oz) can cherries
250 g (8 oz/1 cup) granulated sugar
315 ml (10 fl oz/1¼ cups) Chartreuse or Benedectine liqueur

Peel fresh lychees and carefully remove stones, keeping fruit whole, or drain and stone canned lychees. Remove stalks and wash fresh cherries, or drain canned cherries, and dry on absorbent kitchen paper. Pierce skins of cherries all over with a clean needle or fine skewer.

Have ready 3 or 4 very small, clean, dry, sterilised jars with well-fitting lids. Arrange a layer of cherries in one clean jar and sprinkle with about 1 tablespoon sugar. Arrange a layer of lychees on top and sprinkle with more sugar. Continue to layer cherries, sugar and lychees until jar is loosely filled to neck of jar, do not pack fruit in tightly. Sprinkle with a final layer of sugar.

Fill jar to the top with Chartreuse or Benedictine and seal with a clean lid. Repeat to fill remaining small jars with fruits, sugar and liqueur. Store in a cool, dry place for up to 6 months. Gift wrap for presents.

Makes 3 or 4 small jars.

MINT JELLY

2.7 kg (6 lb.) cooking apples, washed, quartered
juice of 4 lemons
125 g (4 oz/2 cups loosely packed) fresh mint leaves
250 ml (8 fl oz/1 cup) white wine vinegar
sugar, see recipe
chopped fresh mint leaves
green food colouring
mint flavouring, if desired

In a large heavy-bottomed saucepan, combine apples, lemon juice, mint; just cover with water. Simmer until apples are very soft. Add vinegar, simmer 5 minutes more.

Strain mixture through a jelly bag or double thickness of muslin; do not force mixture through. Measure fruit juice and add 220 g (7 oz/1 cup) sugar for every 250 ml (8 fl oz/1 cup) of juice.

In a clean pan, cook juice and sugar over a low heat until sugar dissolves, stirring. Increase heat, boil briskly 5 minutes, without stirring, until proper consistency is reached when sugar temperature reaches 220F. Or, test using spoon method, page 239. Stir in chopped mint and a little colouring and mint flavouring if desired. Pour to within ¼-cm (⅛-in) of top of sterilized jars; cover; seal tightly and store in a cool, dark place.

Makes 2.7 kg (6 lb/12 cups).

TOMATO RELISH

1.5 kg (3 lb.) tomatoes
4 large onions, coarsely chopped
125 g (4 oz/¾ cup) salt
600 ml (1 pt/2½ cups) white wine vinegar
440 g (14 oz/1¾ cups) sugar
6-10 small red chillies
1 tablespoon curry powder
1 tablespoon turmeric
1½ teaspoons dry mustard
1 teaspoon cumin
1 teaspoon fenugreek
2 tablespoons plain flour

Peel, core and coarsely chop tomatoes.

Place in a ceramic or glass bowl, sprinkle generously with salt; cover; let stand overnight. In a large saucepan combine tomatoes, onions and vinegar. Bring to boil; simmer 10 minutes. Add sugar and chillies. Cook, stirring occasionally, until sugar is dissolved. Simmer 5 minutes more. In a small bowl combine remaining ingredients and enough cold water to form a paste. Add to simmering vegetable mixture, stirring to avoid any lumps. Simmer 1½ hours, stirring occasionally.

Pour into sterilized jars. Seal with sterilized vinegar-proof lids. Process for 15 minutes in a boiling-water bath. (Place jars on rack in processing pan. Do not allow jars to touch. Keep covered with 2 inches water while processing.) Store in a cool, dark place – allow to mellow 4 weeks before using.

Makes about 1.9 l (3¼ pt/8 cups).

FRESH MANGO CHUTNEY

2 mangoes
1 red chilli, seeded and finely sliced
30 g (1 oz/¼ cup) cashew nuts, chopped
30 g (1 oz/¼ cup) raisins
2 tablespoons chopped fresh mint
pinch asafoetida
½ teaspoon ground cumin
¼ teaspoon cayenne pepper
½ teaspoon ground coriander
mint sprigs, to garnish

Peel and stone mangoes, then very thinly slice flesh.

Put mango slices in a bowl with chilli, cashew nuts, raisins and mint and stir gently. In a small bowl, mix asafoetida, cumin, cayenne and coriander together, then sprinkle over mango mixture.

Stir gently to coat mango mixture in spices, then cover and chill for 2 hours. Serve chilled, garnished with mint sprigs.

Makes about 250 g (8 oz).

SPICY APPLE CHUTNEY

1 kg (2 lb) cooking apples
2 tablespoons salt
1 whole head garlic
2.5-cm (1-in) piece fresh gingerroot
4 fresh green chilies, chopped
155 ml (5 fl oz/⅔ cup) vegetable oil
2 tablespoons white mustard seeds
1 teaspoon each fenugreek, chilli powder and turmeric
15 whole black peppercorns
2 teaspoons ground cumin
155 ml (5 fl oz/⅔ cup) vinegar
105 g (3½ g/½ cup) sugar

Peel, core and slice apples. In a large glass or ceramic bowl, place apples; and set aside. Peel and chop garlic and ginger, chop chillies. In a large saucepan, gently fry garlic and ginger in oil for 3 minutes. Add spices and cook 5 minutes.

Add apples, vinegar and sugar; simmer until thick. Fill sterilized jars with chutney to within ½-cm (¼-in) of top. Seal with sterilized vinegar proof lids. Store in a cool, dark place.

Makes about 1.5 kg (3 lb/6 cups).

CONFECTIONERY

CHOCOLATE TRUFFLE CUPS

500 g (1 lb) white chocolate
60 g (2 oz/¼ cup) unsalted butter, softened
6 teaspoons whipping cream
4 teaspoons cherry brandy
pink, green and yellow food colourings
4 teaspoons Chartreuse
4 teaspoons apricot brandy
6 pistachio nuts, chopped

Break up chocolate and place in a dry bowl over a saucepan of hand-hot water. Stir occasionally until melted; remove bowl from pan and cool. Place 36 foil cases on a tray, spoon a little chocolate into each one.

Using a fine brush, coat inside of each case; leave to set. Add soft butter and cream to remaining chocolate; stir until smooth. Divide mixture between 3 bowls. Flavour one with cherry brandy and tint pink; flavour another with Chartreuse and tint green, and the other with apricot brandy and tint with yellow and pink colouring to give an apricot colour.

When chocolate mixtures are set enough to peak softly, place each in a separate piping bag fitted with a small star nozzle; pipe swirls of each flavour into 12 chocolate cases. Sprinkle with pistachio nuts and leave to set. Pack in pretty containers.

Makes 36.

HAND-MADE CHOCOLATES

90 g (3 oz) ready-to-roll fondant icing
rose and violet flavourings
pink and mauve food colourings
60 g (2 oz) white marzipan
6 maraschino cherries
6 crème de menthe cherries
6 Brazil nuts
6 whole almonds
185 g (6 oz) plain (dark) chocolate
185 g (6 oz) white chocolate
185 g (6 oz) milk chocolate
crystallised rose and violet petals

Cut fondant into 2 pieces: flavour ½ with rose flavouring and colour pale pink.

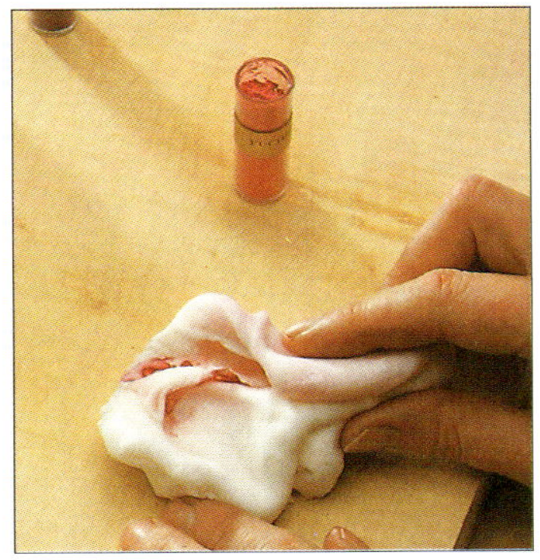

Flavour remaining piece with violet flavouring and colour pale mauve. Roll out fondant to 1 cm (½ in) thickness and cut into shapes using cocktail cutters. Place on a non-stick paper-lined baking sheet. Shape marzipan into various shapes by rolling bite-sized pieces between hands into balls, logs or ovals. Arrange on baking sheet. Leave to dry for several hours or overnight. Pat cherries dry. Toast nuts until golden brown.

Melt each type of chocolate in separate bowls over hand-hot water and stir until melted. Using a fork, dip one prepared centre at a time into chocolate; tap to remove excess, and place chocolate on a paper-lined baking sheet. Leave plain, or mark top with a fork or with piped chocolate. Decorate rose and violet centres with crystallised petals. Continue to dip all centres, giving a variety of white, plain (dark), or milk chocolate.

Makes about 30.

CHOCOLATE TRUFFLES

60 g (2 oz/1/3 cup) sliced almonds
90 g (3 oz/1/3 cup) sugar
750 g (1 1/2 lb) plain (dark) chocolate, chopped
1 tablespoon strong coffee
75 g (2 1/2 oz) butter, softened
2 tablespoons whipping cream
2 liqueurs of your choice
cocoa powder

In a small heavy-bottomed pan, combine almonds and sugar. On a low heat, slowly cook to a pale golden brown, stirring with a wooden spoon until dark brown. Remove from heat immediately and pour onto an oiled plate. Allow to harden.

In a food processor or blender, crush nut mixture to a coarse powder. Melt 250 g (8 oz) chocolate in a bowl or top of a double saucepan set over a pan of simmering water. Stir in coffee; cool slightly. Beat in butter; stir in cream and crushed nut mixture. Divide mixture in half, flavour each half with 1 or 2 tablespoons of liqueur.

Gently roll heaping teaspoons of mixture into balls. Work quickly as chocolate sets fast. Set aside on greaseproof paper; refrigerate until firm. Melt remaining chocolate; dip some truffles and place on greaseproof paper to set. Roll others in cocoa when almost set. Place on greaseproof paper to dry, or place in sweet cases. Store, covered, in a cool place.

Makes about 1 kg (2 lb).

ORANGE TRUFFLES

60 g (2 oz/1/4 cup) butter, chopped
75 ml (2 1/2 fl oz/1/3 cup) thick cream
220 g (7 oz) plain (dark) chocolate, chopped
1 egg yolk
1 teaspoon grated orange peel
2 tablespoons finely chopped mixed citrus peel
2 tablespoons Grand Marnier
Cocoa, sifted

In a small saucepan, combine butter with cream. Cook on low heat until butter melts and cream bubbles around edge. Remove from heat; add chocolate. Cover and let stand until chocolate melts. Stir until smooth.

Stir in egg yolk. Mix in orange peel, citrus peel, and Grand Marnier. Chill until firm.

Form into 40 balls. Roll in cocoa. Refrigerate in an airtight container up to 2 weeks. To serve, place in small paper or foil cases.

Makes 40.

RUM BALLS

RUM BALLS
45 g (1½ oz/¾ cup) cake crumbs
45 g (1½ oz/¼ cup) icing sugar
45 g (1½ oz/¼ cup) ground almonds
2 teaspoons dark rum
1 teaspoon lemon juice
45 g (1½ oz) plain (dark) chocolate, chopped
2 tablespoons cream
ICING
60 g (2 oz/⅓ cup) icing sugar
30 g (1 oz) butter, chopped
30 g (1 oz) plain (dark) chocolate, grated
2 teaspoons dark rum
warm water
Chocolate sprinkles

In a medium bowl, combine cake crumbs, sugar, almonds, rum and lemon juice. Melt chocolate in a bowl or top of a double boiler set over a pan of simmering water. Add to rum mixture to hold together when pressed between fingers. Form teaspoonfuls of mixture into 18 balls. Refrigerate on a baking sheet 4 hours or until firm. To make icing, combine sugar, butter, chocolate and rum in a small saucepan. When chocolate and butter softens, add a tablespoon of water. Warm again and add sufficient water to liquify.

To coat rum balls, insert a skewer in centre of a rum ball. Tilt pan of icing and dip each ball. Let excess drip. To decorate, roll in chocolate sprinkles to coat completely. Refrigerate in a covered container with greaseproof paper between layers up to 10 days.

Makes 18.

CHOCOLATE COVERED PRUNES

12 whole stoned prunes
12 whole Brazil nuts
250 g (8 oz) plain (dark) chocolate

Fill cavity of prunes with Brazil nuts.

In a heatproof bowl or the top of a double saucepan placed over a saucepan of hot water on a low heat, melt the chocolate, stirring.

Dip prunes into chocolate to coat completely. Place on greaseproof paper to set. Store, covered, in the refrigerator.

Makes 12 chocolates.

CHERRY NUT CHOCOLATES

100 g (3½ oz) plain (dark) chocolate, chopped
30 g (1 oz/¼ cup) macadamia nuts or blanched almonds, coarsely chopped
8 glacé cherries, quartered

Grate or chop chocolate.

Toast nuts in a dry frying pan until golden brown. Stir occasionally. Cool. Melt chocolate in a bowl or top of a double boiler set over a pan of simmering water. Stir until smooth. Drop by teaspoonfuls on greaseproof paper and flatten to form thick small buttons. Let partly set.

Sprinkle nuts on outside rim of chocolate. Press cherry piece in centre. Let set; peel from greaseproof paper. Refrigerate in a covered container with greaseproof paper between layers up to 3 weeks.

Makes 30.

PISTACHIO HALVA

185 g (6 oz/1¼ cups) shelled pistachio nuts
250 ml (8 fl oz/1 cup) boiling water
2 tablespoons milk
125 g (4 oz/½ cup) sugar
22 g (¾ oz/4½ teaspoons) butter or ghee
few drops vanilla essence

Put pistachio nuts in a bowl, pour over boiling water and leave to soak for 30 minutes. Grease and base-line an 18 cm (7 in) square tin.

Drain pistachio nuts thoroughly and put in a blender or food processor fitted with a metal blade. Add milk and process until finely chopped, scraping mixture down from sides once or twice. Stir in sugar. Heat a large non-stick frying pan, add butter or ghee and melt over a low to medium heat. Add nut paste and cook for about 15 minutes, stirring constantly, until mixture is very thick.

Stir in vanilla essence, then spoon into prepared tin and spread evenly. Leave to cool completely, then cut into 20 squares using a sharp knife.

Makes about 20 squares.

Note: This halva will keep for 2-3 weeks, stored in the refrigerator.

TOASTED ALMOND TOFFEE

500 g (1 lb/2 cups) sugar
155 g (5 oz/2 cups) low-fat milk powder
few drops vanilla essence
30 g (1 oz/¼ cup) flaked almonds, toasted

Grease and base-line an 18 cm (7 in) square tin. Put sugar in a large heavy-based saucepan with 250 ml (8 fl oz/1 cup) water and heat gently, stirring occasionally, until sugar is dissolved.

Bring to the boil, then boil over a medium-high heat until a few drops of mixture will form a soft ball in cold water. Stir in milk powder and cook for 3-4 minutes more, stirring constantly, until mixture begins to dry on spoon. Stir in vanilla.

Pour into prepared tin and spread evenly. Scatter almonds over top and press into surface. Leave to cool slightly, then cut into 25 squares with a sharp knife while still warm. Leave in tin until cold and firm.

Makes 25 squares.

CASHEW NUT FUDGE

250 g (8 oz/1½ cups) unsalted cashew nuts
375 ml (12 fl oz/1½ cups) boiling water
6 teaspoons milk
155 g (5 oz/⅔ cup) sugar
15 g (½ oz/3 teaspoons) butter or ghee
few drops vanilla essence
few sheets silver leaf

Put cashew nuts in a bowl, pour over boiling water and leave to soak for 1 hour. Grease and base-line an 18 cm (7 in) square tin.

Drain cashew nuts thoroughly and put in a blender or food processor fitted with a metal blade. Add milk and process until smooth, scraping mixture down from sides once or twice. Stir in sugar. Heat a large non-stick frying pan, add butter or ghee and melt over a low to medium heat. Add nut paste and cook for about 20 minutes, stirring constantly, until mixture is very thick.

Stir in vanilla essence, then spoon into prepared tin and spread evenly. Leave to cool completely, then press silver leaf onto surface. Cut fudge into about 25 diamond shapes using a wet sharp knife.

Makes about 25 pieces.

Note: This fudge will keep for 2-3 weeks if stored in an airtight tin.

MARZIPAN FRUITS

125 g (4 oz/1¼ cups) finely ground almonds
125 g (4 oz/¾ cup) icing sugar (or more, if a sweeter flavour is desired)
1 egg white
red, green, blue and yellow food colouring
a few cloves

In a heat proof bowl or top of a double saucepan placed over a saucepan of hot water, place almonds; heat gently stirring occasionally until warmed. Remove double saucepan from heat, add sugar and egg white.

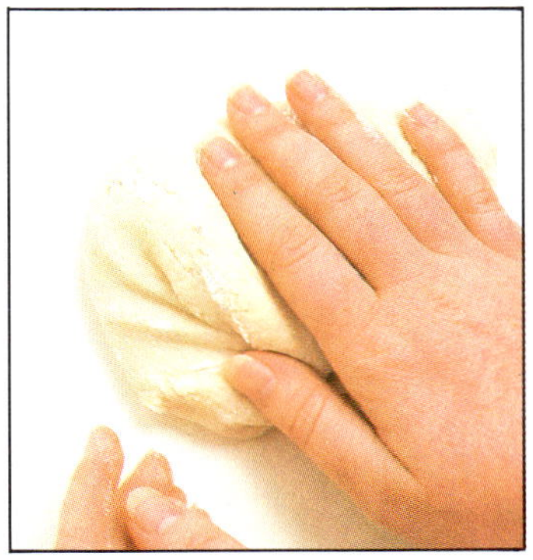

On a work surface, knead almond mixture until a smooth, fairly dry paste. Roll into a ball, cover with a cloth and let stand at room temperature for 15 minutes. Break off small portions and shape into desired 'fruit'. The exact size of the fruit is up to you, but they should never be larger than a small walnut.

You will need a couple of fine-pointed brushes, a saucer for mixing colours, a cup of water and a cloth for wiping brushes between colour changes. Remember, red and yellow make orange, diluted orange will put the base colour on peaches, red and green make brown for the stripes on bananas. Use cloves for the stem ends of oranges, pears and apples. You may make leaves from marzipan or use angelica.

Makes about 250 g (½ lb).

CHOCOLATE MARZIPAN LOG

125 g (4 oz) marzipan, crumbled
45 g (1½ oz/¼ cup) icing sugar
1 egg white
75 g (2¼ oz/¾ cup) dessicated coconut
angelica strips or glacé apricots, halved
45 g (1½ oz) plain (dark) chocolate, chopped

In a medium bowl, mix marzipan and sugar. Knead small amounts of egg white into marzipan mixture. Add additional egg white until a sticky paste forms. Add coconut and knead for 1 minute. If too sticky, knead on an icing sugar surface. Chill mixture 30 minutes.

Form a long roll 30 x 15 cm (12 x 6 in) on plastic wrap. Place angelica strips or glacé apricots along one side. Roll marzipan over to enclose fruit. Wrap well; chill 12 hours.

Melt chocolate in a bowl or top of a double boiler set over a pan of simmering water. Stir until smooth. Unwrap almond roll and spread one side with chocolate. When set, turn log over and spread chocolate on other side. When set, wrap and chill. Refrigerate whole up to 3 weeks. To serve, cut into slices as needed.

Makes 24 slices.

GLAZED APRICOT PECANS

40 pecan or walnut halves
APRICOT PURÉE
60 g (2 oz/½ cup) dried apricots
2 tablespoons icing sugar
30 g (1 oz/¼ cup) ground almonds
1 teaspoon brandy
TOFFEE
250 g (8 oz/1 cup) sugar
75 ml (2½ fl oz/⅓ cup) water

In a small saucepan, cook apricots covered with water until soft. Drain; purée apricots.

In a medium bowl, combine apricots, icing sugar, almonds and brandy. Chill 2 hours before using. Refrigerate up to 2 days. Place a teaspoon of apricot mixture on a nut; top with another nut. Press together gently. Remove excess apricot mixture.

Grease a wire rack and baking sheet. Place wire rack over baking sheet. In a small saucepan, cook sugar and water over low heat. Swirl mixture occasionally until sugar dissolves. Adjust heat to medium. Cook until mixture is a light golden brown. Remove from heat. Quickly drop nuts, one-by-one, into toffee. Using a small spoon, remove immediately; cool on wire rack. Refrigerate in a covered container up to 12 hours.

Makes 20 pieces.

CARAMELIZED FRUITS

140 g (4½ oz/⅔ cup) sugar
5 tablespoons water
about 185 g (6 oz/2 cups) fresh assorted fruit, such as grapes, tangerine sections and strawberries, rinsed if necessary

In a heavy-bottomed saucepan, combine sugar and water. Cook over a gentle heat, stirring occasionally until sugar is dissolved.

Bring to boil without stirring; boil until mixture turns a pale caramel colour. Remove immediately from heat; place in a bowl of warm water.

Carefully dip individual pieces of fruit into caramel. Place on a lightly greased baking sheet or wire rack; allow to cool and harden. To serve, place in petits four cases. Fruit must be eaten within 24 hours. Do not refrigerate.

Makes about 750 g (1½ lb).

FONDANT SWEETS

250 g (8 oz) ready-to-roll fondant icing
pink, green, yellow, mauve and orange food colourings

FLAVOURINGS: 3 marrons glacés
3 pieces crystallised ginger
a few drops of peppermint oil
1 teaspoon each of finely grated orange, lemon and lime peel

Cut fondant icing into 6 pieces. Keep one piece plain and, using food colourings, tint remaining 5 pieces a very pale pink, green, yellow, mauve and orange.

Cut 2 marrons glacés and pink fondant into 8 pieces, wrap each piece of marrons glacés in pink fondant and shape into a neat ball. Repeat with mauve fondant and 2 pieces of crystallised ginger to make oval-shaped sweets. Decorate tops with remaining marrons glacés and ginger.

Flavour white fondant with peppermint oil and roll out to 0.5 cm (¼ in) thickness. Using a small round or crescent-shaped cutter, cut out 8-10 shapes. Knead orange peel into orange fondant, lemon peel into yellow fondant and lime peel into green fondant. Shape each piece into tiny pinwheels, squares, diamonds or trefoil shapes. Or press small pieces of fondant into plastic sweet moulds. Dry out completely on a paper-lined baking sheet.

Makes 40.

KIWI FRUIT JELLIES

1 kg (2 lb) kiwi fruit, peeled and chopped
juice of 1 lemon
750 g (1½ lb/3 cups) sugar
2 tablespoons unsalted butter
250 ml (8 fl oz/1 cup) liquid pectin
green food colouring, if desired
caster sugar, for coating

Line a 23-cm (9-in) cake tin with greaseproof paper. In a food processor or blender, combine fruit, lemon juice and 220 g (7 oz/1 cup) sugar.

Purée. It may be necessary to do this in batches. Pass the liquid through a food mill or fine sieve into a large saucepan. Add remaining sugar; bring to boil, stirring constantly. Boil 3 minutes; add butter; still stirring, boil 3 minutes more. Remove from heat and stir in pectin and a few drops of colouring, if desired.

Pour into prepared tin and allow to set overnight in cool place. Cut into attractive shapes and roll in sugar. Store in a cool place in airtight containers with wax paper separating the layers. Will keep up to 1 week.

Makes about 1 kg (2 lb).

INDEX